AF609594

NAZIS ON THE NILE

The German Military Advisers in Egypt 1949-1967

NAZIS ON THE NILE

The German Military Advisers in Egypt 1949-1967

VYVYAN KINROSS

For Egypt, 'the gift of the Nile'

'Liberty is a dearly bought commodity and prisons and factories are where it is manufactured,'
Mahatma Ghandi, 2,338 days in confinement

NAZIS ON THE NILE
The German Military Advisers in Egypt 1949-1967

Published by Nomad Publishing in 2022
Email: info@nomad-publishing.com
www.nomad-publishing.com

ISBN 978-1-914325-22-9

CIP Data: A catalogue for this book is available from the British Library

CONTENTS

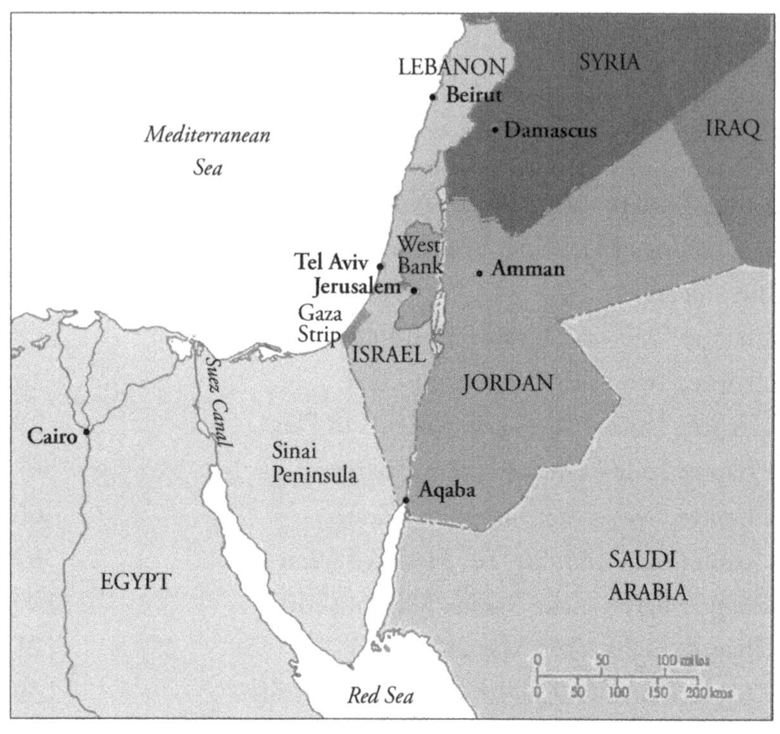

Contemporary map of Egypt and its neighbours to the east *(above)*. The map shows how the 120-mile long Suez Canal connects the eastern Mediterranean to the Red Sea by cutting through the combustible Sinai Peninsula and its border with Israel.

WHO'S WHO IN 'NAZIS ON THE NILE'

THE EGYPTIANS

- **King Farouk Ist of Egypt** and the Sudan, 10th Ruler from the Muhammad Ali dynasty, abdicated 26th July, 1952
- **Muhammad Haider Pasha**, Minister of War & Marine, Commander-in-Chief Egyptian Army, dismissed November 1950
- **General Muhammad Neguib**, Prime Minister and first President of Egypt 1953-1954, Free Officers Movement, removed 1954
- **Colonel Gamal Abdel Nasser**, Prime Minister 1954-1962, second President of Egypt 1956-1970, Free Officers Movement, died 1970
- **Colonel Anwar Sadat**, third President of Egypt October 1970-1981, Free Officers Movement, assassinated 1981
- **Colonel Zakaria Mohieddin**, first head of General Intelligence Directorate 1952-1955
- **Dr Abdel Kader Hatem**, Egypt's first Minister of Information, Deputy Prime Minister, 1956

THE BRITISH

- **Sir Winston Churchill**, Conservative British Prime Minister, 1951-1955

- **Sir Anthony Eden**, Conservative British Secretary of State for Foreign Affairs 1952, Prime Minister 1955-1957

THE GERMANS

Military Advisers

- **Generalmajor Artur Schmitt**, former Afrikakorps commander in Libya and adviser to King Farouk and the Arab League, 1949-1950, resigned
- **SS Standartenführer Dr Wilhelm Voss**, Chief Technical Adviser of Central Planning Board, Ministry of War & Marine, Egyptian Government, 1951
- **General der Artillerie Wilhelm Fahrmbacher**, chief adviser for Egyptian army and paramilitaries, 1952
- **Generalmajor Oskar Munzel**, Head of Tank School and training armoured units, 1952
- **Kapitän zur See**, Baron Theodor Freiherr von Bechtolsheim, chief naval adviser, 1952
- **SS Obersturmbannführer Otto Skorzeny**, Special Forces and armaments adviser, arms dealer, 1951
- **Generalmajor Otto-Ernst Remer**, trainer of Egyptian commando units in the Suez Canal Zone, 1953
- **Major Gerhard Mertins**, Head of training Egyptian paratroops, 1951

Rocket Scientists

- **SS Hauptsturmführer Dr Rolf Engel**, former wartime head of Skoda research centre, Czechoslovakia, head of Egypt's CERVA rocket organisation, 1952
- **Dr Paul Goercke**, electronic guidance expert, Cairo, 1952
- **Wolfgang Pilz**, designer of the Victor sounding rocket, Cairo missile programme, 1959

Propagandists

- **SS Sturmbannführer Dr Johann von Leers**, aka Omar

Amin von Leers, Head of anti-Semitic propaganda, Ministry of National Guidance, 1956

State Security

- **Dr Joachim Deumling**, intelligence adviser, Ministry of Interior, 1950s
- **SS Standartenführer Leopold Gleim**, aka Ali Al Nashar, State Security, Ministry of Interior, 1950s

Bankers

- **Hjalmar Schacht**, Economics Minister of Nazi Germany 1934-1937, financial adviser to Egyptian Government, 1950s

Fugitives

- **SS Standartenführer Walter Rauff**, Head of Einsatzkommando Egypt, adviser to government of Husni Al Za'im, President of Syria, 1949
- **SS Hauptsturmführer Alois Brunner**, deputy to Adolf Eichmann, member of Egyptian SS Group Grand Council, adviser to Syrian Government, resident Damascus
- **SS Obersturmbannführer Adolf Eichmann**, Nazi war criminal, suspected by FBI Director J Edgar Hoover of leading a pogrom against Egyptian Jews in Cairo, 1948. Executed Ramla, Israel, 1962
- **SS Hauptsturmführer Dr Hans Eisele**, Mauthausen concentration camp doctor, resident Maadi, Cairo with Johann von Leers, committed suicide

THE ISRAELIS

Spies

- **Avraham 'Avi' Seidenwerg**, aka Paul Frank, the Mossad, participated in Operation Susannah 1954, escaped arrest
- **Wolfgang Lotz**, 'The Champagne Spy', arrested by Mossad

in Cairo 1965 after his cover as an upmarket horse breeder was blown. Released 1968

- **Waltraud Lotz**, arrested in 1965 with her husband for spying, immersed by interrogators in a bath of ice cold water for night, released 1968

A TIMELINE OF PRINCIPAL EVENTS IN EGYPT

1869: Egypt completes building the Suez Canal in partnership with the French

1882: British Protectorate over Egypt established following the Battle of Tel Al Kabir

1922: 22nd February, UK recognises Egyptian Declaration of Independence

1936: Anglo-Egyptian Treaty concluded

1948: British Military Mission departs Egypt

1948/49: 15th May 1948 – 10th March 1949, First Arab-Israeli War, Egypt defeated

1949: King Farouk and Arab League invite Afrikakorps General Artur Schmitt to review military options

1952: 23rd July: Coup d'état in Cairo by the Free Officers Movement

1952: 26th July, King Farouk I abdicates and leaves the country

1952: New military junta creates the Central Planning Board as vehicle for German Military Mission

1953: 18th June: Egyptian Republic declared, General Muhammad Neguib becomes first President

1953: Internal political parties banned, Liberation Rally Party formed by Nasser

1954: November, Nasser assumes full control of Revolutionary Command Council and government

1956: 13th June: British complete their withdrawal from the occupied Suez Canal Zone

1956: 26th July, Nasser nationalises the Suez Canal Company

1956: 29th October, Israel invades Sinai Peninsula to trigger Suez crisis

1956: 1st November, first laws introduced to curtail civil and human rights of foreign nationals in Egypt, including British, French, stateless and Egyptian Jews

1956: 5th November, Britain and France invade Egypt and take control of Suez Canal

1958: 1st Feb 1958 – 28th Sep 1961: United Arab Republic (UAR) political union of Egypt and Syria

1967: 5th-10th June, Egypt wages Six Day War with Israel and suffers further military defeat

1970: 28th September, Nasser dies aged 52 in Cairo

1973: 6th-25th October, Yom Kippur War, the fourth Arab –Israeli war delivers further military defeat for Egypt

1979: 26th March: Egypt Israel Peace Treaty

INTRODUCTION

The anniversary of the revolution of the Free Officers Movement, an event that changed the course of history for Egypt and the Middle East, falls each year on 23rd July. Revolution Day is Egypt's National Day and the country's biggest public holiday, triggering patriotic parades, celebrations, concerts and speeches.

On that momentous day in 1952, the little known Free Officers led by General Muhammad Neguib and Colonel Gamal Abdel Nasser toppled the British backed monarchy that had held power in Egypt and Sudan for three decades. King Farouk I and his family sailed away into exile and his departure became the catalyst for wholesale changes in a country that was keen to modernise and ready to claim its place at the forefront of a new post-colonial Arab and Muslim world.

'Nazis On The Nile' covers the immediate period leading up to the Revolution of the Free Officers and follows the country's trajectory until Nasser's illness and the consequent start of his political decline after June 1967. During this period, first Farouk, then Nasser turned to German and former Nazi knowledge and expertise to help reinvent and revitalise the Egyptian military and security state and thereby locate a solution to the country's existential challenge.

Who could blame them? Across the 18 years in which Nasser and his fellow Free Officers held power in Egypt, the country was either reflecting on war, planning for it or engaged in it. The disaster of the first Arab-Israeli War from May 1948 to March 1949, in which Nasser himself fought and carved out his military reputation, remained etched in his mind as a source of national shame that could not be expunged but which should never be repeated.

The British and French invasion of Egypt during the Suez crisis of November 1956, and the accompanying Israeli occupation of the Sinai Peninsula came as further outrages, but they also created opportunity. Whilst the surprise attack registered shock and fury, it galvanised the country and helped legitimate its precocious government, a military junta still seeking political and ideological identity. After Suez, Egypt's regional and global profile exploded and it adopted a more assertive and self-confident posture in world affairs.

Nasser's last conflict, which he described as 'the setback' (*al naksa*), was the further humiliation of the Six-Day war with Israel in June 1967. The defeat by a much smaller yet more competent army was crushing enough for him to offer his resignation. His grand gesture was not accepted. The global icon and national symbol of Egypt's renaissance was not allowed simply to walk off the stage but struggled on through declining health until his premature death in 1970 aged just 52.

Over the span of these three defeats by Israel, Egypt was not complacent. Its leadership constantly strove to lessen the shortcomings and vulnerabilities in manpower, equipment and tactics which characterised the state of the Egyptian military during the late 1940s when its forces were judged by Britain as too weak to undertake offensive operations. Both Farouk and Nasser shared the vision of a militarised Egypt, master of a strike force built on an upgraded and expanded hard power base. Both men, as it turned out, were fixated on the same quest to develop the country's military and armaments manufacturing capacity and thus create the means to shape the outcomes of the Cold War struggle that increasingly enveloped the Middle East through the 1950s and 1960s. Within this fixation lay in part the origins of the region's destructive and ongoing arms race.

With denazification in Europe running its course and the emergence of a supercharged recruitment market for specialist military and scientific skills, it was not surprising that significant amounts of the human capital that had gone into constructing the military and security machinery of the Wehrmacht and Third Reich was available for hire. 'Nazis on the Nile' tells the story of how this talent grab unfolded when Egypt set out to harness the know-how and services of a uniquely qualified group of German experts in order to power its military revival. The facts and the truths they portray are sometimes hard to reach in this little visited chapter in Egypt's story. The absence of an official Egyptian account or readily accessible archive of the period compounds the difficulty.

Nonetheless, 'Nazis On The Nile' is a tale of grand vision, practical ambition and noble failure played out against the high stakes background of the new rocket age and the superpower era. The cast of characters is often unlikely, sometimes unsavoury but always compelling. In some cases these historical figures are well rounded and extensively documented, in others more two-dimensional. Still more appear simply as a name on a page or a line in an archive, nothing more than footprints rendered increasingly faint with the passage of time. However, the former generals and sundry military men and specialists who populate these pages are real enough, to the extent that they once inhabited the villas and apartments of Heliopolis, Maadi and Helwan, walked the streets of downtown Cairo and Alexandria, toiled away in hidden armaments and rocket factories and pored over plans in the offices, dusty barracks and ministry buildings of Nasser's new Egypt.

The events portrayed in the book took place during a cathartic period for Egypt, encompassing its transformation from monarchy to republic across the post-colonial and Cold War years that both polarised and weaponised the region. At this time, Britain was losing its grip everywhere in the world and both the United States and the Soviet Union started to take a closer, strategic view of Egypt as a proxy state in the great scheme to play out their own ambitions in the Middle East. The complexities of this geopolitical backdrop infuse the story, as do the growing significance at the time of the global non-aligned movement and the potential of pan Arabism and its promise to coalesce and accelerate the exercise of collective Arab power. Part of this broad canvas is an assimilation of the history that reveals the nuanced ambitions and foreign policy aims of both imperial and Nazi Germany in the Muslim and Arab story from the late 19th century through the two world wars of the 20th century.

On the domestic front, Egyptian government thinking post revolution was driven by big ticket, reforming issues. These included the need to end centuries of feudalism, foreign occupation and the domination of foreign capital, and the incorporation of modern concepts such as social justice and the redistribution of land and wealth into a new political agenda and mandate for change. All these components were pieces of the puzzle confronted by Nasser and his junta, seeking an ideological anchor for their revolution and walking a precarious tightrope between the two poles of dictatorship and democracy.

After an initial cautious welcome by Britain, the government of the Free Officers increasingly became a negative fixation, with a focus on vexed and protracted negotiations for permanent British withdrawal from their Canal Zone bases. Disorder, violence and growing fatalities stalked both Egyptian and British forces operating in the Zone, fuelled by the intervention of German Special Forces veterans who trained Egypt's commandos and irregulars in guerrilla fighting tactics. From late 1954 when he assumed total control of the junta, Nasser was personally demonised as 'the new Mussolini' or 'Hitler of the Nile' and his Revolutionary Command Council was portrayed in foreign media as authoritarian and anti-democratic. Its military make-up and autocratic style was even directly compared with the despised and discredited model of European Fascism.

This reputational damage was driven by Nasser's suppression of all dissenting political voices and opposition parties within Egypt in 1953. It was further compounded by his aggressive handling and expulsion of foreign nationals in the country during and after the Suez crisis in November 1956, including British and French subjects and stateless and Egyptian Jews. In some respects this might have been predictable, simply part of an existing wartime zeitgeist. Internment of German, Italian and Japanese citizens in Britain during World War Two or of British citizens in Nazi occupied France was accepted as collateral damage, part of international conflict.

However, the treatment afforded to Egypt's Jewish population after Suez struck a raw nerve and caused a reputational crisis for Nasser. Parallels drawn at the time by journalists such as Bill Richardson of the New York Post with the machinery and methodology driving the expulsions of the Jews of Nazi Germany in the 1930s caused Nasser damage, some of which became permanent scarring. The direct implication of former German Nazis in the Ministry of the Interior's implementation of Egypt's Jewish expulsions is a subject that has largely lived in the shadows. 'Nazis On The Nile' revisits this episode in the context of the wider Nazi and German influence on Nasser's reforming government during the mid-1950s.

What does the book seek to achieve? I have in the first instance set out to unearth the full extent of former Nazi and German expertise engaged in the building of Egypt's military state after 1949, when defeat in the first Arab Israeli War revealed the need to reform the country's corrupt military culture and replace its antiquated infrastructure and methods. I have attempted to quantify the scale and depth of this penetration of Nazi and German experience and expertise across Egypt's principal government institutions during the years of Neguib and Nasser's junta. These include the Ministry of War & Marine, the Foreign Office, Intelligence Service, the Ministry of National Guidance and Department of Information, the Ministry of the Interior and its state security service. In the case of the Central Planning Board, the administrative vehicle constructed for the German military advisers hired in 1952, I have posed the question: what if the terms of engagement of this mission had been different and the German advisers had been given executive authority and battlefield command during the Suez crisis and the early incursions into Gaza and Israel by the Palestinian Fedayeen? Would there have been different outcomes if experienced and able German commanders had been authorised to lead in the field, a systemic weakness pointed out to Nasser himself in 1954 by former Panzer commander General Oskar Munzel. Records show that, where some German commanders had in fact directed occasional operations in the Canal Zone prior to the Suez crisis, their engagement had deeply troubled British military intelligence.

In the complex and secretive world of arms manufacture and arms procurement, the book attempts to highlight the most significant threads and milestones of the strategy adopted by Egypt in the Nasser years to build hard power and armaments capacity where it could find the opportunities, either at home or abroad.

Whilst its domestic rocket, missile and jet aircraft industry did not finally get off the ground, could the programme have gone further if its efforts had been more focused and less diffuse? After all, precedent had been set by Argentina's development of its first fighter jet, using German expertise, in 1950. Had they received more effective and committed financial and logistical support, would the German scientists and technicians have been left so underpowered and exposed to Israeli efforts to undermine them?

The German knowledge and skills applied in setting up domestic arms production and manufacturing facilities as part of Egypt's new military industrial complex may nevertheless have sown fertile seeds. Over the subsequent decades up to the mid-1980s, some of these went on to flourish under different names, manufacturing and assembling a range of hybrid armaments, jet aircraft and engines. In important respects, the German experts can be seen to have set both the tone and the standards for future arms development where they were unable to make a decisive impact at the time. Operating in a different industrial and technological age, and with new geopolitical dynamics, Egypt's arms factories may even now owe something to their prototypes of the 1950s and 1960s.

The book opens up the question of whether German influence exerted during the Nasser years has survived the ensuing decades to remain discernible in the military, intelligence and security infrastructure of today's Egypt. Is the methodology of state intervention in the lives and freedoms of citizens even remotely reminiscent of long ago imported models and operations first tested in pre-war Europe? In some respects the shape of Egypt's security state could be seen to display a lineage stretching back to the Nasser years when the country's first military junta and its Revolutionary Command Council deployed foreign experts to help plan the security, police and intelligence architecture of its new republic.

As to Nasser himself and the Free Officers Movement he led, there can be no doubt that their bloodless coup d'état and the revolution that followed changed the course of Egypt's history. It became the model for a subsequent age of military coups across the Arabic speaking world, including Iraq in 1958, Syria in 1963, Algeria in 1965 and Sudan in 1969, offering a blueprint for military rule and a model for the state structures and processes to support it. For a moment in time, after international pressure forced British and French forces to withdraw following the Suez crisis in November 1956, Egypt was at the centre of world affairs. President Gamal Abdel Nasser had become the most talked about, charismatic and consequential leader on the global stage. In the decade that followed, it was his German advisers who were instrumental in helping him consolidate his position as the Arab world's pre-eminent statesman. This is their remarkable story.

Chapter One

A DAY OF RECKONING

On 26th July 1952 Sir Michael Creswell, Britain's diplomatic representative in Alexandria, Egypt's second city, sent a telegram to his bosses at the Foreign Office in Whitehall. In it was a message from the American ambassador in Egypt, Jefferson Caffery, which the US diplomat had been having great difficulty getting through to Washington and which he was requesting the British to forward for him. His message read: 'very slow communication, am asking the British to transmit following: King tells me he has been given until noon to abdicate in favour of his son and until 6.00pm to leave the country. He is going. I am telegraphing directly in detail. Caffery'.

The bombshell he was dropping was the news that Egypt's King Farouk I had been deposed in a military coup initiated and carried out by the Free Officers Movement, a small and obscure group of Egyptian Army officers led by General Muhammad Neguib and Colonel Gamal Abdel Nasser. The country was now in the hands of this tightly-knit, secretive band of republican modernisers and under the control of a new instrument of government, the Council of the Revolutionary Command (RCC).

The implications of the coup d'état were far reaching for all Egyptians as well as those foreign powers such as Britain and the US which had carved out a direct or indirect stake in Egypt's future. This decisive moment would in every sense alter the country's trajectory for the coming decades and in the process exert a profound impact on the future of the Middle East. The coup itself was the culmination of a process begun in secret by the Free Officers some time before. No definitive evidence shows that the US had prior knowledge of the coup. However its Central Intelligence Agency (CIA) had been seeking to undermine the British backed monarchy in Egypt and replace it with a more compliant, less corrupt regime. CIA Director Allen Dulles, supported by Cairo Head of Station Miles Copeland Jr and roaming operative without portfolio Kermit ('Kim') Roosevelt Jnr had masterminded 'Project FF' to communicate and liaise with the Free Officers prior to the coup. Roosevelt had personally held three face-to-face meetings with representatives of the Free Officers in Cairo in March 1952 and these and other contacts had resulted in the promise of US co-operation[1].

At the time of the coup, a nominally independent Egypt was still intimately connected to Britain and provided a central pillar of its trading, military and colonial edifice. This still covered much of the globe, though by 1952 the Empire was well into its long retreat. Egypt's central position in the British imperial scheme and world view was anchored in the 120 mile long Suez Canal, designed and built by a Frenchman and embedded by Britain as the femoral artery in its global trading network. The waterway enabled direct access from the eastern Mediterranean through the Red Sea to oilfields and terminals in Iraq and Iran and further eastwards to the commodity rich rewards of India, Ceylon, Malaya and the Far East. Cairo was also an increasingly important hub in Britain's rapidly expanding civilian and military air network which stretched eastwards to Baghdad, Tehran, Singapore and Hong Kong. Thus the importance of securing the Suez Canal was emphasised by the placing of a permanent British garrison along its length, from Port Said on the Mediterranean coast via Ismailia to Suez at the northern end of the Red Sea. The ongoing and unwelcome presence of the British military and their bases in Egypt was the subject of regular and vexed discussions between the British and Egyptian Governments both before and after the coup.

Two days after Caffery's message was despatched, on 28th July, Britain's Foreign Secretary Sir Anthony Eden made a statement in the House of Commons. He told Parliamentarians that the abdication had gone forward and resulted in an Egyptian Council of Regency being set up in favour of Farouk's infant son Fouad, who had been declared king in his place. Eden stressed Britain's reluctance to involve itself in the internal affairs of Egypt. He stated that he did not see the prospect of any disturbance or threat to foreign lives or interests. 'Nevertheless in view of the unsettled conditions which inevitably result from events such as have recently taken place in Egypt, we have thought it right to authorise certain movements of British forces as a precautionary measure,' he said. Eden also told Parliament that, in the existing circumstances, he had ordered British Ambassador Sir Ralph Stevenson back to his post[2].

Stevenson subsequently met General Neguib and Anwar Sadat, another leading member of the Free Officers Movement, on 29th July in Cairo. During the encounter, Stevenson too stressed that Britain had no intention of interfering or intervening in Egyptian internal affairs but pointed out the undesirability of the country being subjected to further constitutional upheavals. In his report of the meeting, Stevenson remarked on General Neguib's lack of fluency in English and the fact that it had been an impediment to being able to assess his views definitively. 'He struck me however as an honest man doing his best in an extremely difficult situation...but I would not regard him as anything approaching a free agent', Stevenson wrote presciently. Nevertheless, brushing his ambassador's concerns aside and without appearing to acknowledge any US role in the coup, British Prime Minister Winston Churchill noted on 26th August: 'We are never going to get anything out of the Wafd or the Muslim Brotherhood. But there might well be a policy in which the United States will join, of making a success of Neguib'[3]. This judgement of Churchill's turned out to be wrong. Neguib, a distinguished and popular professional soldier of mixed Egyptian and Sudanese parentage, was to lose his job as Prime Minister and the first President of Egypt at the end of November 1954 when Nasser seized control of the government. So diminished and desperate did Neguib's position become that he would write to Nasser from house arrest during the Suez crisis of 1956 offering to lay down his life for his country in a high-profile suicide mission against the British and French invaders. 'Please allow me to volunteer on the war front as an ordinary soldier with a fake name under any surveillance you choose, and without anybody's knowledge but those in charge. I promise you on everything I hold dear and, on my honour, to

بسم الله الرحمن الرحيم

بلدة [illegible]
في يوم الاثنين ٢ ربيع الثاني ١٣٧٦هـ
الموافق ٥ نوفمبر ١٩٥٦م

شكرى جدا جدا
وعاجل جدا جدا
و[illegible] تحيا الرئيس

الى السيد الرئيس جمال عبد الناصر

السلام عليكم ورحمة الله — وبعد فقد يظن غيركم أنه هازل أو محاول الدعاية لنفسي أو غير ذلك، ولكنكم تعرفون أخلاقي ومن ميزاتكم الفريدة القدرة على معرفة الرجال. كما أن أي رجل شجاع أو أي وطني صميم يستطيع بسهولة أن يؤمن بصدق ما أكتبه اليكم الآن:

أريد أن نضرب للمواطنين مثلا جديدا على إنكار الذات والتضحية بكل شيء في سبيل البلاد. أريد أن نقف رجلا واحدا ندافع عن الوطن العزيز في هذه الساعة الحرجة.

أريد منك أن تسمح لي بأعز أمنية لي وهي المشاركة في أقدس واجب وأشرفه وهو الدفاع عن مصر فاسمح لي بالتطوع جنديا عاديا في جبهة القتال باسم مستعار وتحت أية رقابة شئت، دون أن يعلم أحد بذلك غير المختصين.

وإني أعدك بأثمن ما أملك أعدك بشرفي أن أعود الى معتقلي اذا بقيت حيا بعد انتهاء القتال. وبذلك تحصلون كل ما لحق بنفسي من آلام. كما تسعدون العدد الكبير من الضباط والجنود المعينين لحراستي والمحرومين مثلي من شرف الاشتراك في القتال وتوفرون مبلغا كبيرا [illegible] ينفق على هذه الحراسة. وانا [illegible] ان اختم حياتي ختاما [illegible]

ولو خامركم أي شك فيما أقول فاني مستعد ان اقوم [illegible]
[illegible] أو ان اسقط بطائرة او مظلة [illegible]

The letter *(above)* written by General Neguib, now fallen from grace to Nasser from house arrest during the Suez crisis of 1956, offering to lay down his life for his country in a high-profile suicide mission against the British and French invaders.

return to my prison if I'm alive when fighting ceases.... all I wish is to end my life honourably and with dignity. Furthermore, if you feel any doubt in my sincerity, I should be prepared to carry out a suicide mission in a torpedo boat, or by crashing an airplane or by strapping on dynamite and falling in a parachute....' his despairing missive read.[4]

In September of 1952 Sir Ralph Stevenson went to see Farouk's cousin, Prince Muhammad Ali, who himself had technical claims to the Egyptian throne and had hoped to succeed. Greatly despondent, Muhammad Ali informed Stevenson that General Neguib, the new Prime Minister, had not called on him and that he now requested His Majesty's Government to ensure that he would be able to leave Egypt and reside abroad for the present, taking with him 100,000 Egyptian pounds. He also wanted guarantees of his future status as a British protected person if his Egyptian passport was withdrawn. Whilst hedging about the money, over which he had little control, Stevenson agreed that the Prince should leave.

Everywhere the patterns and parameters of revolutionary Egypt were being set, a rebirth that would reveal itself through the 1950s and 1960s as a total reimagining of the state. Out would go the large-scale, institutional corruption of a decaying monarchy in colonial harness, under the thumb of the dissolute, capricious King Farouk. In its place the new Egypt would rise, one characterised by a very distinct brand of authoritarian Arab nationalism and socialism, progressive and outward looking, bent on taking its place as an independent, non-aligned country and pan Arab champion in the Middle East.

Egypt's deposed king had gained a reputation over the years more for his eccentricities and excesses than any great state decision-making power. Amongst other collections, Farouk had amassed a huge amount of palace furniture, grand, ornate and baroque, which had become known mockingly as the 'Louis-Farouk' style to mark its gilded opulence, a reference to the Versailles scale of ornamentation on display throughout his homes. Famously this collection-minded monarch, a serial hoarder and surreptitious kleptomaniac, had indulged his penchant for tailor made suits, of which he had over a thousand, rare coins, stamps, pornography including a number of pornographic neck ties, and garages full of classic cars. Alongside his fleet of red

Bentleys nestled a Mercedes Benz 540K given to him in 1938 by another car enthusiast and head of state, the German Chancellor Adolf Hitler.

But though spoilt, petulant and a libertine, Farouk was not entirely frivolous. His identity as a monarch, an Egyptian and an Arab combined with the weight of history, public opinion and domestic political pressure to bear down on him to restore Egypt's place as an independent nation at the forefront of the Arab world. His sense of duty, a flame that flickered only weakly within a famously narcissistic personality, nonetheless became a significant force behind the effort to regenerate his country's sense of pride and carve a definitive path to self-determination. Specifically, the monarch sought a practical means by which to establish political autonomy for a nation state still living under British occupation and pushed further onto the back foot by the establishment of the State of Israel, its newest and most unwelcome neighbour in May 1948. Thus over the final three years of his reign Farouk had been working in secret with his senior political and military advisers to plan the renaissance of Egypt's military and security state, smashed to pieces and humiliated in the first Arab Israeli war fought in the immediate aftermath of the birth of Israel.

On Farouk's watch, the process of reviewing and overhauling Egypt's military assets, its armed forces, leadership and battle plan had been underway since 1949. He had taken the view that the country needed additional specialist help and expertise and that this would have to be sourced externally. Accordingly, his agents had started the process of reaching out to middle men across Europe to locate and sign up foreign talent to help rebuild Egypt's depleted and inadequate hard power base. This group of experts and advisers would help shape a new generation of arms, armaments and military hardware and in time go on to mastermind the design and production of Egypt's first jet engines, fighters and missiles. Farouk's vision was of an Egypt with a clenched fist, its confidence bolstered by the crunch of well drilled military boots on the ground, Egyptian fighter jets in the skies above Cairo, its warships steaming across the eastern Mediterranean and state-of-the-art missiles pointing skywards reaching for the hearts of its enemies. To realise this, he had already started to harness former Nazi and German Wehrmacht military experts and specialists, identifying soldiers, scientists, technicians, arms manufacturers and arms dealers who could help transform his grandiose vision of national renewal and resurgence into a new reality.

The Free Officers were themselves aware of Farouk's scheme and over the coming decades were to take the King's original plan much further and faster. They were to develop their own network of highly connected middlemen and recruiters working through diplomatic channels and front companies in Switzerland to sign up a wealth of scientific and technical talent largely lying idle or underemployed in the post-war hiatus created by the new, divided Germany. By early May 1953, the presence of substantial numbers of German and former Nazi experts in Egypt and their direct intervention in its government's quest for hard power was to become a determining and urgent question amongst the major international players in the struggle for dominance of the Cold War Middle East.

The British at least were initially less aware of this initiative than they might have been. Their post-war focus was on the more general retrenchment and withdrawal of imperial forces and colonial administrations from a growing number of territories now being vacated and handed back to the control of newly independent governments. This process had started with the partition and evacuation of India in 1947 and continued at pace across the rapidly downsizing Empire. In 1948 alone, the British departed from Burma, Ceylon and Palestine. The thorny problem of independence for Sudan, Egypt's southern neighbour, was finally solved in late 1955.

In a telegram concerning events in Egypt he sent to Winston Churchill on board HMS Queen Mary on 26th January 1953, Foreign Secretary Anthony Eden wrote an enigmatic note: 'The evidence we have collected as a result of arresting the seven Nazis is fuller than we anticipated. I propose to make an interim statement on Wednesday'[5]. And so the story of the 'Allemanni', the German and Nazi military advisers in Egypt, was to unfold over the coming decades in all its unlikely and extraordinary detail.

Chapter Two
THE MAN FROM LIMA

"The Nazis may write like schoolboys, but they're capable of anything. That's just why they're so dangerous. People laugh at them, right up to the last moment..."

Christopher Isherwood,
'Goodbye to Berlin', Hogarth Press, 1939

On 29th April 1965, the US Government's Regional Security Officer (RSO) in Lima, Peru sent a lengthy report with several attachments to the Chief of Foreign Operations in Washington. The report contained an account of a recent conversation held by the embassy's Reporting Officer with a Peruvian informant, Cesar Ugarte Jnr. In his conversation and subsequent statement, dictated to a secretary, Ugarte had made some startling claims about the activities of former Nazis now employed by the regime of Egypt's revolutionary President Gamal Abdel Nasser. Central to his allegations was the contention that the Nazi people smuggling network known as Odessa was still highly active and now not only financed but also based in the Egyptian capital, Cairo. Ugarte went on to name a number of prominent Nazis currently on the payroll of the Egyptians and in particular singled out the Nazi racial theorist and propagandist Johann von Leers whom he also claimed had been a recent visitor to Lima.

The immediate purpose of von Leers' visit was to execute his part in a complex currency fraud to smuggle fake copper plates for printing dollar bills out of South America and into France. French Communists had agreed with the Nazi network to use the plates to print a batch of 'queer' dollar bills in a variety of denominations in order to destabilise the currency market both in France and Peru, Ugarte claimed. Von Leers, currently responsible for anti-Semitic propaganda in Egypt's Government Information Department, had arrived in Peru from Cairo on 3rd December 1964 travelling on an Egyptian passport to pick up the copper plates. Once in Lima, von Leers had gone to the Egyptian embassy in Miraflores at 8.00pm on 4th December and held a meeting with the head of Odessa in Peru, one Federico Schwend. On 9th December von Leers had left for Sao Paulo, Brazil and from there had returned to Cairo.

Was all this remotely plausible? The view of US officials in Lima was that it had to be taken seriously. The immediacy of the currency fraud allegations alone required the report to be passed back up the US chain of command. In his accompanying note, the Regional Security Officer wrote that the contents of Ugarte Jr's statement might also be of interest to the US Treasury. But who was Ugarte and where did his information come from? This colourful, quixotic character had been a regular informant of the Americans since 1962. A Peruvian-American dual citizen, he had until recently been employed as technical advisor for public relations to the commanding general of the Guardia Civil y Policia of Peru, a General Quia. His file noted that, amongst other jobs on his CV, he claimed to have been a Los Angeles policeman and an occasional Hollywood actor. The US embassy in Lima had already taken the view that Ugarte sometimes overcooked his information but much of it had nonetheless checked out as accurate over the years and had been useful enough to make him of value. He was, though, a challenging character, judged to be 'over bearing' and had done enough damage to disenchant many of the Americans he had dealt with in Lima, including US Army attaché Colonel John Benson. However, the main Reporting Officer in the embassy had taken the line that, rather than ignoring him completely, he would keep Ugarte at arm's length but continue to glean intelligence from him [1].

The source of Ugarte's information was of interest but remained opaque throughout the process. The Peruvian maintained he had been conducting his own investigation into the Nazi underground movement in South America since he started working at the Guardia Civil in 1961. A mole, whose Spanish accent he judged to be either Venezuelan, Cuban or Panamanian but who also had fluent German, English and Italian, had been in regular telephone contact with him after his appointment to his PR job. Ugarte believed his source to be 'of good background' and almost certainly a disaffected member of the Odessa organisation. This secretive set-up, the 'Organisation der Ehemaligen SS-Angehörigen' or the organisation of former SS members, had reportedly been smuggling fugitive Nazis around the world since 1947 but had never conclusively been proved to exist.

Along with his claims about the Cairo hub of Odessa, Ugarte also asserted that Nasser's government currently employed 3,087 former Nazis hired through the network. The list of these Nazis on Nasser's payroll, all senior members of the Odessa organisation according to the Peruvian-American, was not comprehensive but it contained some high profile names whose various war records, including egregious war crimes made their whereabouts of great interest. Their long standing roles in the reconstruction of Egypt's military and security state and the creation of its armaments industry were also of direct concern to a number of foreign governments, not least the US, Britain, Israel and West Germany and were already known about or hinted at to a great extent inside both Western and Soviet intelligence networks. Based on information from Jewish NGOs in the US concerned about the fate of Egypt's Jews after the Suez invasion of 1956 [2], the Germans and their roles as advisers to the Egyptian government in the Jewish expulsions had also been flagged up as of concern in US Congress on 30th July, 1957[3].

Amongst those on Ugarte's list were some formidable and shadowy characters, many of whom for reasons of convenience or faith, or both, had now converted to Islam and taken Muslim names, a further step towards anonymity in a foreign land where extradition was already next to impossible under Egypt's prevailing legal system. Von Leers himself was now known by his Muslim name Omar Amin von Leers. But others Ugarte alleged were using similar cover included Lt Col Ben Salam, better known as Sturmbannführer Bernardt Bender, former Head of the SS in Ukraine, wanted for war crimes but currently head of

Egypt's political department; and SS Standartenführer Leopold Gleim, former head of the Gestapo in Poland and accused of being in charge of Nasser's pervasive and powerful State Security Cadre (SSC), Egypt's newly created secret police.

For those not in the know it would certainly have appeared extraordinary that such high-profile former and practising Nazis, many of them having been processed through the Allies' patchily successful post-war denazification programme, could be so active in the affairs of another sovereign government and one so seemingly inimical to Western and Israeli interests. But for anyone who had made it their business to follow the trajectory of the Third Reich and its relationships in the strategically vital Middle East before and during the war, it would have been perhaps more predictable.

'Who's Who' in the German Argentine Junta

The story of Johann von Leers is of historical importance in itself but also for the repercussions of its intersections with pivotal characters and era defining events in the Middle East at the time. From 1941 until the end of the war von Leers worked closely in Berlin with Haj Amin Al Husseini, the Grand Mufti of Jerusalem, to mastermind an anti-Semitic, anti-British Arabic language wartime propaganda campaign across the region [4]. Living in Buenos Aires for five years from 1950, he was active in the Nazi and National Socialist exile network in South America and an occasional contributor to Egypt and Argentina's anti-Semitic propaganda campaigns. Resident in Cairo from early 1956, he played a formal part in shaping Egypt's propaganda front and finessing Nasser's effort to expand Egypt's ideological influence in the post-colonial Middle East and non-aligned world until the mid-1960s. Von Leers was well placed to advise Nasser in the construction of the narrative that so successfully exploited the psychodrama and colonial associations of the Suez invasion in November 1956. His hand might also be detected amongst those in the production of the seminal atrocity propaganda film 'The Anglo-French Aggression against Egypt' rushed out for distribution by the Egyptians in December the same year following the British withdrawal from Port Said [5].

His activities must also be seen as part of a wider, systematic initiative to rebuild Egypt's depleted military power base after

1948 that was accelerated by the recruitment of a significant cohort of German military advisers in which he was a peripheral though complementary figure. Nasser viewed this effort as central to building the missing capacity that would enable him to realise his vision of Egypt as the dominant Arab force in the rapidly developing Cold War era Middle East. This worldview encompassed the ability to develop a credible challenge to Israel, see off the debilitating presence of the British with their permanent military bases and garrison along the Suez Canal, negotiate on more equal terms with the new regional superpower of the United States and also make his own arms and industrial deals where required with the Soviet Union. At the same time, he was carving out a dynamic new political and ideological centre ground in Egypt, combining pan-Arabism, socialism, nationalism and Islamic orthodoxy that together brought him unchallenged leadership of a new post-colonial order in the Middle East.

The personal trajectory of von Leers also perfectly illustrates a wider pattern of migration after the war of former high ranking Nazis and German military experts who had served the Third Reich, survived or sidestepped denazification ('entnazifizierung') and needed to relocate from the new Germany in order to sell their skills and build economically viable post-war lives. Over time a well-trodden and carefully curated series of escape routes known as 'rat lines' was developed to help these fugitives, charting a course for thousands after the war out of Germany, across Europe and thence to South America and the Middle East. Both Syrian and Egyptian capitals, Damascus and Cairo, were at different times either stopovers or permanent destinations on these routes. Immediately after the Second World War, the Grand Mufti of Jerusalem, Haj Amin Al Husseini moved to Cairo where he focused the struggle to establish the long awaited Palestinian state with himself at its head. From here the Egyptians and neighbouring Arab states including Lebanon, Syria and Iraq went to war with the newly created State of Israel over Palestine in May 1948. The loss was swift and catastrophic, and provided the catalyst for the revolution of the Free Officers in Egypt in July 1952 and Nasser's escalation of King Farouk's strategy to develop Egypt's hard power and military capacity through the decades of the 1950s and 1960s.

Argentina, Chile, Paraguay and Brazil were amongst those

countries whose well-established German immigrant communities and sympathetic or neutral governments offered fugitives anonymity and employment. Nazi Germany's well planned and executed post-war global footprint rested on the creation of the Auslandsorganisation, a vehicle for coalescing individuals and groups of German origin or extraction wherever found abroad, and keeping track of them through its network of social, cultural and Party organisations. Once in the fold, they were then leant on by the Gestapo. Meanwhile the Sicherheitsdienst (SD) security organisation operated within the same area to gain influence over the indigenous governments which would, in time, be subverted and inclined to make policy favourable to Nazi designs [6].

When the Argentine branch of the Auslandsorganisation was established in 1933 under Dr Gottfried Brandt, it was with the announced purpose of fostering closer commercial relations between Argentina, Brazil and Germany. The CIA estimated that as many as 7,000 Germans had entered Argentina since the end of World War Two and were now living there, among them Auschwitz doctor Josef Mengele [7]. The country's high-profile leader Juan Perón was prepared to make alliances with Fascists as well as those of other political persuasions and wanted to attract up to four million immigrants from Europe. He was also anxious to recruit German expertise to construct Argentina's first jet fighter. Kurt Tank, designer of the famous Luftwaffe Focke Wulf fighter, successfully built Argentina's first jet combat aircraft in 1950, the FMA1Ae 33 Pulqui 11, living and working throughout his time in the country under the pseudonym 'Pedro Matthies'.

The journey taken by Johann von Leers from internment in Germany to Italy and thence to Sweden, Argentina and finally to Cairo and employment by the Egyptian government was one that appears extraordinary for such a close and unrepentant colleague of Nazi propaganda chief Josef Goebbels. Von Leers was a lifelong, die-hard Nazi supporter and proselytizer, a committed anti-Semite and highly organised, prolific and intellectually sophisticated propagandist. An Alter Kämpfer, amongst those who had supported the Nazi Party prior to 1930, he also held the honorary rank of Sturmbannführer in the SS. His work had included the drafting of pamphlets, the writing of books including 'Jewry and Knavery' and 'Blood and Race', and the practical organisation of anti-Semitic education curricula in

German schools. His propaganda work in Berlin from 1941 had created strong connections with the Arab Nationalist cause and cleverly anchored it to German objectives in the region, principal amongst them the securing of vital oil fields in the north of Iraq. At the end of the war von Leers was interned in Germany for 18 months, held by the Americans and then the Soviets. He spent some years after his release in Italy.

It is alleged he was finally helped by Swedish Fascist Per Engdahl (1909-1994) to reach Argentina by ship in 1950 where he took up residence with his wife and daughter in Buenos Aires at Martin Haedo 863, Vicente López, using the name Dr Hans Euler. The detached, spacious pitch-roofed house he chose in this genteel district was set back from the road and protected by metal fencing. The neighbourhood was part of a comfortable, discreet and leafy suburb of the city, just behind the Parque de los Niños and near to Buenos Aires beach. There, he started churning out material for a raft of German language newspapers and newsletters which were circulated amongst Nazi Party sympathisers in South America and Germany. Amongst them were the monthly nationalist publication for Germans in South America called 'El Sendero'; the openly anti-Semitic National Socialist newspaper 'Der Weg (The Way); and Der Arbeitsgeber, the organ of the Federation of German Employers' Associations [8].

But von Leers did not limit his activities to the written word; he became active in propagating the National Socialist cause more widely across South America. His name appeared in a secret US report titled 'Who's Who in the German Argentine Junta' in February 1952. The report contended that expatriate German officers had been working underground to build up a German unit of all branches for service in the Egyptian Army. 'This is apparently part of a widespread organisation to bring German officers and soldiers back into service. The Junta is in touch with the Egyptian Embassy in Buenos Aires' the report stated [9]. The source of the report, 'one who is closely connected with the Argentine police' went on to name von Leers, identifying some of his past jobs, notably as the ideological head of the German National Socialist Students Organisations ('Reichschulungleiter des National-sozialistischen Studentenbundes') after Hitler came to power, along with his parallel careers as journalist and author, together making him 'a leader in Nazi literature'.

In 1954, von Leers' name came up again in a further confidential US report, cited as a member of a committee of German émigrés in Buenos Aires formed to organise the resettlement of Admiral Karl Doenitz in Argentina where this 'legal successor' to Hitler in time might be placed at the head of a Nazi government-in-exile [10]. The group of German exiles in Argentina had their fingers in many pies, among them an attempt to organise a Nazi-style workers' movement in Uruguay against what they saw as the 'Judaizing and corruption in Uruguay which constituted the bastion of the US in this region' [11]. Numbers of other German émigrés in Argentina, many of them former members of the Waffen SS, belonged to a little known lobby group called 'The Centro Europeo of Buenos Aires', founded in the Argentine capital by former Vice-Admiral Joachim Litzmann, which was active against what it saw as expansionist US interests in the country.

By the start of 1955, one of the main sources of income for von Leers was beginning to dry up. The print run of Der Weg, the only remaining Nazi German language newspaper of its type was getting smaller and smaller, reducing to a minimal 3,500 copies. It had first been established in 1946 with a 10,000 print run. The paper was also being printed under increasingly difficult circumstances and staff had been leaving and returning to Germany. Von Leers was left as the only remaining contributor and editor, sometimes writing all the articles himself under different pseudonyms. It was at this moment that he was contacted by General Hasan Fahmi Ismail, military attaché at the Egyptian embassy in Buenos Aires and asked to produce some anti-Semitic propaganda in Argentina on behalf of the Egyptian government. Accounts as to how Ismail connected to von Leers differ. One suggestion is that he was put in touch by former colleague Haj Amin Al Husseini, who after the war had moved from Berlin to Cairo in order to escape prosecution for alleged war crimes committed in the Balkans. Another was that a German exile already in Egypt called Paul Schmitz, known by his adoptive name of Abd Al Majid Amin, made a personal introduction.

Abd Al Majid Amin, who was a language instructor at Cairo University claimed that, as a friend of longstanding, he was responsible for von Leers coming to Egypt and described the propagandist as 'a sincere friend of Islam' [12]. Abd Al Majid himself had been in Cairo since 1952, hired by the Arab League to teach German to senior Arab League officers. In any event, Ismail was so pleased with von Leers' anti-Semitic propaganda work in Beunos Aires that he offered him a job in Cairo on behalf of President Nasser [13]. His role was designated as a political adviser in the Government Information Department, part of the Ministry of National Guidance, where he was tasked with strengthening its anti-Israeli propaganda programme.

To avoid any embarrassment from the appointment, the Egyptian government arranged a cover for von Leers as a visiting professor of language in Cairo University, where he in due course gave some classes. Thus it was that in April 1956 von Leers, his wife Gesine and daughter decided to take this well paid opening in Cairo and left Argentina for the city and a new life [14]. As events transpired von Leers would die in his adopted city of Cairo on 5th March 1965, less than a decade later and a mere three months after his reported trip to Lima to help execute the currency fraud.

New Channels for Nazi Technology

Whilst some of the world's major capital cities including Cairo and Buenos Aires featured high on the list as end destinations for fugitive Nazis and former servants of the Third Reich, the general repurposing and relocation of Nazi technological expertise beyond the war's end went much wider and deeper and was fraught with moral complexities. This leading edge capability struck right at the heart of the new Cold War struggle that characterised the ideological polarisation of the 1950s and 1960s and which pitted the United States and the Soviet Union in direct conflict with each other in a no holds barred fight to become the world's dominant superpower.

These former uneasy wartime allies both harboured expansionist ambitions which could be reinforced and accelerated by technological advances in the fields of rocket propulsion, aerospace technology, product miniaturisation, nerve agents and industrial processes. All of these were specialist fields in which Nazi science and engineering had excelled through the latter stages of the war. This new arms race, one in which Egypt and its revolutionary regime was determined to be a competitor rather than spectator, was central to the struggle for post war power in the Middle East, where the era of British and French domination was rapidly coming to a close and giving way to American ascendancy, Soviet expansionism and Israeli military heft. It was to swallow up thousands of Nazi and Wehrmacht scientists and experts who vanished into a clandestine world whose existence and purpose were kept well outside the public domain. The use of former Nazis and the notion that their skills and knowledge were transferable and even at a premium in this new, high stakes race was deeply problematic and presented a significant moral dilemma for many former soldiers, politicians and patriots in the West whose families had sacrificed everything in the struggle against Fascism.

Perhaps the predominant example of this Nazi talent grab emerged through the story of Operation Paperclip. This hidden programme, initiated by the United States even as the war was ending, co-opted as many as 1,600 German scientists and engineers to work on secret government weapons projects in various locations across America. The highest profile Nazi rocket scientist of the war and inventor of the V-2, Werner von Braun, was co-opted to work on the Apollo Space Programme to beat Russia to the moon and plant the Stars and Stripes. Von Braun, an outstanding technological innovator, in time became visible and popular with the American public through the leading role he took in this programme, to the point that he was due to be awarded the Presidential Medal of Freedom during the administration of Republican President Gerald Ford. But the idea was vetoed after his carefully sidestepped Nazi past was flagged up by one of Ford's senior advisors, David Gergen[15].

As part of 'Paperclip' Nazi scientists and technical experts were put to work on projects that included producing sarin and tabun nerve agents, synthetic rubber, ear thermometers, electromagnetic tape and electrical components. Notorious Nazis soon living and working in the US included Dr Heinz Schlicke, formerly Director of Naval Test Fields at Kiel, Gerhard Schrader and Otto Ambros of the German industrial giant IG Farben and ardent Nazi Kurt Debus, revealed as head of the Launch Operations Centre at Cape Canaveral and, along with 120 fellow German exiles, developer of the Saturn V launch vehicle [16]. Ambros, a former director of the manufacturing giant I G Farben, had been responsible for the industrial plant at Auschwitz and found guilty at the Nuremberg war crimes trials on the count of enslaving and murdering the civilian population.

If Operation Paperclip seemed ambitious and on an unprecedented scale, the Russian talent grab was on a whole other level. In October 1946, 'Operation Osoaviakhim' used 90 trains to transport some 5,000 German scientists and their families, along with all their belongings, to Kuybyshev in south eastern Russia. Set at the confluence of the Volga and Samara rivers, Kuybyshev, now known as Samara, was Russia's ninth largest city. Here, they 'voluntarily' were enrolled on a series of highly technical arms projects which required completion before they could return home [17]. Osoaviakhim was the concluding phase of a Russian initiative started in 1942 to acquire Nazi technological assets and skills. Specialised 'Gosfond' units, the so-called trophy brigade, had been set up to acquire German scientists and the content of their programmes. This move had been formalised by the Russian Government when it issued a decree (No: 874-366SS), ordering the Ministry of Aviation Industry under the supervision of the Head of the Soviet secret police in Germany, Ivan Serov, to deport 1400 German engineers and their families back to the Soviet Union.

To the scientists' astonishment, they soon discovered that the Russians had dismantled and moved the entire BMW factory at Stassfurt and the V2 rocket research and production centre at Mittelwerk Nordhausen and re-assembled them piece by piece. One of the co-opted scientists, Ferdinand Brandner, who had manufactured some of the most sophisticated jet engines in the world for Junkers during the war, found that even his desk within the reassembled factory in Kuybyshev had been put back in exactly the same way and in the same spot [18]. Brandner was to go on to produce the eponymous E-300 turbojet engine in Cairo, where he moved in 1959. It was used in the first Egyptian jet fighter, the HA-300, designed by Willy Messerschmitt for the Egyptian government as part of its secret aerospace programme.

Between them, the Americans, Russians, Argentinians, Spanish and Egyptians were all competing to sign up science and engineering talent which had furthered the rocket and aerospace programmes of the Third Reich during the war. But in the wider fields of military capacity building and training, special forces warfare, intelligence gathering, interrogation methodology, propaganda, information warfare and economic modelling, the full breadth of skills, knowledge and expertise deployed in the 12 year lifespan of the Third Reich's military state was now, to some degree, obtainable on the open market.

For Egypt, needing to rethink its military, armaments and security infrastructure following the disaster of the 1948 war with Israel over Palestine and the ongoing national stain of military occupation by the British, the potential of these resources had obvious if controversial attractions. But how would they tap into such a market? The answer to that question lay in a variety of sources and just a few key individuals. These included reigning British backed Egyptian monarch King Farouk I and subsequently General Muhammad Neguib and Colonel Gamal Abdel Nasser, leaders of the Free Officers Movement which assumed power in Egypt from July 1952.

There was at the end of the war a growing mythology around the international movement of former Nazis through the multiple 'rat lines' and other less formal networks. Over time, some of these proved tangible and others more fanciful. The Odessa organisation, cited in the testimony of Cesar Ugarte Jr as having been started in 1947 in Buenos Aires by Martin Bormann, has never been adequately proven by historians to exist as a standalone entity. Its name, nonetheless, is generally taken to be illustrative of a trend best described as a collective organisational effort amongst former SS members. Franz Stangl, the Austrian policeman in charge of Sobibor and Treblinka extermination camps, claimed when interviewed by Italian journalist Gitta Sereny in 1970 that Odessa did not exist. She found 'no smoking gun' [19]. Stangl and his family travelled via Damascus to Brazil, where in 1951 he got a job with car manufacturer BMW.[20]

However, more robust provenance can be attached to some others, amongst them the organisation 'Silent Help' (Stille Hilfe), set up by Baroness Helena Elizabeth, Princess von Eiserburg in Munich in 1951. The organisation is alleged to have had links with the so-called Vatican rat lines and had two bishops on its Board of Directors, Theophil Wurm of Würtemberg and Johannes Neuhäusler of Munich, along with ex-SS men Wilhelm Spengler and Heinrich Malz, the latter an aide to Nazi security chief Ernst Kaltenbrunner. The complex network was said to involve anti-Communist Catholics, the International Red Cross and also its Islamic equivalent, the Red Crescent [21]. Walter Rauff, high on the fugitive Nazi 'most wanted' lists as designer of the notorious Black Raven mobile execution vans widely deployed against Jews in eastern Europe, used Catholic sources in Rome to help him relocate first to Damascus and then Cairo in the late 1940s, and subsequently on to his end destination in Chile.

By 1948 Cairo, along with Syrian capital Damascus, had begun to feature on the map for Nazi escapers, most often as in the cases of Stangl and Rauff, as staging posts to destinations further afield. Others, amongst them Adolf Eichmann's personal assistant and 'best man' Alois Brunner, were to find steady employment and create a permanent base in one or the other. Over the course of the late 1940s and through the 1950s, as the scale and nature of Nasser's militarising ambitions became better defined, increasing numbers of former Nazi and Wehrmacht officers were to head to Cairo in order to fill the consequent vacancies for experienced advisers and experts as part of a German military mission. The organisation of this influx came inevitably through a variety of sources. One of these, flagged by the CIA in a report compiled in 1953, identified a centre in Munich run by 'colonial expert' Heinz Berthold through which veterans of the Wehrmacht and Waffen-SS were recruited for the armies of the Near East. Another headquarters was known as 'the German Committee' and was located in Beirut under the direction of Count Elmar von Hardenberg. The three-man committee he headed was supposed to screen German refugees entering Lebanon in order to prevent admission of Jewish agents, according to the report.[22]

The CIA believed that Count von Hardenberg had gone into Lebanon with a letter of recommendation from Haj Amin Al Husseini, a totemic Palestinian figure whose cultivation as a close ally was assiduously pursued under a policy established by German Foreign Minister Joachim von Ribbentrop. To formalise this pursuit of good relations, von Ribbentrop had assigned to the task an agent called Wilhelm Keppler, who was a member of the Wissenchaftliche Forschungs GMBH, a scientific research establishment and state corporation set up to cloak deals involving Jewish property and exploitation of occupied countries.

Conspicuous in its success at moving former Wehrmacht and Nazi fugitives around the international chess board was 'Die Spinne' (The Spider), an organisation set up and managed from the Spanish capital Madrid by two major post-war Nazi figures. Former intelligence chief on the eastern front, General Reinhard Gehlen and Special Forces commander Colonel Otto Skorzeny were both destined to exert considerable organisational and personal influence in the project to establish a German military footprint in Egypt and the countries of the Middle East. Skorzeny in particular was to go on to play a major role in the military training and rearmament of Egypt through the early 1950s, first as an adviser to King Farouk and then successively General Neguib and Nasser. As Johann von Leers and his wife and daughter boarded the plane that would take them from Buenos Aires to Cairo this effort was already well underway and growing in scale with every passing month.

Chapter Three
THE BLACK KNIGHTS IN PLAY

'The more I read the news from Egypt, the more I like the Neguib programme which I hope Ali Maher will express in constitutional form. We ought to help Neguib and Co all we can, unless they turn spiteful.'

Winston S Churchill, Prime Minister's Personal Minute, 26th August, 1952

On 13th February 1950 a newspaper reporter strolling along the Champs Élysées in Paris spotted Europe's most wanted man sitting brazenly outside a café drinking Pernod, accompanied by a girl. With great presence of mind and a nose for a scoop, he took a snapshot of the chatting couple. Thus he was able to both identify and place Otto Skorzeny, sometimes dubbed 'Hitler's Triggerman', sometimes 'the most dangerous man in Europe'. Skorzeny in the flesh presented an unmistakable figure, a six foot four titan weighing some 20 stone, with a face marked from ear to chin by a scar that was a souvenir of his early Austrian army duelling days. But his reputation more than matched his physical persona. Amongst other daring feats as commander of Hitler's Special Forces, this larger than life action hero had deployed gliders as part of 'Operation Oak' to rescue Italy's imprisoned leader Benito Mussolini from a windswept mountain top in the Gran Sasso raid of September 1943. He had worn an American uniform to lead a clandestine attack on US army units during the last ditch Battle of the Bulge in the Ardennes in 1944, codenamed Operation Greiff, an act that was later to be investigated as a war crime. To compound his formidable backstory Skorzeny had supposedly walked out unchallenged from Darmstadt Internment Camp in Germany in July 1948 having declared: 'I shall escape how and when I please, and you shall never find me.' [1]. In time, Skorzeny would be revealed as a ubiquitous intelligence agent, double agent, informant and 'go to' source for every government active in the region including Israel. Skorzeny and his networks would play a part in Egypt's move to build a modern military industrial complex and help it claim its place as the predominant Arab force and powerbase in the post-colonial Middle East

Now in the aftermath of the post-war realignment in Europe, when it was still possible for fugitives to bypass government bureaucracies struggling to keep up with the mass migration of refugees, missing paperwork and antiquated records, Skorzeny was known to be operating Die Spinne (The Spider), an escape network for former Nazi and German officers seeking to relocate from Europe. The operation was gaining increasing attention amongst Western intelligence agencies. Their information showed Skorzeny was running the operation in partnership with General Reinhard Gehlen, one of Hitler's most powerful wartime intelligence chiefs and the man who alone held the keys to the network of former Nazi agents still in place in post-war Russia and Communist East Germany. Finding Skorzeny and tracking his movements was thus significant on multiple levels.

The appearance of 'Scarface' Skorzeny in broad daylight on the Champs Élysées caused an immediate rash of newspaper headlines in France. The French dailies splashed on the shock and outrage that Hitler's 'No 1 killer' was at large in the French capital and the news was also avidly read across the Channel. The scandal caused two former British Special Forces officers to decide to track down Skorzeny, confront him and get a career-defining exclusive interview in the process. That same Saturday night, the two managed to get aboard a freight plane leaving London carrying frozen fish bound for the Paris restaurant trade and once in the French capital they checked into a hotel. The next day, venturing out to the Rue de Rivoli, they found they were featured in the English Sunday newspapers now on sale on Paris newsstands. Accompanying photos identified and billed them as 'the hunters of Scarface'. They had themselves been outed by a nosy English journalist in London.

One of the two soldiers turned reporters was Major William Stanley 'Billy' Moss, who himself was a legitimate contender for Boy's Own adventure magazine status. A Coldstream Guard and member of the Special Operations Executive (SOE) during the war, Moss had been responsible in April 1944, along with Major Patrick Leigh Fermor, for kidnapping General Heinrich Kreipe, the head of the German garrison in Crete and trekking back with him, assisted by Greek partisans, through the mountains to a secluded cove where they had boarded a boat for Cairo.

He was to write about this extraordinary mission after the war in his book 'Ill Met by Moonlight' [2], later turned into a film starring British actor Dirk Bogarde [3]. In their quest for Skorzeny, recounted in a later article for the BBC Listener Magazine [4], Moss and his companion Captain Michael Luke embarked on an ultimately fruitless chase across Europe, often in contact with representatives of The Spider and sometimes only a hair's breadth away from Skorzeny himself. On one occasion, they tracked him down to a hotel at St Germain-en-Laye just outside Paris to find that he had departed in haste two days previously. His hotel registration document gave his name as Rolf Steiner, an Austrian born in Vienna on 12th December 1909. The details echoed Skorzeny's own place and date of birth of 12th June 1908. They then followed a lead to the picturesque ski resort of Mégève south of Geneva where they were told that Rolf Steiner had left hurriedly 24 hours earlier, giving no forwarding address.

In time, tipped off that they had themselves become pawns in a much larger game being played by Western and Russian intelligence agencies, they nonetheless continued to follow up contacts in The Spider network, even meeting Skorzeny's blue-eyed girlfriend and learning the 'minutest details' of the organisation's structure. A letter that Moss wrote to Skorzeny and which he asked the network to pass on to the peripatetic and elusive Special Forces chief was eventually answered from Egypt where Skorzeny was staying in Heliopolis, an upscale suburb in the north-east of the Egyptian capital. Whilst he was finally to abandon the chase for the mercurial German, the wider significance of the Egyptian connection seems to have escaped Moss.

At the time, Skorzeny was establishing initial contact with the regime of Egypt's British backed monarch King Farouk I, still marginally on the throne and seeking German expertise to help him rebuild the country's military capacity after the defeat of the 1948 war with Israel. By now Skorzeny had already set up a permanent base for himself, his wife Ilse and The Spider network in Madrid, with the tacit approval of the Fascist sympathising Spanish government and helped by the Spanish Nazi organiser Clarita Stauffer. Through an informant who had been introduced to Skorzeny there sometime in October of 1950, the CIA learned that the Austrian was living at Calle Lopez de Hoyas 70, going by the name Rolf Steinbauer and passing himself off as an industrial engineer developing solar heat for use in heating houses and hot water [5]. In fact, according to the informant who was an adviser to the Spanish government on electronic landing and approach systems for Spanish airfields, Skorzeny may have been doing more than simply passing himself off as a heating engineer but actually embracing his new career, taking on a number of agencies for specialist German companies in the country. He certainly made no effort to keep a low profile in Madrid, opening an office in Mentora Street and enjoying cocktails on the roof of his flashy apartment in the city's exclusive El Viso neighbourhood.

The informant recorded his belief that Skorzeny moved to Madrid from Paris in August 1950 because of his fear of Communist reprisals, noting that there had already been five attempts on his life. At that time, it emerged, Skorzeny was also anxious to open up contacts with the American authorities to support 'a German group' which he professed to control, and which he imagined might become instrumental in any resistance movement required to stand up to a Russian invasion of post-war Germany [6]. Whilst Skorzeny was physically impressive and possessed a massively energetic and dominating character, the CIA noted that it was his wife Ilse Countess Finckenstein who might be the more intellectually astute of the couple. In time, Ilse was to become a confidante of Gamal Abdel Nasser, Egypt's future President and the dominant figure in the Middle East during the Cold War years.

It was also significant that Ilse's principal sponsor, protector and 'uncle', Hjalmar Schacht, President of the Reichsbank and Economics Minister under Hitler in the 1930s, started a private import-export bank in West Germany after the war and became a visitor to Cairo and adviser to the Egyptian government on economic and industrial development, as he did to a number of other governments in the Middle East including Syria. Schacht's name was to be linked in both media and political contexts as an important yet somehow unsavoury figure pulling the financial levers that enabled the development of Egypt's manufacturing and industrial base through the 1950s.

Skorzeny and the Egyptian Mission

Otto Skorzeny was to become a pivotal figure in the deployment and operation of German military expertise in post war Egypt and he fulfilled a number of direct and indirect roles in his efforts there to broaden his influence, practical input and earning power. Alongside intimate knowledge of the Wehrmacht's special operations and sabotage tactics learned on both the western and eastern fronts where he had commanded 150 Waffen SS Panzer Group, he could act as a signpost and rallying point for former colleagues with skills that were in demand in a Middle Eastern marketplace which was expanding. He was in effect both a market maker and prime mover who was in a unique position to help service the demand for a broad mix of military specialists and resources, from infantry and tank professionals to guerrilla training, intelligence gathering and arms manufacture. In doing so, his organisational power, motivational skill and personal charm were to exert a meaningful influence on the leaders of the Revolutionary Command Council which assumed power in Egypt.

Britain was not at first set against Neguib and Nasser's revolutionary regime in Egypt, prepared more or less to wait and see what this new era might deliver for the Egyptian people and thus for Britain and the US. British Prime Minister Winston Churchill wrote in a note in August 1952: 'I am not opposed to the policy of giving Neguib a good chance provided he shows himself to be a friend. I hope he will do something for the fellahin, but we must not be afraid of him or be driven by the threats of cowards and curs from discharging our duty of maintaining the freedom of the Suez Canal for all nations until we can hand it over to some larger, more powerful combination'[7].

But the British government was less certain of the motives or mandates of German military advisers, among them some defiantly unrepentant Nazis, hired by the new Egyptian government. The British political and military establishment felt a certain visceral paranoia about the potential of these authoritarian thinkers to act against British interests in the country and more widely across the region. This was especially true in the case of the British military occupation of the 120 mile long Suez Canal Zone, where a permanent garrison of up to 80,000 British forces still provoked deep anger and resentment amongst the new government and the Egyptian people who wanted an end to the permanent foreign military presence on their soil.

Skorzeny travelled back and forth from Spain to Cairo as surreptitiously as possible. Like thousands of other former Nazis, he was declared entnazifiziert (denazified) in absentia in 1952 by a West German government arbitration Board, which meant that he could also now travel from Spain into other Western countries on a special Nansen passport for stateless persons. His movements were regularly tracked by US and British diplomats and intelligence services. In 1955, the year before the Suez crisis, his name appears in an Annex to a memorandum prepared by the British Embassy in Bonn for the US government, providing details of known German advisers to the Egyptian army since 1953. Listed as one of nine active arms dealers, Skorzeny is said to have visited Egypt from November 1952 to January 1953 offering arms and advice to the Egyptian government on commando training.

The CIA tracked one of his visits to Cairo between 13th and 29th January 1953, when it reported that General Neguib invited him to establish an Egyptian Military Academy for Air and to direct the formation of commando forces, both requests which he refused, according to the agency. 'Skorzeny nevertheless may well be acting as consultant on this general program. Two training centres for Egyptian commandos already exist, it is said, where recruits are being instructed by German officers, for possible guerrilla warfare against the British', the agency reported [8]. Skorzeny was also reported by the British to have carried out a reconnaissance visit to the Canal Zone to advise on commando and sabotage tactics [9].

These visits were corroborated by further British government reports of his activities, one top secret Annex to a memo in

May 1953 confirming that 'there is abundant evidence that German ex-officers and technicians are training and advising the Egyptians at all levels. A reliable report also states that recently some Germans, including Otto Skorzeny, who came to Egypt on a commercial mission, carried out a reconnaissance of the Canal Zone' [10]. The British War Office recorded at the time that an experimental brigade group of the Egyptian Army, with a strong team of German instructors, had been stationed in Huckstep Barracks on the eastern outskirts of Cairo, possibly to be used in the role of a mobile battle group. It also noted that about 1,000 armed soldiers from Muslim Brotherhood regiments, led by Germans, had already been infiltrated into the Canal Zone [11]. The hand of Skorzeny is seen everywhere in the insidious infiltration into the Canal Zone by irregular forces, some 'disguised as civilians in *jalabiyyas*'.

In truth, Skorzeny was perhaps uniquely qualified to both advise on and direct sabotage operations in military conflict zones. His experience was extensive and officially recognised and documented as such. In its appraisal of the German Intelligence Service compiled in 1945, the Counter Intelligence War Room at the Supreme Headquarters of the Allied Expeditionary Force identified Skorzeny as Head of Sabotage in Militaerisches Amt IV (Foreign Intelligence) reporting to Walter Schellenburg and Head of Sabotage for Militaerisches Amt (Military Intelligence) under the overall command of Ernst Kaltenbrunner[12].

The document confirms that by the summer of 1944, the organisation of all German sabotage and political subversion had come under the control of Otto Skorzeny who, at that time, was already Head of VIS, the sabotage section of Amt V1. Skorzeny had his headquarters in Schloss Friedenthal near Oranienburg just north of Berlin. The function of Skorzeny's sabotage services was twofold: to threaten Allied lines of communication by sabotage and fomenting political trouble; and to mount military operations of a special type which the regular army would not normally undertake.

To that end, he had at his disposal three entire units dispersed throughout Germany, SS Jaegerbataillon 502, SS Jagdverbaende and the Frontaufklaerungs-Kommandos and Trupps of Mil Amt. D[13]. But this former Obersturmbannführer in the Waffen SS, though he stood out from the crowd, was simply the outlier for a phenomenon whose reach was to extend much wider and deeper into post-revolutionary Egypt. Furthermore, his direct engagement in the country's affairs was not simply tactical but closely aligned with the changing nature of Egypt's status as a sovereign power and its regional leadership in the prospective family of Arab states.

The Arab League and its First Approach

The crisis precipitated by the Arab defeat in the first Arab-Israeli War of 1948 over Palestine provided a moment of catharsis and the trigger for deep psychological and existential changes in Egypt's world view. The war itself, in which the Egyptian army was intimately engaged and during which Gamal Abdel Nasser made his reputation as an officer on the front line by holding the much fought over Faluja Pocket, endured from 15th May 1948, the day after the creation of the State of Israel, until 10th March, 1949. At the end of the war, the peace settlement that followed a comprehensive Israeli victory left the new Jewish state in control of 77 per cent of the land mass of Palestine. Only Jordan, which by agreement with the Israelis had moved its forces into the West Bank and East Jerusalem emerged with any temporary territorial gain, a move which was the subject of subsequent objections by Egypt.

The other states in the Arab coalition, among them Iraq, Lebanon, Saudi Arabia, Syria and Yemen were left militarily weakened and with less political leverage as a result of the defeat. Egypt in particular, with its north eastern border abutting Gaza and the Sinai Peninsula to the east was left more exposed and vulnerable to the ambitions and reach of the newly proven Israeli military juggernaut. The Egyptian monarchy, traditionally enabled and supported by the British and now increasingly opposed by the Americans, had presided over what Egyptians perceived as a military debacle and national shame.

Egypt's ruler at this time of national crisis, King Farouk I, would not necessarily have topped a list of candidates tasked with achieving national redemption. Often lampooned as a lover of the high life (he had 1,000 bespoke shirts in his wardrobe and a large collection of Bentleys, all painted red so that Egyptian police could identify him when speeding), he was the 10th ruler of Egypt from the Muhammad Ali dynasty and the penultimate

King of Egypt and the Sudan, succeeding his father Fuad I in 1936. As events transpired, he was soon to be overthrown in the Revolution of the Free Officers in July 1952 and forced to abdicate in favour of his infant son Ahmed Fuad, whose rights and status were preserved in the short term by a Regency Council.

However, one immediate outcome of Egypt's military defeat in early 1949 was the excuse it provided for Farouk to progress a plan to carry out radical reforms in the army, which by evidence and consensus was simply not up to the task. This process of reform began immediately in the aftermath of the war with the sacking of Muhammad Haider Pasha, Egypt's military commander-in-chief and Minister of War and his cohort of senior officers who were deemed responsible for the defeat. Rather than build back the armed forces in isolation, Farouk and his government were initially attracted by the potential benefits of adopting a more collegiate approach to the development of regional hard power. The guiding principle behind this thinking was the modernist and politically fashionable notion of pan Arabism, an idea which at the time encompassed the strategy of Arabic speaking countries within the region acting together to achieve greater critical mass across the economic, political and military spectrum. Part of this analysis rested on the creation of a more unified post-war Arab powerbase that could challenge Western imperialism, end colonialism, face off growing Communist ambitions in the region and provide an effective response to the new threat of Israel and its ally the United States.

This idea first became formally encapsulated in the creation of the Arab League, which came into being on 22nd March 1945 following the adoption of the Alexandria Protocol in 1944. Alongside extended economic and political co-operation, the League signed a mutual defence treaty, in part to stop Jordan's agreement with Israel over the division of Palestinian land after the 1948 war. This was the altered landscape which provided the rationale and trigger for Farouk and his generals to look outwards for the kind of professional support they felt was needed to help rebuild Egypt's military and security state in a way that could meet the new post 1948 realities of the region. There were, though, other compelling forces in play at the time which helped drive Farouk to seek external help. Britain's Military Mission to Egypt was withdrawn in 1948, a major cause of Egypt turning towards the Germans as advisers to its armed forces.

There had been deep ties connecting British military leadership, equipment and methodology with the development of Egypt's own military capability for half a century. This relationship had started in 1889 at the Battle of Tukshi near the Sudanese Egyptian border, where a British trained Egyptian army had successfully defeated an invading dervish force. Thereafter the Egyptian army had been further developed by the British to comprise a total of 15,000 men, combining infantry, cavalry, artillery and transport. A military academy was set up to train Egyptian officers to fight alongside a number of British officers seconded to the Foreign Office on two-year contracts. In 1937, Britain sent a mission comprising 32 officers and NCOs to Egypt. By 1939, this had grown to 51 officers and 98 NCOs. Part of the mission's remit had been to establish training schools for artillery, armour and engineering, along with founding a staff college to train the first cadres of senior Egyptian officers. By 1947, it was estimated that the Egyptian army possessed 188 of this new generation of qualified staff officers. After the war, however, it was rumoured that some disgruntled Egyptian army officers targeted the British military mission, accusing it of providing Egypt with low quality armaments and poor training in an attempt to dominate the Egyptian armed forces.

In 1951, three years after the British Military Mission had departed, the governing Wafd Party unilaterally abrogated the Anglo-Egyptian Treaty of 1936, which limited the British to 10,000 troops plus auxiliaries in the Suez Canal Zone. This caused a further loss of opportunities for the Egyptian military to secure British technical advice [14]. However, it was not until the Anglo-Egyptian Agreement of 1954 that Britain agreed to withdraw all of its troops.

The arrival of Mr Goldstein

'The Arab League Secretariat determined that the best elements and the ones who were most knowledgeable, in fact the authors of modern mobile warfare, were the Germans,' according to Mahmoud Sabet, son of Arab League spokesman Adel Sabet, a cousin of King Farouk and the man charged with carrying out the mission [15]. In due course, acting for the Arab League, Sabet began to cast around for a senior member of the German Wehrmacht who would carry sufficient authority and experience to analyse Egypt's military predicament, assess its challenges and thus be qualified to make recommendations as to the make-up, training and deployment of future armed forces.

He found and appointed Artur Schmitt, a professional soldier and former senior commander in Germany's Afrikakorps. Schmitt had fought valiantly in the Libyan desert during the war, subsequently being awarded the Knight's Cross. Promoted to Generalmajor in late 1941, he was posted to North Africa and served under 'the Desert Fox' Erwin Rommel, initially in charge of Rückwärtiges Armeegebiet 556 (556th Rear Army Area) for Panzergruppe Afrika. In November, he became the commander of the Bardia Axis Division in the Sollum-Bardia sector. In January 1942, following a prolonged offensive against Bardia by South African and New Zealand units, Schmitt was forced to surrender his forces to the South Africans, the first German general to do so in the Second World War. He became a prisoner of war and following his capture was held in Canada until 1946, when he was transferred to Britain, finally being released in 1948 [16]. Schmitt, a rather upright, severe and unsmiling figure arrived in Cairo on 11th July 1949, using the enigmatic name 'Herr Goldstein' and checked into a modest hotel in a nondescript Cairo suburb. His first request was to undertake a study of the conditions of the Egyptian army on the ground, which he rapidly criticised for its organisation into entirely separate teams for tanks, artillery and infantry.

In his view this tactic alone would make it difficult to hamper any attack and he judged the strategy to be incompatible with methods of modern warfare. He also requested to see all the reports relating to the war with Israel in order to carry out a thorough analysis of the defeat.

Schmitt quickly started to draw some initial conclusions from his analysis. None of them were particularly flattering and thus made uneasy listening for the Egyptian High Command. The main orders issued by army commander Haidar Pasha were rejected as mistaken, the overall strategy was labelled as wrongheaded and he accused those managing the war in Palestine of having been conducting it by 19th century methods. In a dramatic turn of events, Schmitt asked to visit the Golan Heights personally to see conditions for himself. In due course he was able to look out from the high plateau directly into Syria in order to assess the battlefield on the Syrian front [17]. After his trip to the Golan Heights, Schmitt wrote in a letter to Sabet: 'Defeat (in 1949) was a consequence of Egyptian leaders' inability to take advantage of the early stages of fighting to wipe the State of Israel off the map with a blitzkrieg of two weeks at most'.

In more positive tones, Schmitt proceeded to draw up initial recommendations to rebuild a much stronger, sounder Egyptian army founded on modern operating procedures, using up to date strategy and arguing for massively upgraded technical capability in armour, artillery and the air force, proposing an inventory of no fewer than 2,000 aircraft. However, Schmitt's recommendations, founded though they were in military orthodoxy and considerable experience, were at first side lined and then blocked. Egypt's generals, many of whom were themselves deeply implicated in the inefficiencies and corruption of the pre-war Egyptian military, could not get past his scathing criticisms and commenced a co-ordinated campaign to lobby against him, impeaching both his character and professional credibility. Schmitt in turn became disaffected by what he saw as the machinations of the generals to undermine him and his mission. He denounced the campaign in 1950, resigned his position and returned to Germany. This signalled the end of Schmitt's direct engagement with the question of Egypt's military capacity and the Arab League's 'Arab army'.

He was, though, destined to be a controversial figure back home in West Germany. In 1966, he became a candidate for the far-right National Democratic Party (NPD) in the Bavarian state parliament and his campaign material used controversial images of him in his Wehrmacht uniform, which unashamedly featured swastikas on the cap badge and the Knight's Cross.

The Spider's Web Expands

At the same time as Otto Skorzeny was making his first fact-finding mission to Cairo, the 'Spider' organisation was also extending its sphere of influence into the United States and Latin America. Immediately after the war, spymaster Reinhard Gehlen had spent time in the United States being debriefed by the CIA about the network of agents he had built in communist Russia and the future East Germany during his time as Lieutenant-General and Intelligence Chief of the Wehrmacht Foreign Armies East Military Intelligence Service. First posted to the Eastern Front in 1942, Gehlen was preparing estimates on the enemy order of battle and had reached the conclusion as early as 1943 that the German cause on the Eastern Front had already been lost. Gehlen's pessimistic analysis had reached Hitler himself, who relieved him of his command in the last days of the war [18].

Aware of the value of the information he had collected on the Soviet order of battle and the network of agents who had been feeding it to him, Gehlen had consulted with senior members of his staff and made plans to continue their efforts against the Russians after the inevitable capitulation of the German Army, but in co-operation with the American Army. 'General Gehlen consequently cached his files in the Bavarian Alps and withdrew to that area in the final days of the war. He subsequently surrendered to the Americans and after his initial POW debriefings presented his plan for the continued collection of order of battle information of the Soviet Armies', the official US report stated [19]. In the account of Gehlen's initial interrogation written in 1952 by his interrogator John R Boker, the American confirmed that the process of recovering Gehlen's documents took two weeks of physical digging.

'Operating from the 3rd Army Headquarters at Bad Toelz and the 3rd Army Intelligence Center at Freising, we were able to locate these men and through them the documents which they had concealed between floors of remote foresters' lodges and buried or otherwise cached. By the middle of 1945 we had succeeded in reconstituting General Gehlen's key members and staff, all of his important documents and were very much aware of the goldmine we had found', he wrote [20].

Managing to convince his US captors that the deployment of the Soviet armies so deep inside Europe constituted a threat to Western civilisations, Gehlen persuaded his case officer Boker to fly him and his whole team back to Washington in August 1945 for further debriefings. The 'goldmine' Gehlen had with him in the plane included files on Soviet tank production, the strength of the Soviet Army, Soviet manpower studies and estimates of probable Soviet demobilisation policy. It was in discussion with the Gehlen team at the Interrogation Center at Ft Washington Overlook at Alexandria, Virginia that the US took the decision to let him continue his efforts against the Soviets. Funded with $US 2.5million of government cash, he reunited his units and formed the Gehlen Organisation which he ran between 1946 and 1949.

Thereafter, with the support of the CIA, he 'devoted his full energies to legalising his organisation as the West German Federal Intelligence Service' in 1956. He thus became the founding President of West Germany's BND intelligence agency (Bundesnachrichtendienst) and a pivotal figure in the clandestine ideological manoeuvring which underpinned the unfolding Cold War struggle in Europe. Gehlen was considered by insiders to be the principal architect of the new Egyptian Intelligence Service, someone who did not himself appear very often but who had a direct hand in appointing his partner Otto Skorzeny to take a more active role. A small, intense looking man, whose receding hair and slight frame gave him a somewhat unmilitary bearing, Gehlen might be best described as nondescript and unremarkable, a perfect cover for the intelligence business. This quiet, unassuming family man whose principal passion had been for riding horses remained over the course of his turbulent life enigmatic and largely reticent, judged to be 'in all things essentially conservative'.

As quiet and unassuming as Reinhard Gehlen may have been, Otto Skorzeny was quite the opposite. This giant personality blazed a trail across multiple continents during his career as a gun for hire and the public face of The Spider network alongside other shady post-war Nazi networks such as the Bruderschaft, always on the move, open for business and looking to sign up new clients. He made several appearances in Argentina, where he was pictured with Juan Perón, with whom he allegedly held discussions about the establishment of a Fourth Reich and for whom he acted as an adviser and consultant; in Ireland in the 1950s where he bought a house in Curragh, County Kildare; in his post-war base in Madrid; and in Egypt, where both he and his wife appeared increasingly at ease with his Egyptian employers in Cairo.

Skorzeny and The Spider attracted some unlikely admirers and supporters on the way. One of them was Harold Keith Thompson, a mysterious New Jersey born businessman and PR man who spent much of his time in the late 1940s and early 1950s as the principal US advocate for the network [21].

Thompson, something of an eccentric already known to US intelligence agencies, was allegedly a Nazi agent in the United States, having been appointed via a special order signed by Hitler himself. Through his right-wing political and lobbying activities, Thompson became an acquaintance of Skorzeny, about whom he remarked: 'he was not an intellectual. He was a get-it-done type, a soldier. Very daring. He would take on anything.' According to Thompson: 'Skorzeny played a significant role after the war in the escape routes….'

It was also noteworthy that in 1952 Thompson set up the US Committee for the Freedom of Major General Otto-Ernst Remer and began bombarding anyone who would listen with announcements and press releases advocating on his behalf [22]. Remer was leader of the controversial West German Socialist Reich Party (SRP), which attracted many former Nazis and neo-Nazis. He had come to global attention as the officer who had broken up the conspiracy to assassinate Hitler and other leading Nazi officials by countermanding orders issued to arrest Josef Goebbels and others during the July 1944 plot, a dramatic day in the German capital on which he and Skorzeny had first met.

In March 1953, he left West Germany for Egypt, sidestepping a further prison sentence for rabble-rousing, and arrived in Cairo without a visa, invited by head of the German Military Mission in Cairo, Dr Wilhelm Voss with the support of the Egyptian Consul-General in Hamburg, to help train Egyptian commando units for Canal Zone fighting [23]. In Cairo, he was helped most immediately by Major Gerhard Mertins, paratroop advisor to the Egyptian Ministry for War, at whose house at 7, Qasr Al-Qahira, Kubbah Palace District, he first stayed.

Between them Voss, Mertins and Skorzeny were to become central figures in the new era of German military influence in Egypt as the 1950s started to unfold. Remer, however, was at first refused permission to stay in the country and was evicted. Under an assurance provided by Otto Skorzeny, he was temporarily allowed back whilst he tried to organise employment in Spain or South America. In September 1953, giving the Egyptian secret police the slip, Remer 'went to a place of entertainment in Heliopolis. He became completely intoxicated and caused a scandal. He was arrested by the police and the Egyptian authorities demanded that he leave the country immediately' [24]. Remer's vulpine good looks, his fastidiousness in dress and petulant and narcissistic personality made him easy to dislike but hard to ignore. Despite repeatedly falling foul of the authorities, he seems to have been finally accepted, given a small stipend of 50 Egyptian pounds per month (worth $US 138 at the time) and gone to work for the Egyptian government on establishing an Egyptian system 'similar to that of the Nazis in Germany'.

As well as the Americas, The Spider network reached into the Soviet bloc, attracting friends in East Germany. At the same time, Jewish NGOs in the United States were tracking Thompson's activities. One of them, Prevent World War 111, reported that the firm Dürer Verlag, publisher of the Nazi newspaper Der Weg (The Way) had a United Nations correspondent in New York: 'he is H Keith Thompson, describing himself as a journalist and public relations counsel' [25]. The NGO reported that on October 11th 1956Thompson sent a telegram to Admiral Doenitz 'to mark the occasion of his release from 11 years of illegal confinement by the Allies for war crimes'. In this telegram, Thompson allegedly referred to the 'despicable Nuremberg proceedings brought about by the criminal co-guilt of the USA and world Jewry'[26].

Claims, counter claims, allegations and rumours were to follow closely behind Skorzeny throughout his extraordinary life, both during the Second World War and long after it. Perhaps because of his unsavoury associations, questionable alliances and active interventions, he remained a figure of enduring interest and source of concern for all those whose radar screens he chose to cross. Already a longstanding asset for the CIA, in 1964 Skorzeny was recruited by the Israeli Mossad intelligence agency to provide information on German rocket scientists and engineers working on Egyptian arms projects. Mossad agent Avraham Ahituv in time confirmed that he had recruited Skorzeny in September that year in a Madrid restaurant where Skorzeny had agreed to 'an exchange of views' under which he would provide the necessary information in return for a valid Austrian passport, a writ of lifetime immunity from prosecution and a price on top of that. Thus Europe's most wanted man in time embarked on a secret operation to betray his former colleagues which remained hidden for years. Claiming that he was gathering a team of former SS officers to plan the implementation of a Fourth Reich, Szkorzeny leant on the German scientists to provide details of the missile programme by invoking their secret Wehrmacht oaths, a strategy that largely succeeded in giving the Israelis what they wanted [27].

Later on in the 1960s, Skorzeny is said to have set up the Paladin Group, which he envisioned 'as an international directorship of strategic assault personnel that would straddle the watershed between paramilitary operations carried out by troops in uniform and the political warfare which is conducted by civilian agents' [28]. Refused a passport to live in Ireland where he had bought a home and thought he might settle, an unrepentant and defiantly Nazi supporting Skorzeny died of lung cancer on 5th July 1975 in Madrid, aged 67. In 2011, his personal archive containing over 2,000 documents, press cuttings, home movies, letters and official papers and that of his wife Ilsa were put up for the sale by the Spanish family to whom they had been bequeathed and bought by a US writer, Ralf Ganis. Many of their secrets have yet to be revealed, including the details of Skorzeny's post-war recruitment by the CIA and the alleged involvement of the Spider network in the assassination in 1963 of US President John F Kennedy. Amongst those secrets may lie further evidence that reveals the true extent of his post-war involvement in Egypt's internal affairs.

Interviewed in 1973 at his holiday home in Majorca in the Balearic Islands, Otto Skorzeny made no attempt to sidestep his Nazi allegiances or his past: 'I accept the fact that, as is the obligation of every soldier, I helped prolong the war by carrying out orders. It will be history that decides if I was right in doing that. Enough time has not passed. But of course, I don't personally regret it. I can assure you that I would make exactly the same choices.' [29]

The defeat of Nazi Germany signalled for Skorzeny the end of his professional army career and the start of a precarious life on the move as an internee, sometime mercenary, intelligence agent, businessman, powerbroker, networker, conspirator and disruptor. It must at times have seemed to this inveterate adventurer and risk taker that his immediate prospects were bleak. But no more than two years after establishing an alternative life in Madrid and making his first exploratory visit to Cairo, his horizons had become massively expanded. In Egypt, he had found a country whose new leaders and their high ambitions, their organisational conceits and administrative weaknesses perfectly suited his rare combination of talents, knowledge and esprit, an almost miraculous conjunction of timing, location and opportunity in which he could put them all to good use.

Chapter Four
DR VOSS TAKES CHARGE

'The presence of the Germans provides the Council of the Revolutionary Command with just that amount of confidence which might well lead them into dangerous ventures.'

British Chiefs of Staff Committee,
C.O.S (53) Memoranda 201-290, Vol 111, 1953

The departure of Artur Schmitt in 1950 was a setback to King Farouk's plans to advance Egypt's military renaissance, exposing in the process some of the more intractable views and vested interests in the upper echelons of the armed forces. Too many of the old guard remained hidebound by tradition and personally threatened by the uncertainties of reform. This initial roadblock did not deter him. As he cast around for successors to Schmitt he was already working on plans to create an armaments industry in Egypt to fuel the expanded military machine he had in mind. This manufacturing revolution was to include the design and construction of the country's first fighter jet aircraft and ballistic missiles, both weapons to which he attached symbolic significance and which he felt might provide a game changer in the region's new balance of power. In the Spring of 1952, just before the military coup, Farouk entered into an arrangement to set up an independent company to manage the construction of jet engines, rockets and jet aircraft. The new venture known by its French acronym CERVA (Compagnie des Engins à Reaction Pour Vol Accéleré) was incorporated as a joint military-civilian firm with research and development facilities located at the Almaza airbase outside Cairo. CERVA had a Board of directors headed by a low profile and generally elusive Frenchman, known as the Comte de Lavison[1].

Over the course of 1950 and 1951, German outliers including the professional soldiers Otto Skorzeny, Artur Schmitt and the paratroop commander Gerhard Mertins had found their way through a variety of networks including the German Committee in Lebanon to the Egyptian capital, where they successively stepped in to fill the gap left by the withdrawal of the British Military Mission in 1948. This trend was acknowledged by the British Chiefs of Staff Committee, which registered in 1953 its awareness of German advice being increasingly sought by the Egyptians at the time [2].

It judged, however, that this influence was at first occasional rather than systematic and did not coalesce into a coherent strategic force until the military coup of the Free Officers in July 1952 forced the abdication of King Farouk. 'Thereafter, the military regime has come to place an increasing value on their services', it recorded in an internal analysis [3].

Within days of the military coup on 23thJuly 1952, the new regime under General Muhammad Neguib had created a government agency called the Central Planning Board to co-ordinate a programme of military reconstruction. It offered former Nazi and SS Standartenführer Dr Fritz Wilhelm Voss, a past Chairman of the Hermann-Goering-Werke in Germany and wartime head of the prestigious Skoda Werks munitions factory in Pilsen a job as its Director and as lead consultant to the War Ministry. Dr Voss explained his remit thus: 'the Germans are in Egypt to help in the building of factories, to conduct research and to train the forces on land, at sea and in the air'[4]. This was true though somewhat paraphrased the full story. At the time, the British did not have comprehensive information on the overall numbers or individuals to be employed in this work by the Egyptian Ministry of War & Marine, and it took them some while to find out the detail. The structure of the Central Planning Board was simple. It comprised two basic elements. The first, under the direct control of Voss, was to operate in the military sphere with the support of General Wilhelm Fahrmbacher, the distinguished and highly experienced former artillery general in the Wehrmacht, who had fought in western France until the bitter end of the war. Dr Voss' main concern was the recruitment and direction of the advisory group, in particular with arms manufacturing and research. General Fahrmbacher was to be in charge of training the Egyptian ground forces, para-military forces and guerrilla units. The British considered rightly that, of the two, Voss would wield more influence with the new Revolutionary Command Council because he would be running a military planning office. A third operation, more random and not formally directed by the Central Planning Board was the involvement of former German prisoners-of-war and mercenaries 'who may not be directly under General Fahrmbacher and are being utilised in unknown numbers by the Egyptians for the training and in some cases leading of guerrilla and sabotage groups' [5].

At first, the British thought there were some 80 Germans employed by the new Central Planning Board but based on reports that the Egyptians were paying a monthly bill of 13,000 Egyptian pounds for this expertise (about £411,000 today), the initial estimate was revised upwards. Recruitment was handled through the Egyptian Consulate-General in Frankfurt, co-ordinated with a German recruitment mission. British assessments of the recruitment process were of the view that no East Germans were involved and that the West German government had little knowledge of what was going on and, even if they had, no way of controlling it. This lack of knowledge within the West German Federal Government about events involving its nationals in Egypt and their roles as military advisers, alongside an apparent lack of will to act upon it in any case, was to become a major issue in Anglo-German relations. In due course this blind-spot was to be the subject of a meeting in London on 5th May 1953 between British Prime Minister Winston Churchill and West German Chancellor Konrad Adenauer, at which Adenauer finally committed to try and bring some tangential influence to bear on the military advisers despite the prevailing official view at the time that they were private citizens delivering on purely commercial overseas contracts. Adenauer's West German government stressed to Churchill at the meeting that the advisers and experts were in no way an extension or instrument of West German foreign policy in Egypt or the Middle East.

From its initial attempts to identify individuals in the group, the British believed that most of the German recruits were former professional soldiers of the officer class with no especially strong political associations. There were however a number of ex-Nazis and SS officers, among them Dr Voss's own assistant Colonel Sepp Tiefenbacher, a former SS Standartenführer, and Dr Rolf Engel, a rocket scientist, former joint head of the research centre at Skoda's Pilsen factory and a Hauptsturmführer in the Waffen SS. The Germans were in Egypt not for love of the Egyptians, the assessment stated, but 'many find in their work an outlet for their organising ability. Some are simply adventurers who are prepared to work for a Government which values their services and gives them easy money. Finally, they may have the feeling that the British are on their way out and that there is chance of re-establishing the German position in the Middle East '[6].

Big Picture Thinking

As with many adviser client relationships, the one struck between Egypt's new military hierarchy and Dr Wilhelm Voss in its initial stages ascended a steep curve of customer delight before it plateaued in 1954 and then descended in July of the same year into increasing acrimony and disillusionment. Voss was a proven organiser and industrial heavy hitter, a man who was capable on one hand of big picture thinking and on the other of retaining an impressive command of the detail, a skill set with which Egyptian management culture at the time was not widely blessed. An engineer by training, Dr Voss was hyper efficient, knowledgeable and above all industrious.

Voss took charge of an initial group of some 30 scientists, arms specialists and technical experts in the first wave of arrivals. They were employed across the spectrum of Egypt's nascent arms industry as advisers to the Development Directorate of the Ministry of War and Marine. Alongside the Ministry, the Physikalische Arbeitgemeineschaft (FAG) organisation was set up in 1951 to provide a vehicle through which elements of the arms manufacturing business could be channelled. Armaments advisers in Voss' team identified on a British list supplied to the Americans in 1955 included rocket scientist Dr Rolf Engel, Kurt Hanisch who had served on the V2 rocket development programme at Peenemünde, chemist and high explosives expert Professor Dr Georg Romer and ballistics and munitions expert Dr H Andrea, a wartime employee of the German Ministry of War Production and adviser to German industrial giant I G Farben [7]. These experts were spread across a number of facilities, including rocket and aircraft production at Egypt's two aircraft factories at Helwan and Heliopolis and a small arms manufacturing plant in a Cairo suburb with the cover name of 'the Masr Car Company'. They were also involved in boosting the local production of shoe mines and improved types of flame throwers. In time, Voss was to bring some order to these activities and involve himself closely in importing German systems and processes to help establish the new Egyptian armed forces operating manual.

Though experienced and efficient, Voss proved to be a polarising and abrasive figure who was to make powerful enemies in the Egyptian regime, amongst them future President Gamal Abdel Nasser himself. After the war, Voss' name first appears in a coded message from the Headquarters (HQ) of the Ninth Allied Infantry Division on 25th June 1946. Officers there issued a request for him to be picked up from his home in Tegernsee, Bavaria and transferred to a civilian internment enclosure in Munich codenamed 'Dustbin'. Whilst a guest at Dustbin, where he was in the hands of the Enemy Personnel Exploitation Section of the Allied Field Information Agency ('T' Force), he compiled two reports, one on details of the mines which had been produced at the Skoda Combine Werks and a second concerning compasses at the Bruenner Combine Werks. Voss was subsequently asked in March 1947 to provide further details to supplement both of these reports, one concerning what more he knew about the supply of technicians from Skoda to supervise the emplacement of coast defence and heavy static guns supplied to Czechoslovakia and other countries [8]. By the time the request was sent Voss had been transferred again, this time to the International Military Tribunal in Nuremberg where he was also to receive medical attention for an undisclosed condition [9].

Dr Voss was an unrepentant Nazi and convinced Nationalist, according to British assessments. His political record was relieved by his apparently humane behaviour whilst at Skoda, the primary reason why the Czechs released him after the war. However, he experienced great difficulty in passing through the denazification process because as an arms manufacturer he was classed as a war criminal. In the summer of 1950 Voss was finally tried and sentenced to five years' deprivation of his civil rights plus two years imprisonment as a war criminal, but was successful in appealing this sentence. He visited Egypt for the first time in April 1951 and returned there later the same year having entered into a two-year contract with the Egyptian government [10].

In addition to his role in setting up arms manufacturing and research facilities in Egypt as head of the Central Planning Board, Voss was responsible for recruitment and deployment of suitable experts to populate and deliver the strategy. It was in this aspect of his role that he started to encounter problems and where his abrasive style might have contributed to his upending. According to a German ex-Abwehr informant in Cairo, Voss fell out with Colonel Ernst Zolling, principal adviser on intelligence affairs to the Central Planning Board. Zolling was sacked in early 1954, and Voss was instructed to find a successor in October 1953. Zolling sent highly damaging reports about Voss and his coterie to the Gehlen Organisation in Germany, a factor which may in turn have influenced his Egyptian paymasters. As a substitute for Zolling, Voss managed to recruit Dr Joachim Deumling, a former SS Obersturmbannführer and officer in the Reichsicherheitshauptamt (RHSA), the Nazi Party security establishment which operated the Gestapo. Deumling was subsequently posted to the Egyptian Ministry of the Interior where he worked to Colonel Zakaria Mohieddin, head of Egypt's first intelligence agency, the Egyptian General Intelligence Directorate. According to the CIA, Deumling's work came in for high praise from Zakaria, who was receiving sufficient credit from it that a shift in the balance of power of the Egyptian ruling clique may have resulted. Deumling kept his journey to Cairo as low profile as possible, beyond the sight of the Allies, eventually being joined there by his wife Liselotte and three daughters Ingrun, Grauke and Gisela [11].

In 1953, Voss was floating the idea of starting a Nasser Youth organisation along the lines of the Hitler Youth, as well as starting up an overall Egyptian security authority. He was also in the process of proving the efficacy of regulations for Egyptian infantry training, which were being tried out by the third battalion of the Egyptian Test Combat Brigade at Huckstep Barracks outside

Cairo. This training was under the auspices of Colonel Kurt Ferchl, a former prisoner of the Soviets and suspected Soviet agent at the end of the war. The CIA had noted in 1953 that Ferchl, a General Staff Corps officer in 1941, was captured by the Russians and, contrary to the usual treatment given high-ranking German officers, was liberated in 1950. The Agency remarked: 'in such cases, there is room for suspicion that some pledges of co-operation may be involved in obtaining release' [12].

In consequence, the West German ambassador in Cairo believed that Ferchl was collaborating with the USSR by maintaining contact with Russian agents, a situation which he found highly alarming. Ferchl's work in embedding the regulations was supervised by Lt-Col Mueller and a Lieutenant Schaup. Both the Operations Department and Training Centre of the Brigade in due course approved these regulations.

Something of a revolving door policy operated amongst the Germans at this time. The contract of armament and equipment adviser Lt Col Herbert Bochmart was not renewed in 1953 and a successor, Otto Ellendt, was found by Voss. One of Voss' closest associates, Joachim Hertslet, a member of the Nazi Party and former official of the Nazi controlled import-export trade organisation Wirteschaftsgruppe Gross-Ein-und Ausfuhrhandel, had failed to take up an invitation by Egypt's Ministry of the Interior for a visa before May 1954 but finally applied for and received one in that month[13]. Under the recruitment process, the German advisers were typically given two-year renewable contracts. The Egyptian government paid the relocation costs for them and their families, offering salaries paid in Egyptian pounds and insurance policies valued in deutsche marks. The Wehrmacht veterans remained German citizens and in their capacity as advisers did not have the right to give direct orders or command troops. The German advisers were in general popular and respected figures in Egypt; collectively they were referred to by Egyptians in their circle as the 'Allemanni', the direct Arabic translation of 'Germans'.

Nasser regarded the contribution of these German experts as just one part of a much wider overhaul of the armed forces and within months of the coup he had encouraged large numbers of career officers schooled in traditional military methods and procedures to take early retirement, increased the pay of those remaining and improved the pay and working conditions of the rank and file, creating an overall much more attractive career path in the military. He also made a start on a comprehensive building programme of military infrastructure that included new ammunition and aircraft factories and new quays and harbours for the navy' [14].

It was in their strictly defined role as advisers that one of the principal clues may be found to the longer-term influence of these professional soldiers and armaments experts. The 'Allemanni' had no executive authority so were not directly empowered to implement or enforce any recommendations they were making. Thus like all consultants, even those at the highest level, they wrote reports, attended meetings and conferences, strategized, advised on best practice, devised training programmes and oversaw exercises. They developed relationships with their opposite numbers and acted as mentors and sometimes confidants. Many of their recommendations were listened to closely with great respect and implemented as far as possible by the Egyptians. However, a comprehensive assessment of their long term influence on the make-up, performance, strategy and tactics of Egypt's reforming military and security state was hard to assess in the early 1950s when the sweeping cultural shift was only just getting underway.

One area in which they were to make a swift change was in the linkage of military force with mobility and speed as a combat tactic, an approach to the conduct of land war that had been pioneered and mastered by the Wehrmacht in Europe and North Africa during 1940 and 1941. The Experimental Brigade of the Egyptian Army at Huckstep Barracks outside Cairo was identified by the British in 1953 as undergoing an organisational development consistent with German advice, being an independent brigade group, fully mobile and with its own armour and artillery component, a transition perhaps in response to Artur Schmitt's initial criticisms. There was also evidence that this brigade had been trained to use anti-aircraft artillery in a ground role, a particularly German tactic which had been used to devastating effect during the Normandy landings in 1944. 'It may be expected that the influence of German thought on Egyptian tactics and organisation will be to produce a more flexible and mobile force', the British assessment declared [15].

The role of Dr Voss as the Chief Technical Adviser to the Egyptian Government and Head of the Central Planning Board in Cairo was to come under severe pressure in 1954. In June of that year the German weekly news magazine Der Spiegel ran a highly damaging article about what it claimed was the double game being played by Voss in his collaboration with the Secretary of State for Foreign Affairs in the West German government, Professor Walter Hallstein. The paper alleged that Voss and Hallstein's relationship was damaging Anglo German relations as well as German Egyptian relations. Voss, it claimed, had written a letter in March 1953 to Lt Col Kamal Abdel Hamid, Egyptian Minister of War and Marine. In the letter he claimed he had established contact with the Supreme Command of the West German forces in order to obtain for use in Egypt the latest service regulations and instructions relating to the organisation, command and tactics of the new German army. Centred on his network of personal connections in the German forces, Voss claimed he had secured a private agreement to supply these highly valuable and secret documents, which would be accessed only by him and his 'emissaries'. To that end, he sent his deputy Colonel Kurt Ferchl to Bonn to pick the documents up and prepare the information for use by the Egyptian forces.

'I have given instructions for the immediate evaluation of this material in order to make it available to all experts concerned and to submit it for the benefit of the Egyptian Forces together with our special suggestions,' he wrote [16]. At the same time, in Cairo it was being said that Voss and his team were full of praise about their close relationship with the top levels of the Federal Ministry of Foreign Affairs in Bonn. The Head of the Political Department, Ambassador Herbert Blankenhorn even asked him to drop by personally when he was in town. However, officials of the German Ministry of Foreign Affairs in Cairo were warning German industrialists and officers against co-operating with Voss and his team. They were being clearly seen as agents of a foreign power who had been receiving, for months, communications and telegrams in code sent between the German Embassy in Cairo and Bonn Central Office.

The straw that broke the camel's back was Voss' insistence to the Egyptians that they should pay the considerable expenses incurred by Colonel Ferchl during his week's trip to Bonn, including a stay in a hotel, when he went to pick up the promised material from his personal contacts. Der Spiegel questioned how well advised Secretary of State Hallstein had been in valuing his relationship with Voss above the one he had with the German Ambassador in Cairo. The paper exposed what it described as a growing rift between the Central Planning Board and the Free Officers Government, especially with Nasser. Whereas Voss had maintained good relations with Neguib and his team, it now seemed clear that Lt Colonel Nasser preferred to deal with the German ambassador. After Nasser's assumption of power in November 1954, the influence of Dr Voss was accordingly minimised and the new rulers dismissed many of the German group of experts which then numbered about 60. The British took the report in Der Spiegel particularly seriously because of the proven quality of its sources, noting the fallout between Voss and Nasser and that Voss had appeared to maintain a direct correspondence with Hallstein. They also noted that things had deteriorated to such a degree that Nasser was quoted as saying about Dr Voss: 'he is a liar and you may quote me' [17].

The Legend of General Wilhelm Fahrmbacher

With his outstretched arm gesturing across a huddle of giant concrete pens at the German submarine base at St Nazaire, standing next to the legendary 'Desert Fox' Field Marshal Erwin Rommel, General Wilhelm Fahrmbacher looked every inch the wartime Wehrmacht military commander. In his leather coat and stiff, weather worn peaked cap this artillery general with the firm jaw, authoritative poise and Knight's Cross at his uniform collar, matched almost perfectly the stereotype of the classic World War Two German army professional officer class. In this case the image had a certain prescience, as Fahrmbacher was to end his career in the German army defending the submarine base at Lorient on the Atlantic coast of France, part of Hitler's famed 'Atlantic Wall' designed to keep allied forces out of France and thus ultimately out of Germany itself.

Five years or so after the war Fahrmbacher was to become a key figure in the Central Planning Board in Cairo. Settling in to a dusty office in a military barracks at a sprawling camp south of Heliopolis in north-east Cairo, he was to refocus his considerable talents on shaping Egypt's future land forces. But in 1945 with the allied armies charging through France on their way to the Rhine and Berlin beyond, he could not have known his military career was to end in foreign employ in a vast, ancient and teeming city at the crossroads of the Middle East and Africa. Nor could he have guessed that his role as defender of the last town in France remaining in German hands in May 1945 would in time create his legend as the most stubborn German holdout of the war. On 8th May 1945, VE Day, the 25,000 strong garrison at Lorient under Fahrmbacher's command was still fighting on, ignoring allied appeals to surrender and orders from Admiral Karl Doenitz, now in charge of Germany's remaining armed forces to lay down their arms. Bypassing Lorient in 1944, the invading Allied forces had given up trying to attack the well defended base and decided it should be left to wither on the vine and swept up at a later date.

Fahrmbacher, an ageing artillery general of the old school who had put in some serious time on the Russian front during Operation Barbarossa in 1941, had other ideas. He had shown extraordinary ingenuity and imagination in managing to keep the encircled garrison fed for over a year, doing deals with local French farmers and even raiding Allied food supplies. But his most extraordinary feat was in the continued supply to his men of 'Komissbrot', the bread that kept the German army marching. Aware of the effect on morale if the bread supply in the town was to run out, he had been supplementing the dwindling German army ration of flour with sawdust ground down from railway sleepers that underpinned the track which snaked its way into town [18]. Slowly but progressively over time, Fahrmbacher had worked with his regimental Quartermaster to pull up the requisite number of sleepers every day and then ground them into sawdust. This was mixed with the army flour in increasingly unfavourable proportions. The Quartermaster's daily report on the state of sawdust supply was allegedly the first thing that Fahrmbacher asked for when he woke. Three days after Germany formally surrendered on 7th May, only one sleeper remained. Finally, on 10th May, the veteran general from the Russian Front admitted that the game was up and surrendered the garrison and the town[19].

Something of Fahrmbacher's stubbornness, dogged determination and courage was evident in the picture taken on the occasion of his surrender to US forces outside the town. Cutting a lonely figure as he stood to attention in a nondescript field surrounded by the US and French surrender parties, Fahrmbacher looked the complete German professional soldier that he was, dignified in defeat, both immaculate and incongruous amongst the dressed down Allies spread out across the long, unkempt grass and proliferating weeds.

But Fahrmbacher's association with the town of Lorient was not yet over. Not long after his surrender, the 62 year old general found himself serving five years in a Parisian jail for having disfigured French property. Not only was desecration of the railway sleepers part of his transgression of the French criminal code, but he had also allegedly disfigured French state postage stamps for the garrison to use, overprinting them with the word 'Lorient'. On his release from French custody in 1950 Fahrmbacher, needing both employment and professional purpose had little hesitation in signing up as a key member of Egypt's Central Planning Board, attracted to the idea of steady employment and the opportunity to implement his ideas at such an elevated level. To some degree his reputation preceded him. The Israelis and the British in particular noted his appointment with concern. The general had over 35 years' experience, was a formidable artillery officer and had served in both world wars in addition to helping organise the Reichswehr militia of the Weimar Republic. On 13th December 1952, the same year he arrived in Egypt, the taciturn Fahrmbacher was interviewed along with Dr Wilhelm Voss by Associated Press. 'Quiet spoken, white haired Fahrmbacher appears to be concerned mainly with the training of Egyptian units in the field. He talks with pride of 'his boys', the AP correspondent noted. 'The Egyptian army is now fit', the general told him. [20]

The Israeli spy Avraham Siedenwerg, operating in Egypt under the cover name 'Paul Frank' met Fahrmbacher for the first time in his office at an army general headquarters near Heliopolis 'filled with maps, filing cabinets, documents and an air of seriousness' in February 1954. Fahrmbacher stressed to the young Israeli spy just how much work the Egyptians needed to do to improve performance. Speaking with fire and passion, the veteran blue-eyed, white haired German general told Frank of his plans for creating an Egyptian strike force of 15 divisions, based on the old Reichswehr structure of 1933. But he cautioned this was a hard task since 'Egypt needs another seven to eight years before they can sustain the logistics of large fighting groups. Until then, I think that small groups, not more than company strength, should be built to expertly man their few modern weapons.'[21]

From the start, Fahrmbacher became an authentic figure of authority in Egypt, backed up by a team that contained enough serious players to worry the British who were still trying to assess the impact of the German experts on British operations along the Suez Canal zone. Amongst the heavyweights that worked for him were General Oskar Munzel, the former tank commander and now adviser on armoured warfare; Colonel Albert Brierlein, infantry training adviser; Major Gerhard Mertins, paratroop adviser; and Colonel Ernst Zolling, a former Afrika Corps officer and expert on desert navigation who moved to Cairo with his wife Elisabeth[22].

At the time of Fahrmbacher's arrival, the Egyptian Armed Forces comprised an army of some 80,000 spread across two infantry divisions, two armoured regiments, two armoured car regiments, two independent infantry brigades, a parachute brigade, anti-aircraft formations and coast defence units. It was felt that the effects of the military coup in July 1952 had cut two ways. On the one hand the fact that it had managed to maintain internal control had boosted the army's morale. On the other, the handling of army formations was thought to be poor and the dismissal of many officers for political reasons was thought to have been detrimental to efficiency and training [23]. The Egyptian Air Force, though it looked substantial on paper, was thought to have an effective strength of only some 20 jet fighters, with poor air control. All of these aircraft were in the Delta except for one squadron of Furies on the Palestine border.

The Senior Management Team

Generalmajor Oskar Munzel, Fahrmbacher's effective Number Two in rank, was a highly decorated Wehrmacht tank officer who had commanded both the 14th and 2nd Panzer Divisions in the Second World War and fought at two of the great tank battles on the Eastern Front, Moscow and Kiev, winning the Knight's Cross in the process. He had also been commanding officer of the 6th Panzer Regiment during its successful breakthrough of the Stalin Line, near Dubno in 1941.

Munzel's army career was stellar and his authority in the field of tank warfare was impossible to challenge. To that extent, he was an extraordinary catch for the German military mission. A cavalryman to his core, he had joined the German army in 1917 and was one of the few officers permitted to stay on in military service after the defeat of the First World War. After the collapse of the Third Reich Munzel was interned for two years until 1947 and eventually arrived in Egypt in 1951. He was to spend the next four years, most of them uneasy ones, under contract to the Egyptian War Ministry.

Munzel was in most respects unprepared for and unhappy with the conditions he found in Egypt, including the equipment, resources and training of the tank units. Israeli spy Paul Frank, in his campaign to get close to the German advisers recalled his first meeting with Munzel at a Cairo poolside. The former Panzer commander cursed the atrocious performance of the tanks he was now responsible for. He recounted the story of Independence Day that year on July 23rd 1953 when the new government had commemorated the fall of the Farouk regime by staging an impressive procession of 40 tanks. 'Would you care to know how many passed the tribune, Herr Frank? Twelve! Can you believe 12 out of 40? And one lost a track and almost ran down the saluting stand…a thousand times I've tried to beat into their dead heads that pretty paint and big identification numbers do not a fighting panzer force make!' The general concluded: 'It is my opinion, Herr Frank, that the Egyptians will never have an army' [24].

In a letter from the British Embassy in Cairo to the Foreign Office on 6th February 1953, the Chancery summarised a conversation the military attaché had held with General Munzel in which the General confirmed that he was not minded to extend his contract when it came up for renewal. Munzel gave the impression that 'as the German advisers have no executive powers… he considered the attempt to train Egyptians in modern weapons was something of a waste of time. He also expressed the view that the Egyptian Army was really training to fight the Jews and had no intention of being committed in a larger conflict against the Russians. He was struck by the bitterness of Egyptian feelings against the British ' [25]. Munzel reportedly left his job on bad terms with his former employers after a personal confrontation with Nasser during which he slammed his fist down on the desk in front of him before storming out of the office. After his departure, Munzel was to be replaced by another German tank expert, Ernst-Günther Gerhartz, who was to become the only dedicated tank specialist in the German military advisory group and chief expert at the Egyptian army's tank school.

It may have been that Munzel's standards and expectations of Egyptian capacity were simply too high. When he closed the door on his time in Egypt, this dedicated, experienced and committed professional joined the new West German Bundeswehr when it was founded in 1955 and served as commander of its tank school, later to become inspector of all tank forces. After leaving the new German army in 1962, he was to go on to head up another German military advisory group, this time in Taiwan. Munzel's credentials as a formidable military strategist of blitzkrieg style tank warfare were further evidenced by his writing a book 'Panzer Tactics: Operations in the East 1941-1942' which became a textbook for tank commanders. The value of Munzel's skills and strengths as a front line tank commander and strategist, and his loss to the Egyptian mission, were underlined by his later work for NATO forces being formed to face off against the Soviet Union as the Cold War got further underway.

Baron Theodor Von Bechtolsheim

The Egyptian Navy of the early 1950s appeared as the poor relation or at least the junior partner in Egypt's Armed Forces, its ships rarely seen outside port and its sailors perceived as lacking equivalent glamour and military relevance. Whilst its fleet did not have great striking power, it could still marshal 10 frigates, three armed patrol boats, seven coastal minesweepers and 17 motor torpedo boats [26]. The British assessed that its effectiveness in the event of conflict would be almost negligible, principally owing to the loss of British training facilities, the removal of British trained officers and the deterioration of equipment.

The man placed in charge of changing all this was a former Captain in the German navy and a nobleman to boot. Kapitän zur See, Baron Theodor Freiherr von Bechtolsheim was another *bona fide* war hero who had taken the long road from post-war Germany to Cairo seeking steady work after the war. A professional sailor who had joined Germany's navy, the Kreigsmarine in April 1923 von Bechtolsheim was a holder of the Iron Cross and the Knights Cross. This slim, stocky figure with his oval face, long upper lip, high forehead and dark hair was a survivor of numerous successful naval sorties, among them convoy patrols, escort missions and mine operations.

During the Allied invasion of Normandy in 1944 von Bechtolsheim, now a Flotilla Commander, had led his destroyers into battle against the invading fleet. Just north-west of the Isle de Bas, he had engaged the British 10th Destroyer Flotilla in several battles between 7th and 10th of June. During these engagements, his command ship was fatally hit but von Bechtolsheim managed to save all his crew from the sinking vessel, an act of gallantry that was rewarded with the Knight's Cross. Though a legitimate war hero, von Bechtolsheim was also more than his naval rank and status suggested. In fact, he harboured the kind of secrets that made the final year of his war both difficult to explain and inconvenient for his future career and the security of his wife Ruth and their four children. On his way back to Germany after the sinking of his ship off the coast of France, von Bechtolsheim had been told that for his next posting he would be given command of the prestigious warship the 'Prinz Eugen'.

Instead in an unwelcome move he had been bounced into a much more high profile and potentially precarious role, one closer to the seat of power and one which he tried but was unable to refuse. Von Bechtolsheim's boss Admiral Balzer appointed him Liaison Officer between the German Naval High Command, the Oberkommando der Marine (OKM) and the Military Section of the Intelligence Service, the Militarischen Amt (Mil. Amt) of the Reich Main Security Office, the Reichssicherheitshauptampt (RHSA)[27]. Specifically, the German Navy had identified a need for more effective liaison between the OKM and the head of foreign intelligence, SS Brigadenführer Walter Schellenburg and the Chief of the RHSA, Dr Ernst Kaltenbrunner. Post the July 1944 plot to assassinate Hitler, the atmosphere within the intelligence community was febrile and a purge had taken place of some leading figures, creating vacancies.

One of von Bechtolsheim's jobs was to process requests from German Intelligence to place secret agents on submarines bound for the United States, where they would carry out missions. At least two Portuguese agents, one named Mesquita Lello, had already been successfully infiltrated into the US via submarine from Bremen four months before the end of the war. Placed under arrest on 24th May 1945 in Kiel whilst on board the ship 'Oranjefontein' von Bechtolsheim was taken to Kiel prison and interrogated by two naval officers. Thereafter, he was subject to numerous further interrogations and moved between internment camps for months as the Allies tried to extract information from him concerning three German agents whose fate remained unknown, Heinz Stahl, Willi Palow and Albert Ladis, along with other details of his work.

Von Bechtolsheim was unable or unwilling to give his interrogators what they were after, forcing them to conclude in a report on July 1st 1945: 'he made no apparent effort to disclose his connections with the RHSA; a man of his mental calibre should not be allowed to get away with the excuse that he did not realise this interested us' [28]. Generally though, this high-born English speaking professional, whose brother Anton had been German military attaché at the embassy in London before the war, was given the benefit of the doubt. 'He is a regular naval officer and comes of a good family; his bearing is accordingly good and he realises that imprisonment and interrogation is an evil necessity' the report stated.

In a letter she wrote to the British authorities 'respectfully' pleading for his release from detention, Ruth von Bechtolsheim emphasised that her husband had been a destroyer officer for the last eight years 'without having anything to do with the German Abwehr' before in June 1944 'being commanded as a Liaison Officer.' After his release von Bechtolsheim disappeared into the post-war free for all and economic chaos that engulfed Germany. But in March 1952 he resurfaced on the radar screens of the intelligence services when a letter he had written from an address in Alexandria to a former naval colleague in Hamburg, Admiral Meisel was intercepted. By this time he had jumped the fence and had joined some of his former colleagues as a military adviser in Egypt.

The letter revealed some of the cultural frustrations he was already experiencing in his role: 'here one has to act much more slowly than in Prussia and the Oriental sloppiness irritates me again and again, while here they just shake their heads about it. Malaish!' Reunited with his wife and children in Egypt where life was generally congenial, von Bechtolsheim had to develop a watchful eye on predatory 'Southlanders' intent on seducing his 19 year old daughter [29].

In his role as architect of the Egyptian navy, tasked with teaching it new skills, he had only three specialists to help him, one each in torpedoes, mines and dockyard engineering. The British believed that, whilst all the men were competent in their particular fields, they had been able to achieve almost nothing and their reports showed increasing frustration and disillusionment. It was felt that, with German supervision the Egyptian Navy would be able to operate some of the Motor Torpedo Boats or lay a minefield in Alexandria Harbour but not much more. On his mission to assess the German military team, the ubiquitous and persistent Paul Frank also met von Bechtolsheim on a visit to Alexandria, Egypt's principal and ancient port city on the eastern Mediterranean. As they talked together after dinner one evening, Frank remarked that en route to Egypt from Italy he had noticed three warships performing battle manoeuvres and commented: 'I thought they might be Italian or Egyptian until I saw the blue and white flag of the Israelis.' The Baron seemed taken aback by the suggestion. 'Oh yes, the Israelis. They are bloody efficient. You could never encounter the Egyptian navy so far out to sea. They are afraid to steam beyond sight of land.'[30].

The initial verdict on German influence

Asked to pronounce on the effectiveness of the interventions of the German advisers in Egypt up to 1953, the British Chiefs of Staff were clear that some damage to British interests had been done and more was quite probably on the way. 'The peculiar combination of a military dictatorship with advisers from a race whose taste is authoritarian must inevitably increase the latter's influence' their report suggested. This view echoed the racist stereotyping of German national character traits picked out by influential WW1 British psychological theorist Wilfred Trotter in his book 'Instincts of the Herd in Peace and War', a work which had famously described the German character type as being closest to the wolf [31].

The report also drew the British government's attention to the fact that General Neguib was a German speaker and the consequent possibility that he and his officers shared an admiration for German military efficiency. In a meeting with the British military attaché in Cairo, noted to London, General Oskar Munzel had expressed his view that Neguib actually modelled himself on Adolf Hitler. As further evidence of this wider permeation of ethnic stereotyping, the British Chiefs of Staff cited the pattern of the Egyptian Liberation Movement, the plans for training of students in schools and universities and the philosophy of the Revolutionary regime as all being consistent with German thought. 'What is certain is that the German advisers are giving direct and valuable assistance in the production of warlike material and in the training and organisation of the Egyptian Army and para-military forces', the report summarised. With a clarity of foresight into the near future, the British Army Chiefs' verdict was that some of the German advisers 'are engaged in training and preparing Egyptian military, para-military and minor naval forces for sabotage, terrorism and assassination roles directed against the British forces in Egypt. Although they hold no executive positions in the Army, Germans are expected to lead some of the guerrilla units into action'[32]. Whilst British fears focused on the implications of military threat to its forces and trading interests in the Suez Canal Zone, the activities of the German advisers and former Nazis in Egypt was also causing acute alarm at the new West German Embassy in Cairo. Here, its diplomats were increasingly aware that a group of citizens were operating in Egypt without official licence and with little regard for the consequences for the new state's reputation.

Chapter Five
GUERRILLAS IN THE ZONE

'Down With the Pashas, and up with the Fellahin.'

British Prime Minister Winston Churchill
to Foreign Secretary Anthony Eden,
7th September 1952
(TNA/PREM 11/392/86940 Prime Minister's Personal
Minutes)

As early as December 1952, only five months after the military coup of the Free Officers, the British Government was holding internal discussions about the nature of a new defence agreement with Egypt. It calculated that a comprehensive settlement would involve agreeing terms on which Britain could withdraw its forces from the Canal Zone, secure Egypt's participation in a Middle East defence organisation, and put in place a programme of both economic and military assistance to Egypt [1]. In a secret analysis of the prospects for such an agreement, Britain's Defence Department proceeded from the premise that only Egypt could provide the full means of support for a military base that would be required for the future viable defence of the Middle East. The definition of a base in this context meant not only supplies, stores, depots and airfields but also the ports, transportation, logistics and labour that would make it functional. Without such fundamentals, realistic defence would not be possible. Therefore

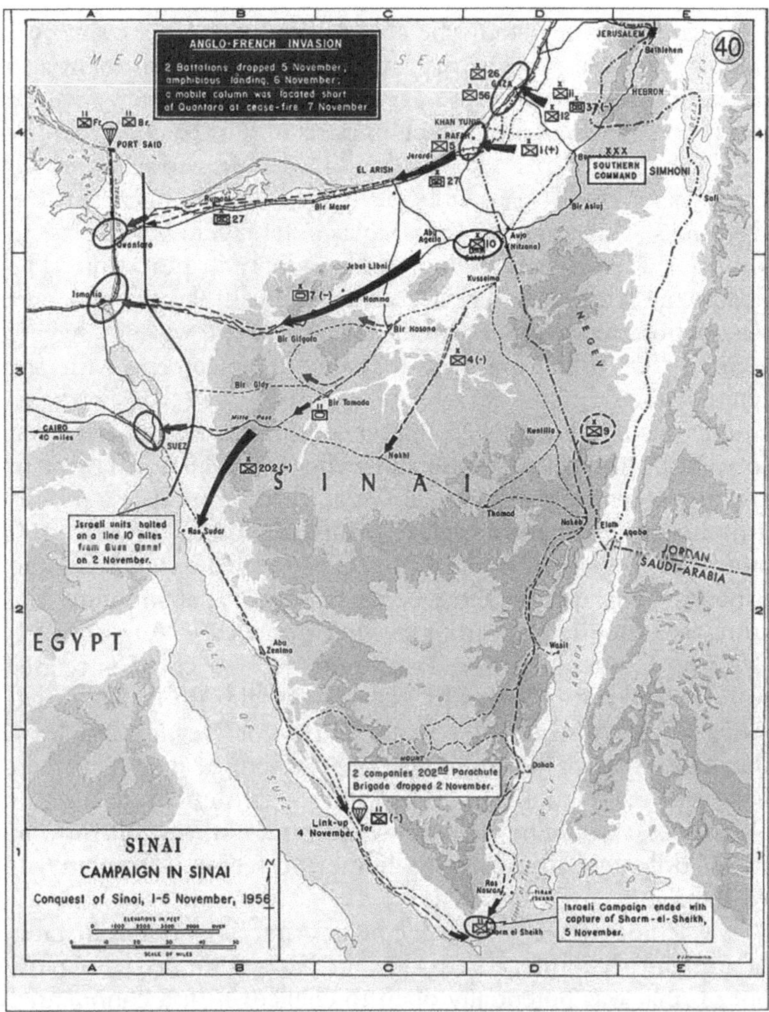

A British military map of the Suez Conflict of 1956 *(above),* showing the movements of the British, French and Israeli forces.

concessions would need to be made in order to secure Egyptian support and co-operation. It was not considered realistic that the Egyptian Air Force would be able to supply sufficient air cover to guarantee military security and the Defence Department also decided that as part of the agreement the British navy would need access to the major Egyptian ports of Port Said, Alexandria and Suez. The paper set out the different scenarios on which concessions could reasonably be made, all contingent on the Egyptians accepting that British personnel would have access to any agreed base for inspection and resupply in peacetime. The document strongly asserted that the British should not start negotiations with the Egyptians in any event without having secured 'the fullest possible measure of agreement with the United States' [2].

This position was arrived at after consideration had been given to vacating the existing base along the Suez Canal in favour of creating an entirely new one at Gaza, to accommodate a mobile armoured division and a brigade group, at a cost of between £100 and £200 million. The Gaza 'project' was ruled out as being too expensive but also on there being no case for abandoning the stores and supplies kept in Egypt. In a note of 17th August 1952, Winston Churchill wrote: 'I am quite sure we could not agree to be kicked out of Egypt by Nahas (Mustafa Al-Nahhas Pasha, twice Prime Minister of Egypt), Farouk or Neguib and leave our base, worth £500 millions, to be despoiled or put in their care, and make another highly costly establishment at Gaza or elsewhere. It would be far better to clear out of the whole show in the Middle East after bringing home and selling what materials we have got,'[3].

It was not public knowledge at the time but the legal status of the British military garrison and bases stationed along the Suez Canal was potentially open to challenge. In a confidential memo of 13th March 1953, British Foreign Secretary Anthony Eden had drawn the Cabinet's attention to this when he pointed out that the present strength of the British forces in the Canal Zone numbering some 80,000 was only permissible under the terms of the Anglo-Egyptian Treaty of 1936 if the strengthening of the garrison had been undertaken because Britain's rights were threatened by Egypt's repudiation of the Treaty. However, this did not cover the British position if questions were asked as to why the permitted maximum number of 10,000 troops provided for in the Treaty had been exceeded in the years up to 1951. 'We should be on somewhat shaky ground if accused of having failed to observe the Treaty by having too many troops in Egypt in the period between the end of the war and October 1951 when Egypt repudiated the Treaty' he wrote [4].

Whether the status of the British garrison in the Canal Zone was legal or not was a question only of academic interest to the soldiers and airmen stationed at intervals along its 120 mile length, which ran directly north to south from Port Said to Suez. As their numbers grew over the years of tenure their living conditions had become nothing less than squalid and dreadful, a situation in time recognised in Britain as a national disgrace. During 1953 and into 1954 the appalling conditions of the British troops manning the Canal Zone bases became critical. Thousands of soldiers and airmen, many of them National Servicemen with no previous experience of military life at all, were permanently living in inadequate tents or sub-standard housing, suffering from intense heat, with poor sanitation, persistent and debilitating illnesses, under constant harassment from locals and with little sense of military purpose.

'It really was an open sewer - it was pretty filthy. If anybody fell in the Sweetwater Canal... they had to have the full treatment for rabies, injections in the tummy and everything. It was the early days of anti-mosquito spraying of their breeding grounds in canals, swamps etc and all the waters around were being constantly sprayed by the public health people. So nobody got the traditional malaria. But there was a lot of 'gippy tummy' (diarrhoea) - that was a fairly constant thing,' remembered Second Lieutenant Kenneth Baker, stationed in the Canal Zone between 1953 and 1954 [5]. The living conditions and consequent low state of morale amongst the British was widely known and would have been helpful to the Egyptians and their German instructors planning a campaign to infiltrate and degrade the Zone's military assets.

Disease, poor diet and terrible living conditions might have been prevalent problems but so was the existential danger to life in the Zone. This stretched from Port Said on the Eastern Mediterranean due south, passing near the town of Ismailia in the central section and through Suez at the southern entrance where it fed into the Red Sea at Port Tewfik. The canal's design and construction, by French engineer Ferdinand de Lesseps in 1869, incorporated three natural lakes including the substantial Great Bitter Lake and Lake Timsah in the course of its north south connection of the Red Sea to the eastern Mediterranean. With military camps, warehouses and ammunition dumps spread out across the length of the canal, limited air support and few patrol boats, the British garrison had a huge amount of ground to cover. It was everywhere exposed to sniping and incursion by small groups of guerrilla fighters, whose debilitating effects grew over time and increased exposure.

In January 1952 three battalions of the Parachute Regiment were deployed west of Suez alongside other British forces to deter an Egyptian Army advance against the Suez Canal. Tension was such that One Para was on stand-by to conduct a possible airborne operation against Cairo, supported by Three Para and a Squadron of the Royal Tank Regiment, if British nationals were threatened. In time, the conventional threat eased but attacks against British military establishments in the Canal Zone increased while the Egyptian Police made matters more threatening by refusing to co-operate in maintaining security. Events came to a head during resistance to a cordon and search operation in Ismailia the same month during which four Egyptians were killed and 12 captured for the loss of one officer. The 1st Lancashire Fusiliers meanwhile fought a bloody battle to occupy a police barracks, supported by a Centurion tank, resulting in the killing or wounding of 95 Egyptian policemen at a cost of four dead and one wounded [6]. Sixteenth Independent Parachute Brigade in due course assumed responsibility for all of Ismailia and the surrounding district, mounting patrols, setting up cordons, carrying out searches and carrying out guard and convoy duties. It was fully committed on such internal security duties for two years.

'If you went to Korea you knew where the front line was but in Egypt you didn't know who the enemy was, so eventually you began to think everyone was the enemy and if they were in the front line of fire, that was just too bad,' remembered National Serviceman Emmanuel Clark. 'We'd lost two or three guys to snipers so when we caught one, as soon as he divulged where the others were, I watched an officer shoot him. He was about 16, I think...but nobody bothered' [7]. Eric Osborne, a furniture restorer from Somerset, was 18 when he was called up. Within 48 hours of finishing training, he was despatched to Suez. 'I was on death row for three months', he recalled when describing his job of driving a ration truck along a road that lay in parallel to the canal. Trucks travelling along the road were regularly ambushed and it soon acquired the reputation of being the most dangerous road in Egypt. 'I knew I had to do it…it wasn't an adventure, it was just something I had to do. I have heard of people say 'fancy fighting over a body of water' but we had a perfect right to it and it made me grow up,' he recalled. Nonetheless, the National Servicemen drafted for duty at Suez gradually started to lose the esprit which was a general leftover from the Second World War, an enterprise in which everyone engaged had felt some common sense of purpose in the cause of a national effort.

'In January 1952 we were told we were going to Ismailia. Word had come through from Special Branch that… it was the police who were sniping at us. So we were going down to the Bureau Sanitaire, which the police were occupying. As we were going in the lad aside of me, he just went "ooh" and down he went. So I looked and all his side was out and he was dead… He was a new draft, he came over to Egypt and I think he'd done about six weeks' intensive training in the desert and then he copped it. A nice lad. I don't know what he was hit with, but we were told afterwards that the police were using dum-dum bullets so that would rip up rather than just going in. I think the best way to explain how I felt was in a daze really, it was something I just can't pinpoint how I felt, but I know I was shitting myself, I was frightened. I think anybody that says that they weren't is telling lies. The old soldiers knew what it was about, but I was bewildered,' recalled Private Eric Pearson, who was stationed in the Canal Zone between 1951 and 1952 [8].

Between 1951 and 1956, there were 450 British military fatalities in the region. So poor were the conditions and so abject the state of morale and health amongst the British troops that their marginal existence amidst the heat, flies and disease of the Canal Zone became the subject of a major parliamentary debate in the British House of Commons on 11th March 1954. Speaking at length about the increasing unsustainability of the situation in the Canal Zone, Labour Member of Parliament for Blackburn East, Barbara Castle forced the problem out into the open. In a lengthy and provocative speech, she questioned the entire purpose of the British occupation.

'The theory is that they are supposed to be defending a lifeline of Empire. In practice, they are spending all their time watching the depots and trying to protect our installations and property from the depredations of the local inhabitants. Local thugs specially trained for the work….are lying in wait at night to attack our men, hoping to catch them off their guard, and jumping on vehicles and attacking drivers and escorts from behind. It must be the strangest kind of soldiering in all our history to have our soldiers spending their time defending themselves and British property from the local inhabitants on whose friendly co-operation we should be completely dependent in time of war.

She drove her point home: 'To the sense of danger which the men must have is added the sense of futility. In addition to his normal duty, every man does two nights guard duty a week watching for an enemy who ought to be an ally if this base is to have any military sense at all. It is not surprising that a tour of duty in Suez is considered the worst assignment that the Army can offer. In fact, despite the additional dangers, the soldiers would rather be in Korea or Malaya'. Castle administered her coup de grâce: 'It is not surprising that our men in the Canal Zone consider themselves to be the forgotten Army of 1954 sitting as they are in a concentration camp, doing a job which has no military sense. It is no wonder that commanders on the spot want the Government to reach a decision which will end this uncertainty. No wonder, too, that the War Office is worried and that the Secretary of State for War is worried, as I appreciate he is.' [9]

Operation Rodeo Evacuation Plan

The Anglo Egyptian talks finally got underway with a measure of goodwill and co-operation on both sides. However, beyond the choreography of formal negotiations and diplomacy each side was making preparations for the eventuality that the talks might break down. If they did so, the British did not want their civilians in Alexandria and Cairo and military forces along the length of the Canal Zone to be surprised and fatally compromised. To that end a contingency plan, codenamed Operation Rodeo, was put in place for activation at 48 hours' notice. Alternative versions of this plan were computed to accommodate different timings.

This required pre-emptive military intervention to secure designated access routes, supply lines, installations and port facilities to enable the British to manage an orderly withdrawal of civilians. Rodeo was prompted by solid intelligence information rather than existential angst or instinct alone. At the beginning of August 1952 assessments of the position in Cairo recorded that whilst things were currently quiet, by October the Anglo-Egyptian issue would be in full focus, at which point the situation could undergo 'a very sudden and violent change for the worse' within weeks.

The Commander-in-Chief (CIC) of Middle East Land Forces General Brian Robertson emphasised that, where possible, the state of readiness should be lengthened. 'In the Canal Zone we are aware of the presence of a number of dangerous elements who could very quickly cause a lot of trouble especially if they were reinforced and supplied with additional arms from the Delta.' The memo declared that 'were an Egyptian ultimatum to be issued and backed up by the use of its armed forces, then 'our present plans would not be suitable'[10].

Subsequent intelligence on the movement of Egyptian forces across the country proved the overall priority of this warning. By 14th May the following year a summary of the military position showed a wholesale re-deployment of the Egyptian Army had been taking place in order to resist potential British military intervention both in the Delta and the Canal Zone [11]. To that end, Egyptian units had already taken up positions at the main Suez Canal crossings at Firdan, Ismailia, Ferry Point and Kubri, and the garrison at Kantara East had been strengthened. The Egyptian army had placed two infantry companies on the southern approaches to Alexandria across the Cairo-Alexandria road, positioned the best part of an armored brigade across the Cairo –Suez desert road at Almaza; and placed the army's experimental brigade group, along with its German instructors, on the eastern outskirts of Cairo. Other units additional to the Egyptian Army were also reported to be on the move. About 1,000 armed members of the Muslim Brotherhood (IEM) regiments, led by Germans, had already been infiltrated into the Canal Zone; and there was a build-up of paramilitary forces, supplemented by regular soldiers, operating in civilian clothes.

The reasons for the inspection visits of Otto Skorzeny and other German military advisers including Major Gerhard Mertins and General Otto Ernst Remer to the Canal Zone in early 1953 now became abundantly clear. The particular skills offered by the German specialists in guerilla tactics, paramilitary operations and sabotage had been rolled out in training and were now shortly to be put to the test. German instructors, having devised and implemented the training, were not in all cases going to stand aside when the action started but would be leading from the front. Some of the Germans involved in training for this irregular type of warfare were not attached to the Central Planning Board in Cairo and were thus not subject to any control from Dr Voss, General Fahrmbacher or members of his team that might have limited or directly influenced their role. These freelancers comprised a motley crew of former Afrika Korps POWs, mercenaries, soldiers of fortune and Wehrmacht veterans.

However Otto Skorzeny himself was still very much a central figure. Having turned down a full time position in Egyptian employ, he was now operating as a consultant to the Egyptian Government across a number of fronts including arms dealing. He was also in practice Egypt's most senior adviser on Special Forces and irregular warfare, skills he had honed in campaigns and special missions for the Third Reich during World War Two from Italy and France to Russia and the Balkans. As far back as 1944, then Head of German Special Forces Skorzeny had contemplated using frogmen to sink ships in the Suez Canal in order to disrupt British shipping but had been prevented from acting on his plan by the Allies' total control of the Mediterranean. He described the formation of Arab demolition parties and setting them to work as one of his most promising yet dubious ambitions.

Skorzeny was aided in this work by Major Gerhard Mertins, a specialist Luftwaffe 'Fallschirmjäger' paratroop officer, holder of both the Knight's Cross and Iron Cross and an integral player in the successful conclusion of the meticulous operation to spring Benito Mussolini from captivity in the mountains of Gran Sasso in 1943. This experienced and daring paratrooper who by now was residing at 11, Abd Al Wahid Pasha Street in Heliopolis was in charge of developing the Egyptian army's first paratroop regiments, a task in which he was assisted by two further Wehrmacht paratroop specialists, Captains Richter and

Steimel. This top team, under Otto Skorzeny's oversight, was in due course to extend its training to include elements of Egypt's first Palestinian Fedayeen (self-sacrificer) fighters. They were to be deployed in a low-intensity guerilla campaign against Israel from May 1954. The Fedayeen were in time to launch border raids from Egypt into Gaza, to other parts of Palestine and even further afield into Jordan and Israel itself.

Through this strategy of persistent and clandestine cross-border incursions, Nasser hoped to demoralise the Israeli civilian population which he calculated might then lean on its government to hand back some of the territory annexed during the 1948 war. Inspecting a Fedayeen training camp south of Cairo in Beni Suef in the previous year, Nasser encouraged Palestinians not to give up their hopes and dreams that they would one day return to their homeland. Claiming that history was on their side against the West and that Palestine would one day be liberated, Nasser told them: 'our future goal is to achieve the greatest homeland at some stage in colonialism's departure' [12].

Playing to German Strengths

The field of irregular warfare and special operations was one in which the German advisers were to deliver some of their highest value work during their time in Egypt. Egyptian Army General Abdel Moneim Khalil, a principal instructor at the Egyptian Army infantry training school from 1947 to 1954, remembered the Germans coming to train Egyptian soldiers: 'They taught them to conduct Blitzkrieg-type, lightning war, special operations and also night combat' [13]. This high risk style of military engagement which encouraged pre-emptive action, daring and independent decision-making played to the strengths of the German Special Forces tradition and was to have an enduring impact on Egyptian military strategy and tactics in the coming decades. The British certainly felt that it was in the field of sabotage training in Egypt that German influence was at its most serious from the British point of view. British intelligence had evidence that regular army personnel 'of all ranks on a wide scale' were being trained in sabotage, terrorism and assassination roles, but that Germans had also been detailed to train para-military guerrilla formations and particularly the Muslim Brotherhood (IEM). The British believed naval training had included underwater sabotage and frogmen tactics [14].

The Muslim Brotherhood (Al Ikhwan Al Muslimin) was the first modern Islamic mass movement, founded in March 1928 by school teacher and iconoclast Hassan Al Banna in the Egyptian Suez Canal city of Ismailia. The Brotherhood, which was to go on to play a central role in modern Egyptian and wider Islamist political events, aimed to achieve a complete spiritual rebirth ('nahda') of society under Islam. Its strong message, highly developed organisational skills and binding individual commitment of members meant that by 1949 it had expanded across Egypt from a standing start to incorporate some 2,000 branches. The Brotherhood's tight, hierarchical structure based on a proliferation of self-contained, independent cells promoted an efficient system for recruiting, training and multiplying cadres.

By 1937 it had developed a military wing called Al Katai'b (The Battalions), or 'the formations'. These Battalions, referred to by the British in their reports as the Kateibas were typically composed of one to four sub-groups of 10 members, each subgroup being headed by a deputy (Mandub), to whom the local members pledged an oath of strict obedience, discipline, and secrecy. The Muslim Brotherhood, whilst it would later recalibrate to pursue representative political ambitions within Egypt, was focused in 1953 on increasing the internal influence of its own Guidance Council and on the expulsion of imperialism in all its forms from Egyptian territory.

The Brotherhood was known to have demanded Egyptian government action against the British as soon as any talks broke down. The British had evidence that a tour of the Canal Zone by 30 Kateiba leaders and a German adviser in April 1953 had resulted in 1,000 Ikhwan members being organised into parties to enter the Canal Zone in terrorist, sabotage and assassination roles. In addition, a further 600 members were operating independently in the Suez area and were believed to have already taken part in some practice attacks [15]. The total strength of the Kateibas was estimated at 5,000 to 6,000, organised into specialist rifle, wire cutting and demolition squads, the German influence most visible in training in the use of explosives, sabotage and mobile Commando style operations.

However, British analysis also showed that the Ikhwan leadership was anxious that no action would go off at half cock before they had reached an understanding of what the Egyptian government was going to do. The desire to expel the British was only surpassed by their need to challenge the Government. 'The Ikhwan is suspicious of Government intentions, fearful of the results of uncoordinated action and nervous of the efficiency of British preparation', the report stated [16]. For the time being, large scale Ikhwan action was held back whilst its leadership played a waiting game. The British, watching closely the comings and goings into the Canal Zone were hyper sensitised to unusual movements and reported with some certainty the appearance of numbers of 'bad characters' on the move and thus did not consequently rule out the possibility of individual acts of sabotage and terrorism by Ikhwan members. The British also observed that the general state of Egyptian security in the Canal Zone was so uncertain that acts of sabotage and terrorism should be expected regardless of any deliberate policy triggered by the Egyptian Government.

Word reached British intelligence that one German officer who had been lecturing at a meeting of the Ikhwan in March 1953 had revealed that the Egyptian Army was not expecting to stop a British advance to Cairo and into the Delta. Instead it planned to fight delaying actions in the fields and villages along the Tel-Al Kabir to Cairo road and mine the roadside, desert tracks and areas of desert around the Cairo to Suez road, which was expected to be the main line of advance. Thereafter, the plan was for small Egyptian units to attack the extended British forces as well as camps and installations in the Canal Zone. British analysts felt it was possible that this plan was also of German origin.

A second German officer, who had been training Ikhwan paramilitary units in sabotage techniques since the start of 1953 claimed that the Egyptian action would be triggered by the British failure to evacuate the Canal Zone unconditionally. At this point, a three stage plan would be rolled out: infiltrators would first be planted in camps and installations; second, sabotage operations in these installations would begin on a given signal; and thirdly guerrilla bands, in touch with each other via wireless, would be sent from the Delta to attack British forces. By the third week of April, he claimed, the first stage of this plan was complete, something which confirmed British fears that the Germans were known to possess detailed plans of a number of camps and installations in the Canal Zone, including 9 Base Ammunition Depot at Abu Sultan and its sub-depot at Lake Timsah. The relevance of this was that the early stage of the planning involved the destruction of British reserves of ammunition [17].

On the last day of April the British received reports of a German technician working in the Fayid Power Station having been found in possession of a number of detailed photographs of the installation, its machinery and nearby diesel-oil tanks. Under interrogation, he admitted that he had been in touch with Egyptian Army Intelligence officers and members of the German advisory group in Cairo. He also confirmed that approaches had been made by Egyptian Intelligence to other German workers but refused to give further details. As a result of this incident, the technician and 16 other Germans employed in the Canal Zone were dismissed and flown out of Egypt immediately. Further detailed photographs of the power station were found amongst the possessions of the wife of one of them and close inspection of these convinced the British that the photographs had been taken to assist acts of sabotage [18].

From the beginning of May, the British picked up further signs that members of the Kateibas were finding their way into the Canal Zone. 'From these instances, it is clear that at least some of the Egyptian plans for organising sabotage and guerrilla warfare in the Canal Zone are based on German initiative and advice, and envisage the use of Germans in their execution,' the report stated [19].

At the same time as the German instructors were training the Kateibas of the Ikhwan, they were also committing energy and resources to training the Egyptian government's Liberation Units, the activist units of Nasser's new political party, the Liberation Rally. These anti-British groups of civilians, managed through the Egyptian Ministry of the Interior, were formed with the objectives of consolidating the power of the Revolutionary Command Council and driving the British out of the Canal Zone. British military intelligence picked up evidence of infiltration by Liberation Unit members together with Egyptian Army officers in plain clothes, but took the view that the numbers were not sufficient to be at unit or even sub-unit level. One report they received concerned 24 Egyptian Army officers including three Lt-Colonels who had recently returned to Cairo after a plain clothes reconnaissance of the Zone. The British also acknowledged that Egyptian Army personnel had infiltrated their installations, that some sabotage plans had been worked out and that 'Germans have been concerned in their preparation though steps have already been taken to neutralise these plans' [20]. Between Egypt's regular and special forces, the Kateibas of the Muslim Brotherhood and the armed civilian Liberation Units, it was unsurprising the British felt that powerful and destabilising forces were increasingly ranged against them in their bases and airfields that straddled the 120 mile length of the highly vulnerable and exposed Canal Zone, even as they tried to negotiate a way out of the fix.

The new Egyptian Government had been placing some hopes on applying leverage to the negotiations with the British through the involvement of the Americans. US Secretary of State John Foster Dulles made a visit to Cairo on 13th May 1953, when he met with General Neguib, Foreign Minister Fawzi and senior Egyptian military leaders. The Egyptians had manoeuvred a breakdown in the talks prior to the arrival of Dulles in the hope that they could get American support against the British position, but they were disappointed by Dulles' response and his reluctance to offer any American intervention. This failure left the Egyptians casting around for some face-saving device which they could deploy in order to re-engage with the British.

In the event the Anglo-Egyptian talks nonetheless progressed, driven in part by British domestic political pressure and were concluded on 19th October 1954. This led the way for British withdrawal of all its forces from the Canal Zone progressively through 1955. It was not long after the departure of the last British troops at the start of 1956 that Nasser was to nationalise the Suez Canal Company and precipitate the Suez crisis of November that year when British paratroopers would find themselves to world condemnation fighting Egyptian forces and civilian militias to the death in the streets of Port Said.

Pursuing the German Connection

With the withdrawal of Britain's Military Mission from Cairo in 1948, the way had been left open for alternative military advisers, technical experts and procurement specialists to step in and fill the gap left behind. The scale of this shortfall in expertise was brought into sharp focus by the overwhelming defeat suffered by Egypt and the Arab coalition in the first Arab-Israeli War of 1948-49. Egypt's Government, first under King Farouk and latterly the Free Officers now harboured radically revised military and security ambitions that required upgrading, training and equipping a new generation of Egyptian military forces. If this reconstitution was to be convincing, these forces would need to be backed by modern infrastructure, a new generation of weapons, contemporary military methodology and a new style of leadership. To compete with Israeli regional military dominance, Egypt would need to far exceed the traditional limits of its prior military thinking to embrace a vision that included its own fighter jets, ships, tanks, ballistic missiles, rockets and even in time nuclear weapons.

The Arab League's attempt to float the idea of a pan-Arab army, bringing together Arab neighbours and allies to construct a federal military powerbase and counterbalance to Israeli force in the region did not progress past the first inspection of Egypt's forces in 1949 by Afrikakorps veteran Artur Schmitt. However, as events transpired, Schmitt was an outlier for the recruitment of substantial German military expertise under the umbrella of Dr Wilhelm Voss and his Central Planning Board, the principal conduit for German military and security support in Egypt through the early 1950s.

As had been revealed by Arab League envoy Adel Sabet, Egypt turned towards the Germans because they offered the pre-eminent model of how best to organise and conduct modern mobile warfare. Wehrmacht methodology and operating procedures, notwithstanding defeat in the Second World War, remained the best in the world. And more to the point, many German veterans along with rocket scientists, arms dealers, security experts, engineers and chemists were available at a reasonable price on the world recruitment market. It was unsurprising that the Egyptians began the process of realising this military vision by procuring a core of assets assembled from this wide and deep talent pool.

There were however, other historical reasons that made Egypt's decision to reach out to German military professionals both logical and consistent. One of these related to Germany's supportive relationship with the Muslim and Arab world first carved out and defined in the last decade of the 19th century. This commitment to support Islamic identity and purpose against

British and French interests in the Middle East developed into an alliance between imperial Germany and Ottoman Turkey during the First World War and Germany's active intervention in Turkey's military campaigns against the British in Mesopotamia, Palestine and the Dardanelles, all of which proved so destructive to British military aspirations and its reputation for military competence.

And second, the collaborative relationship that Nazi Germany had fostered with Arab nationalists and Islamists during the 1930s and through the Second World War offered a counter to British and French colonial dominance of the Middle East. Nazi Germany's support for a Palestinian national homeland during the war and its prosecution of a remorseless Arabic language propaganda war against the British and the Jews between 1941 and 1945 cemented its anti-British stance in the region and poured further fuel on the fire of its Nazi fostered anti-Semitic ideology and race war against the Jews. The post-war influence of former Nazis in Cairo was one contributing factor in the extension of this ideological, territorial and race war which was to endure in Egypt and the Arab world through the 1950s and beyond.

Chapter Six
TRAINING THE FIRST FEDAYEEN

'The incidents by the Egyptian commandos on Saturday disturbed Israel's confidence. Forty eight hours after Israel had shelled Gaza, the Egyptian commandos were in Migdal firing their guns. This surprise paralysed the Israelis. The commandos were able to fire their guns and throw hand grenades in the city centre. The commandos left the city on fire. This incident means that the war does not only include firing on border raids but reaches the heart of Israel and places which they thought were out of reach. The continuous incidents made Israel realise that there were a great number of commandos inside their territory.'

'Voice of the Arabs' (Sawt Al-Arab) radio broadcast from Cairo, 9th April 1956.

Some time in the early hours of 7th April 1956, 100 Fedayeen fighters slipped across the Egyptian border into the Gaza Strip and under cover of darkness dispersed into smaller groups once further north and inside Israeli territory. Later that day, they struck a number of targets in different locations with total surprise and maximum impact, then vanished back into the Gaza Strip from where they had emerged. Gathering information from multiple sources inside the attack zone, the stunned and furious Israeli authorities informed the United Nations Truce Supervision Organization (UNTSO) later that day about the extent of the damage done by the raids. The Fedayeen had carried out a number of acts of sabotage and attacked seven vehicles in the area between Beersheba and the Gaza Strip; they had blown up a water installation at Migdal; and also thrown a hand grenade into a house in Ashkelon, a town well beyond the northern end of the Gaza Strip further up the Israeli coast. The attacks had resulted in two Israeli civilian fatalities along with numerous further wounded and injured. In a despatch on April 8th to the Foreign Office in London, Britain's Consul-General in Jerusalem, Thomas Wikeley, reported that UNTSO Chief of Staff Lieutenant-General Edson Burns had cancelled his visit to Rome planned for later that day, asked for an immediate interview with the Israeli Prime Minister and also issued an appeal to Egyptian President Gamal Abdell Nasser to order the cessation of all Fedayeen attacks. [1.]

Israeli analysis of the attacks over the subsequent two days, made clearer by the number of tracks discovered, led them to the view that all the 100 Fedayeen fighters on short range missions had returned immediately to the Gaza Strip. However, a further 80 fighters on longer missions were making their way eastwards to the Jordanian border, in some cases even passing through the Israeli capital Tel Aviv. Two groups who had been pinned down by Israeli forces in the coastal town of Rishon LeTsiyon south of Tel Aviv had slipped through a police cordon and resumed operations, causing nine further Israeli casualties on the evening of 11th April. These details, passed on to the Foreign Office by British Ambassador in Tel Aviv Sir John Nicholls, revealed the true extent of what was rapidly escalating into a crisis [2]. A second group of seven Fedayeen who had been attacking the Faluja Road were seen crossing the border back into Jordan on the night of 11th April. From here they were returned to Israel, as the Jordanians did not want to offend Egypt by imprisoning them.

Wikeley was again in touch with the Foreign Office in London on 10th April to report that a member of his staff had witnessed a bus in Jordanian controlled east Jerusalem carrying a number of passengers in khaki uniform, to be told that they were Egyptian Fedayeen. The staff member was subsequently informed that the group left by air from Jerusalem to Egypt and that an Egyptian colleague was present at the airport when they departed. Wikeley was worried that if the information was confirmed, the subsequent Israeli response would create great difficulties for Jordan whose official policy was to prevent infiltration from Jordan into Israel. Wikely had also taken a call from the London Times correspondent in Israel. In an off the record briefing with the Secretary General of the Israel Ministry of Foreign Affairs, the journalist was told that the Egyptian Fedayeen were being sent into Jordan, from where they were despatched on raids. The Israelis understood that the Jordanian Government was trying to prevent this abuse of their territory but was being handicapped by pro-Egyptian elements in the Arab Legion, Jordan's British financed army.

British Ambassador to Egypt Sir Humphrey Trevelyan sent his own appraisal of the situation to Whitehall on 11th April. Parsing the facts from his conversation with General Burns, he was able to give a full account of the now fast becoming infamous Gaza incident. Egyptian army units had opened fire on an Israeli patrol. This led to shelling of an Egyptian village by Israeli 25 pounder guns in order to extricate the patrol. This in turn led to retaliatory shelling by the Egyptians of a kibbutz; and thus the subsequent despatch of Egyptian commandos in retaliation for the casualties. Trevelyan reported that Nasser had confirmed to American colleagues that he had in fact ordered the commandos in, with instructions to cause as many casualties as the Israelis had caused in Gaza. He was reluctant to sign up to any cease fire arrangements until he was certain that all Egyptian Fedayeen would be out of Israel by 12th April. Trevelyan wrote: 'Nasser did not explicitly either admit that that he had sent commando troops into Israel, nor explicitly agree that he would liquidate this operation, but he implied he would do this' [3]. Subsequent efforts by UNTSO, pursued in further meetings and discussions with Nasser and the Israeli Government now focused on trying to tighten up Articles in the Armistice Agreement, most especially Article 2(ii), which related to the cessation of all firing along the border. The Gaza incident illustrated just how volatile the border had become, how porous it was to those who could exploit its weaknesses and the extent to which Egypt had developed the capacity to export irregular war to its immediate neighbour.

Training Para-Military Forces

The development of a para-military capability in its modernising military strategy was intrinsic to Egypt's ability to take on what it saw as a fully realised British army of occupation as well as to confront the existential threat represented by the military capability of its new, and assertive neighbour Israel. Alongside revitalised conventional armed forces and a new generation of armaments, the para-military capability would offer the country an alternative means of applying force of arms, one moreover which had already been widely proven as effective in revolutionary insurgencies in the Middle East, not least by the Zionists in Mandate era Palestine and by Arab irregulars under the command of T E Lawrence during the Arab Revolt of the First World War against the Ottoman Turks.

Without experience of developing this kind of strategic and tactical capability, Egypt's Revolutionary Command Council turned in 1953 to its German advisers to plan and construct a suitable model. In January of that year Otto Skorzeny had been in Cairo where, as a guest of General Neguib, he had been invited to establish an Egyptian Military Academy for Air and to direct the formation of commando forces. Whilst the CIA reckoned he had turned down both requests, it had reported that Skorzeny might well be acting as consultant on the general programme: 'two training centres for Egyptian commandos already exist, it is said, where recruits are being instructed by German officers, for possible guerrilla warfare against the British'[4]. The British had already reported that Skorzeny had carried out a reconnaissance visit to the Canal Zone to advise on commando and sabotage tactics[5].

On 5th August of the same year, Sir Frank Roberts, Deputy-Under Secretary at the Foreign Office had written in a commentary to an intelligence report on the training of para-militaries in Egypt: 'a significant point is the assistance given by German advisers to the Muslim Brotherhood in the training of sabotage squads. No doubt (Gerhard) Mertins is in charge of this. I understand that we have asked the German Federal Government to get him removed' [6]. Roberts went on to say: 'I saw a rather significant report the other day to the effect that the German advisers, with the exception of Mertins, were getting very disturbed about the possibility of being involved in trouble between us and the Egyptians.' The expertise and advice of both Skorzeny and Mertins were subsequently seen as instrumental in the development of Egypt's para-military forces, which through the 1950s spanned the Muslim Brotherhood

Kateibas, the Liberation Units formed to defend the Canal Zone (and later to form the nucleus of a new Egyptian Home Guard) and latterly the Fedayeen. The idea driving the formation of an elite Palestinian fighting force of Fedayeen 'self-sacrificers' was to get round the restrictions applied to Egypt's use of regular armed forces in the Gaza Strip, precluded by conditions in the Armistice Agreement established after the 1948/49 Arab Israeli War. To partially circumvent this, the Palestinian border police was formed in 1952 and hundreds of volunteers started training for the force in 1953.

Late in the following year, larger scale Fedayeen operations into Gaza were mounted from Egyptian territory. The Egyptian Government supervised the establishment of formal Fedayeen groups to launch raids into Israel, allegedly under the control of Egyptian Army Intelligence Chief General Mustafa Hafez, after an Israeli raid on an Egyptian military outpost in Gaza in February 1955 during which 37 Egyptian soldiers were killed. At least two of the German instructors of the Palestinian Fedayeen units were separately identified as Wilhelm Boerner, a former SS Untersturmführer known by his Muslim name of Ali Ben Kashir [7] and Erich Altern, a former Gestapo agent known by his Muslim name of Ali Bella[8]. The history of these cross-border raids and retaliatory action by the Israelis became increasingly contentious and bloody. In 1956, Israeli forces entered Khan Younis in the Gaza Strip. In the course of carrying out searches for weapons and unauthorised personnel, 272 Palestinians were killed allegedly as a result of 'refugee resistance' [9]. Whilst Nasser was reluctant to enter into a second fully fledged war with Israel before he had concluded that Egypt was ready, a lower intensity guerrilla campaign offered the option of attrition, the erosion of popular support amongst Israeli civilians for a government seen as unable to protect them and the eventual return of land appropriated in 1949.

The true extent of the strength, organisation and threat of para-military forces training in Egypt in 1953 alarmed the British. In the report commented on by Sir Frank Roberts, the General Staff Intelligence HQ of the British Forces in Egypt delivered a downbeat summary in August 1953 of the general situation [10]. Whilst their report suggested that internal divisions between the Muslim Brotherhood and the Liberation Units might render the para-military effort less effective overall, the extent of its general advance was nonetheless surprising. The authors confirmed that there were a number of Muslim Brotherhood camps specialising in training for mine laying, explosives and sabotage; a dedicated camp controlled by the Muslim Brotherhood in every major university in the country; and up to 90 separate camps for Liberation Units, many of them run by or alongside the Egyptian Army. In all, the para-military training operation was most likely turning out an estimated 5,000 men per month but in any case no fewer than 4,000.

In detailing the training itself, the report differentiated between preliminary and advanced courses, the latter lasting for at least two weeks and focusing on training in mines, explosives, flamethrowers, support weapons, mortars and town fighting. Men chosen for this advanced training would often then be selected for commando units in which they would serve alongside army units and practice in jeeps for mobile raiding parties. 'Courses vary in length but average a fortnight, though courses for advanced training are often longer. Members usually wear overalls and a German type peaked cap. There has certainly been considerable German influence if not assistance in training. This has given rise to increased attention paid to and probably more effective techniques in the use of explosives, sabotage and mobile commando type operations. Such assistance is probably more apparent at IEM (Ikhwan El-Muslimin) than at Liberation Unit establishments,' the report warned [11].

Most camps, especially in the Cairo area, had access to local army rifle ranges, though ammunition supplies were assessed by the British to be stretched and the quality of marksmanship poor overall. Whilst discrete Fedayeen training camps were not referenced in the report, it addressed the topic of the Muslim Brotherhood volunteers directly: 'it must be remembered that these Kateibas have been in existence for some considerable time, have had operational experience in Palestine and during the last troubles and, being true volunteers, are likely to reach and maintain a higher standard of efficiency.' The threat from para-military forces was not limited to the Canal Zone but would present a widespread threat of guerrilla type ambushes and sniping at British troops operating in towns and villages, the report further warned.

A German general in Gaza

The decision by Egypt to reach out to the German professional military class to replace British knowledge, expertise and resources after 1948 was driven by logic and experience as much as opportunism. German military culture embraced the theory and practical application of modern organisational development, leadership theory, strategy and tactics, training methodology, advanced standard operating procedures and a style of mobile modern warfare that was still widely recognised as both proven and cutting edge.

Some of its most able practitioners, unemployed since the Second World War and having negotiated denazification or internment, were available on the open market or by special negotiation at affordable rates. There was a reasonable prospect that the right selection of experts would help realise the kind of step change that Egypt felt might tip the balance of power in the region back in its favour and enable the Egyptian military to compete on a more equal footing with Britain and Israel. But the connection would also serve a dual function. The former Wehrmacht and Nazi German cohort offered access to a wider and deeper network that would enable Egypt to scale up its military economy, access much needed international finance, manufacturing expertise, industrial regeneration and offer a gateway to arms and munitions suppliers and dealers.

The Egyptian leadership had also studied history closely, not least on its own doorstep. The choice of German military expertise was entirely consistent with comparable decisions and precedents created successfully in the region before. Some two generations earlier, prior to and during the First World War, imperial Germany had fulfilled precisely the same function for Ottoman Turkey, the predominant Muslim military and political power in the region and ascendant for the previous four centuries. In a bid to take on and contest British and French ambitions in the Middle East and pursue their own economic interests, most especially in access to oil supplies in northern Iraq and trade networks beyond the Persian Gulf, the Germans had reached out the hand of friendship to Ottoman Turkey and the wider Muslim world as far back as October 1898.

This was the pivotal moment when Kaiser Wilhelm 11 ('Al Hajj Wilhelm') had made a high-profile, expansive visit to Jerusalem in order to promote his world view. In consequence, Germany had been invited to establish a military mission in the Turkish capital Constantinople prior to the war. Some of its most formidable military strategists and thinkers, including the preeminent giant of Prussian military theory, Field Marshal Colmar Von Der Golz, had subsequently worked with the Ottoman military leadership for years to upgrade the antiquated Turkish army and bring it into the modern fighting world.

In the near past the Egyptians, themselves under British occupation, had thus witnessed at first hand one of Germany's most famous wartime generals tread the scrub and dust covered hills of Gaza, commanding the Ottoman army in the Palestine and Sinai campaign of 1918 as the Turks tried to stem the advance of Britain's revitalised Egyptian Expeditionary Force (EEF) under General Sir Edmund Allenby. A Prussian general in the classical style of the time, Otto Viktor Karl Liman von Sanders (1855-1929) presented a slim, moustachioed, upright and open faced figure, with his high forehead and direct gaze. Looking surprisingly youthful for his years Liman became a familiar figure in Gaza and was most often pictured in the uniform of a Turkish marshal with the distinctive kolpak fur hat that signified the rank and a medal at his collar. A career soldier and previously commander of Germany's 22nd Division, Liman was assigned by Kaiser Wilhelm 11 to Constantinople where, in 1913 he was appointed to head the German military mission to the Ottoman Empire. The Ottomans had for many years operated a close partnership with the Germans to modernise their antiquated army, and Liman was to be the last in a long line of advisers to take on the job. To further fuel the alliance Enver Pasha, a declared Germanophile, had come to power as part of a Triumvirate running the Ottoman government after a military coup in 1913. Now appointed War Minister, Enver had been Turkey's military attaché in Berlin from 1908 to 1911. At the age of only 31, he found himself in charge of Turkey's military modernisation programme and his strong empathy and contacts within the German leadership cemented the relationship between the two countries.

Much as Dr Wilhelm Voss was to replicate the model some 40 years later as Head of the Central Planning Board in Cairo, Liman arrived in Constantinople in December 1913 with 40 officers to become Inspector-General of the Ottoman army. He immediately started on the process of reorganisation, putting Germans as advisers into key positions. The military mission with its German head became the third most important command centre in Turkey after the Sultan and Minister of War [12].

Unsure who to side with in the coming war, the decisive factor for the Ottoman leadership was the realisation that they needed the military heft and the influence of a major European power to bolster their opposition to Russia. Ottoman Turkey thus signed an alliance with Germany in July 1914 and the British and French declared war on this alliance in November the same year. Later that month, the Ottoman Sultan in his role as Caliph called for all Muslims in the region to rise up in a formal jihad, or Holy War, against the Allies. Liman von Sanders found himself in charge of the Ottoman 5th Army at the Gallipoli Peninsula leading six divisions containing over 80,000 of Turkey's best equipped and trained soldiers. The decisions he made at Gallipoli, which the British and Australians invaded in force in April 1915 were to cement his reputation as a formidable military commander in the field and carve out a famous victory for the Sultan against an over confident, poorly led Allied Army. In 1918, the last year of the war, Liman assumed command of the Ottoman army during the Sinai and Palestine Campaign, replacing the German General Erich von Falkenhayn who had been defeated by Allenby at the end of 1917. Now on the back foot in the later stages of the war, Liman could do little more than sit in defensive positions and wait for the British to attack. First he lost the iconic city of Jerusalem which General Allenby formally entered on 11th December 1917; then his entire force was destroyed at the decisive Battle of Megiddo (Aramageddon) in Syria and Liman barely made good his own escape from the field. This decisive battle ended the fighting in the campaign and opened the way for the post-war settlements made in the region at the Paris Peace Conference in 1919.

The larger-than-life, generally unpopular Colmar von Der Golz (1843-1916) had been fighting with the Ottoman army that was simultaneously confronting and halting the British invasion of Mesopotamia, now modern day Iraq. The 6th Indian Army under General Sir Charles Townshend landed in Basra and Abadan in November 1914 to secure the oil supplies shipped from there to Britain via the Persian Gulf and Suez Canal. The oil was vital to fuel the British navy and much of British industry, and thus critical to the war effort. Having surprised the Turks and achieved this initial objective with relative ease, British forces set out in a motley flotilla of flat-bottomed boats and paddle steamers, nicknamed 'Townshend's Regatta' up the shallow and marshy Tigris and Euphrates rivers to capture Baghdad.

Undone by a combination of overconfidence, weak supply lines, disease, a nightmare trinity of flies, sand flies and mosquitoes and unexpectedly fierce opposition, they were brought to a sudden and expensive halt by the Turkish army at Ctesiphon, 50 miles south of Baghdad, under the leadership of the bespectacled and moustachioed Von der Golz. The battle of Ctesiphon was officially declared a draw though the British retreated back down the river nursing terrible casualties and with completely inadequate medical facilities to treat the wounded. They came to a halt 100 miles south of Baghdad in a loop of the river Tigris at a small, nondescript town called Kut Al Amara. Here, Townshend decided to make a stand and allow his wounded along with the cavalry to depart the town while he bought time from his Ottoman pursuers. He took the view that the town was defensible and ordered his garrison of 14,500 men to dig in for the long haul until British forces could come up the River Tigris to relieve him.

The infamous siege of Kut was to last from November 1915 to April 1916, and resulted in the slow starvation and death from malnutrition and disease of thousands of British and Indian soldiers. Golz laid careful and effective siege to the British position moving the Turkish 6th Army south of the city to take up positions straddling marshland either side of the Tigris which he reasoned would impede the advance of British relief columns. Three separate British expeditions tried to relieve the city of Kut at a cost of 23,000 casualties. In the end they came close enough for the garrison to hear the tantalising sound of their artillery, but they were ultimately unsuccessful. On 29th April, 1916, the 11,800 remaining men of the garrison of Kut surrendered and began a long and infamous march northwards to Baghdad and then central Anatolia into a captivity from which many never returned. During this long and terrible trek, British officers were able to travel in relative luxury by train whilst the rank and file marched with little food and water for hundreds of miles, half-starved, stripped and often beaten by Arab irregulars who were left in charge. Most infamously, General Charles Townshend himself lived out the rest of the war in a congenial villa on an island in the Bosphorus, treated by the Turks as a military hero. His failure to lobby for fairer treatment for his soldiers was to sink his reputation after the war and he retired into obscurity. The owlish and schoolmasterly Golz with his wire rimmed glasses, heavy jowls and fastidious sartorial elegance died in Baghdad from typhus just two weeks before the surrender. In accordance with his Will, he was buried in the grounds of the German Consulate in Tarabya, Constantinople, overlooking the Bosphorus.

Between them, Liman von Sanders and Colmar von der Golz provided role models for the Turks, operating as foreign military commanders in a high-functioning, modernised Ottoman army, responding in the field to military challenges with contemporary strategy, tactics and command structure. Golz was the first to establish the German military mission, von Sanders the last to lead it. Of the two, Golz was credited as a major theorist of war and his writing massively impacted the organisation of the huge Ottoman military machine, which was to be put under intolerable pressure on too many fronts and would collapse as a consequence by the end of the war.

This sometimes dislikeable Prussian Field Marshal, who was never able to shake off responsibility for some of the civilian atrocities committed by the German army in its invasion of Belgium in 1914, wrote a number of standard works of military theory and strategy. Die Operationen der II. Armee bis zur Capitulation von Metz (The Operations of the Second Army until the surrender of Metz) and Die Sieben Tage von Le Mans (The Seven Days of Le Mans), were both published in 1873. Léon Gambetta und seine Armeen (Léon Gambetta and his armies), published in 1877 was translated into French in the same year and is widely considered to be his most influential work.

The new regime's leaders however 'adored the head of the German army's training mission, General Colmar von der Golz, as their father figure and viewed his writings on war as sacred texts'[13]. Golz spent 12 years on his project to reorganise the Ottoman army, achieving some notable reforms including lengthening the period of study at military schools and adding new curricula for staff courses at the War College. The 'Golz generation' of army officers would go on to become highly influential in both Ottoman political and military life, embracing his 'nation in arms' theory as the basis of its understanding of war. Ironically Golz did not get along with the last mission leader von Sanders, nor was he liked by the real power in the Ottoman Government, Enver Pasha.

An appraisal of the impact of the German military mission on the evolution and performance of the Ottoman army up to and during the First World War forms a critical part of the analysis of the German military advisers within Egypt's Central Planning Board from 1952. In some respects it may be judged as a direct successor although all-important distinctions differentiate the status and role of the two. The German advisers working directly for Nasser and Neguib in the early 1950s were not representatives of the West German Government in any sense and thus were not helping execute West German foreign policy in the region, in fact somewhat the reverse. Nor were they empowered to command troops in the field, as had been Sanders, Golz and Von Falkenheyn. Their rules of engagement confined them to advisory and consulting roles, organising, planning and training, only maintaining a clandestine and occasional presence in the field. In this major respect, it remains impossible to know how the events of the Suez invasion in November 1956 might have played out differently if German leadership had been directly engaged in or even directing the defence of Port Said or repelling the invasion of Sinai.

Or later the following decade, whether the crushing defeat of Egypt by Israel in the Six-Day War of June 1967 might have had a different outcome for a combination of the same reasons. The Egyptians were totally surprised by the tripartite invasion of Egypt in early November 1956 by Israel, Britain and France and seemed to have no prior intelligence or information on which to have acted differently. This failing was down to weaknesses in Egyptian intelligence and the secrecy of the British, French and Israeli plan. In any case, by that time many of the first wave of German military advisers in Egypt had already departed, leaving the question more about the legacy which they had bequeathed than the action they had missed.

Islamism and German Foreign Policy

On the morning of 31st October 1898, Kaiser Wilhelm 11 vacated his tents in a luxurious camp supervised and arranged by the travel firm Thomas Cook just beyond the walls of Jerusalem, preparing to enter the city through the Jaffa Gate. The event was redolent with symbolism. Imperial Germany was reaching out the hand of friendship and solidarity with Ottoman Turkey and by implication the 300 million Muslim and Arabic-speaking inhabitants of an 'Orient' which stretched from the North African Maghreb in the West to the borders of Iran in the East and Yemen and the smaller independent sheikhdoms in the Arabian Peninsula to the south. The German Emperor riding on a horse through the Jaffa Gate into the Old City to meet the city's assembled dignitaries presented a potent image not lost on the photographers and publicists who were there to record a definitive moment in modern German foreign relations.

Even a cursory analysis of the motivation underpinning such a visit suggested that the goodwill was to be made manifest through an action plan to mark the new alliance between the Kaiser and the Ottoman Sultan, Abdul Hamid 11. Accompanying Kaiser Wilhelm was his little known though ubiquitous and highly influential adviser on Muslim affairs, Max Von Oppenheim.

It was von Oppenheim, an accomplished archaeologist and member of the banking dynasty, who was the strategic thinker with a vision of imperial Germany acting alongside the Muslim world in opposition to the French and British in the Middle East, and thereby furthering German economic interests in the region. Oppenheim, who gained a reputation as Germany's version of Lawrence of Arabia, believed that the Kaiser and the German Empire stood to gain from the relationship by aligning German foreign policy with pan-Islamism and the Islamist political movement.

As an attaché at the German Consulate in Cairo, Oppenheim developed the theory which drew direct comparisons between the positions of the Papacy in the Christian Church and the Caliphate in the Muslim faith. He came to the view that the Caliphate no longer possessed the equivalent unified constituency in Islam as the Papacy did in Catholicism and thus it needed strengthening. He believed that the desire amongst Muslims to end the domination of Christian countries in the region, most particularly Britain, France and Russia over Muslim majority lands required Islam's 'command to unite and make their societies follow their precepts'.[14] Pan-Islamism represented for Von Oppenheim the most effective way of undermining the British, French and Russian colonies in the region, destabilising them and causing the Arab people to rise against colonial subjugation. As part of this vision, he failed to recognise that the Caliph, an Ottoman Turk, had in reality only a fragile grip on the region's Muslims, many of whom were ethnic Semites, Arabs who had been living under exploitative and often humiliating Turkish rule for four centuries. And further to that, he did not anticipate the Arab Revolt of 1917 championed and supported by the British, but carried out by Sharif Hussein of Mecca. Hussein was an Arab and a Hashemite, thus a direct descendant of the Prophet and fully able to mount a legitimate 'counter-jihad' from the Arabian Peninsula whose major holy cities of Mecca and Medina were still occupied by the Turkish army.

The German-Turkish alliance nonetheless produced a series of outcomes which formalised and strengthened the relationship between the two partners. The Berlin-Baghdad Railway, started in 1910 was planned and built to provide a land bridge linking German interests in Europe with their furthest colonies beyond the Persian Gulf. The railway represented an outstanding feat of engineering that negotiated some of the most inhospitable terrain in central Anatolia. But it ran into technical trouble and the line stopped at Mosul in northern Mesopotamia before being finally completed and reaching Baghdad in 1940. A second outcome of the Kaiser's visit was the establishment of the German military mission in Constantinople, which would endure until the end of the First World War. Von Oppenheim, as part of his strategy to promote the cause of pan-Islamism, also set up two prisoner-of war (POW) camps outside Berlin where he sent all Muslim soldiers from Allied armies captured on the Western and Eastern Fronts. Halbmondlager (Half Moon Camp) and Weinbergslager were in due course to turn out the first cohorts of jihadists trained to serve German interests whilst employed in Ottoman armies. The German war time propaganda machine also cranked out a dedicated strain of material aimed at turning Muslim soldiers in the British and French armies, from Mesopotamia to the Western Front, away from their colonial masters and towards the Turks.

Haj Amin Al Husseini, Grand Mufti of Jerusalem

In the disaster of the First World War for Germany, with its national humiliation, loss of territory and impossibly high war reparations lay the seeds of the National Socialist and later Nazi philosophy which would grow through the wilderness years of the 1920s to deliver Hitler and the Nazi Party to power in 1933. The ascent of Fascism and the eclipse of liberal democracy were played out in countries across Europe with the strident figures of Benito Mussolini, Franscisco Franco and Adolf Hitler becoming Europe's predominant statesmen. Across the Mediterranean in the North African Maghreb, the attractions of Fascism found echoes in the formation of the Young Egypt Party, the Green Shirts, a Falangist political movement which for a while was copied in Syria and Lebanon with its equivalent Brown Shirts. These parties offered a home, especially for young army officers, to those who believed authoritarian government, primary loyalty to the state and conspicuous nationalism might offer a way out of British and French imperial subservience and colonial occupation.

Future Egyptian President Gamal Abdel Nasser, looking for a solution to what he saw as Egypt's perpetual subjugation was at one time a member of the Green Shirts and an early enthusiast for the Nazi Party's approach to harnessing national unity and purpose in a common cause. The system of Mandatory governments set up in the Middle East after the war by the League of Nations left Britain and France in charge of overseeing the transformation of former Ottoman territories to independent states, including Iraq, Greater Syria, Transjordan and Palestine.

It was the case of Palestine especially, and its fight for national identity against the British and the Jews which first attracted the attention and then the support of Nazi Germany as the 1930s progressed. The Palestinian nationalist leader Haj Amin Al Husseini, Grand Mufti of Jerusalem, was to become a constant thorn in the side of the British as he led an insurrection in Palestine in 1936 and lobbied extensively for external support for his fight. From the start of the Second World War, Amin was exiled from Palestine to Baghdad but in October 1941 found his way to Italy, where he met with Mussolini and Italian Foreign Minister Galeazzo Ciano. Declaring a joint pact which pitted the Arab nation against the British and their allies in the Middle East, Amin went on to Berlin to meet Hitler and plead the case for Nazi support to liberate Palestine and defeat the Jews, fast becoming ascendant in the country. Hitler received him with cautious respect but would not commit to a military move against the British in Palestine. After the halting of Rommel's Afrikakorps in Egypt in 1942 he would not have been able to act directly, but in any case saw Palestine as a sideshow compared with other more pressing fronts opening up in the war. However, he was fully prepared to enter into what became a rapidly escalating and vicious anti-Semitic, anti-colonial propaganda war against the British and the Jews in the Middle East, exhorting Muslims and Arabs to rise up against their British oppressors and defeat the threat posed by international Jewry [15].

Amin was invited to make his home in Berlin where he resided during the war years. This immensely powerful, energetic and well connected Palestinian grandee with his mild manner, enigmatic smile and piercing gaze worked closely with Arab colleagues in Berlin, including deposed Iraqi Prime Minister Rashid Ali Al Gaylani to develop written and spoken content for Nazi driven Arabic language propaganda dispersed across the region. In collaboration with a young Egyptian in Berlin, Dr Abdel Halim Al Naggar, he helped developed radio as the most effective and far reaching propaganda tool in the region to promote the Arab nationalist message. His closest Nazi Party colleague in the German capital at the time was the racial theorist and propagandist Johann von Leers with whom he worked closely to develop rabidly anti-Semitic material to deploy in his war of race hate against the Jews of Palestine. Both Amin and Gaylani received substantial allowances from the German Foreign Office whilst in Berlin, according to an FO official called Carl Berthold Franz Rekowski, who had dealt with Amin over expense payments totalling 50,000 marks a month, more than twice the annual salary of a German Field Marshal. According to Rekowski, the Nazi Government planned to use both Arab exiles to control their respective countries when the Germans had conquered them, although as a believer in a pan-Arab state, Amin's closest contacts were with the SS rather than the Foreign Office.

After the war, Amin Al-Husseini was hunted for war crimes he was alleged to have committed in the Balkans, amongst them the recruitment of the Bosnian Muslim 'Handschar' Waffen SS

Division. He also did an alleged deal with Hitler under which he agreed to actively aid the Nazi cause in return for no further Jews being moved from Europe to Palestine. After the war, this was interpreted by some as having made a contribution to worsening the scale of the ensuing Holocaust. Amin was also accused but never convicted of having visited the Sachsenhausen concentration camp at Oranienburg, north of Berlin which he had sized up as a potential model that might be exported to Palestine.

Amin was saved by two former Nazi collaborators who had worked for him during the war. One was Husain Sulaiman Djozo who he had hired as an instructor at his SS imam training school and who went on to be the Bosnian SS Division's chief imam. Tito's Communist government pardoned Djozo because it needed a Muslim leader who it knew would follow orders. His other saviour was Abd ar-Rahman Azzam, the post-war Arab League's secretary general. Azzam threatened an Arab boycott against Yugoslavia unless Al-Hussaini was taken off the list [16].

Aided by the decision of the French not to prosecute him, Amin made good his escape from Europe and fled to Cairo where he was welcomed as a hero. Here he set about planning along with Gamal Abdel Nasser, Anwar Sadat and other members of the Free Officers movement for the first Arab Israeli war of 1948 to reclaim Palestine. Looking to continue the propaganda front against the Jews after the war, Amin was also said to have issued the invitation to Johann von Leers in Buenos Aires in 1955 to come to Cairo and take up a position as head of anti-Semitic propaganda at Egypt's Ministry of National Guidance, which Leers did in February 1956. There is no doubt that Amin's network stretched far and wide across the Arabic speaking world. His luxurious villa in the Maadi district of Cairo provided a haven for former Nazis and Wehrmacht officers arriving in the city while he played a central role in co-ordinating activity, enabling meetings and keeping the case of Palestine at the front of the collective mind. Amin also kept up his contacts with old German comrades, many of them now escaped from Europe. In Cairo, he was especially helpful to former Wehrmacht and Nazi expatriates who he assisted to obtain the paperwork needed to start a new life. Some he even helped convert to Islam. Amongst them was the racial theorist, ideologue, propagandist, pamphleteer, author, journalist, agitator and recent refugee from Buenos Aires, Johann von Leers.

Chapter Seven
THE ROCKET MEN OF CAIRO

'The Egyptian Ambassador told me today that...the third development which had given pleasure in Cairo was Her Majesty's Government's decision to release 15 jet aircraft to Egypt, of which he had heard from the Chief of Air Staff. This was the third and he hoped it would not be the last favourable development in Anglo-Egyptian relations. As the Ambassador had heard nothing from Cairo about the jets, I told him of the communication which Sir Ralph Stevenson had been instructed to make to General Neguib.'

William Strang,
Permanent Under-Secretary at the Foreign Office,
12th November 1952
TNA/PREM 11/392/86940/Prime Minister's Personal Minutes.

Throwing up clouds of thick, cloying dust and shards of gravel, the column of 70 Israeli tanks and armoured vehicles crossed the Sinai border into Egypt heading north-west for the main Egyptian airfield at Al Arish. It was shortly after midday on 30th December 1948. They first captured a satellite airfield just south of the main field. Then the column hit some resistance from Egyptian forces. It was held up by a small detachment from the main Egyptian army position still being held between Rafah and Gaza, which had been bypassed by the Israeli column in the advance. Whilst the position stabilised, a second Egyptian detachment which had withdrawn from the nearby town of Auji in the face of the Israeli advance remained unaccounted for and off the radar. The Egyptian forces at Al Faluja and those between Rafah and Gaza were assessed as being intact and in possession of a week's worth of supplies.[1] The key to the Egyptian forces maintaining their defensive position was the continued possession of Al Arish airfield. Loss of this would cut off air cover for their main forces along with air support for the soldiers occupying Al Faluja. Loss of Arish itself would sever the lines of communication between Rafah and the Suez Canal, making the situation of the main force precarious. The complex tactical situation made it tough for the battlefield commanders to be definitive about any situation in the tangled terrain of scrub, dune and shallow hills. But somewhere inside the developing 'Faluja pocket' was Gamal Abdel Nasser, future President of Egypt. A career army officer and deputy commander of the Egyptian troops occupying Al Faluja, he was about to enter into a fight for not only his life but also the making of his political future. In time, events at Al Faluja were to have a direct bearing and symbolic significance which between them would cement his reputation as first-class combat soldier and Egyptian popular hero.

The account and analysis of this fighting in the middle of the first Arab Israeli war was contained in a secret despatch from the Military Attaché at the British Embassy in Cairo to the War Office in London on 30th December 1948. It described just a vignette, though as it turned out a historical one, of the way the war was going at the end of December that year when the Egyptian forces were still managing to put up some resistance. However, the war was already headed the wrong way and would continue to do so until it ended in a humiliating and comprehensive defeat for Egypt in March 1949. In his despatch from Cairo, the Military Attaché also highlighted a critical issue that was to dominate Egyptian military planning and thinking for the next two decades. 'The Ministry of Defence has appealed for active help and equipment from British forces. This appeal was first made by the Minister and his military and air staffs, not by the Egyptian government, presumably in order to avoid raising the 1936 Treaty implication,' he wrote [2]. And went on: 'The Ministry has been told informally that these implications seem inevitable and that we must have formal notification of the present position from the Egyptian Government. They are evidently anxious to know the answer we would return to a request for help before they ask the question in order not to be placed in a position in which it would become publicly known that an Egyptian request for help had been publicly refused' [3].

The despatch highlighted an essential though awkward truth. Egypt's position as a military power was made precarious amongst other reasons by its lack of arms and armaments. Much of the armed forces' equipment on land, sea and in the air was antiquated, of poor quality and in short supply. The country had little industry or arms manufacturing capacity, irregular procurement processes and patchy logistics. Both the Military High Command and the monarch, King Farouk, were aware that this combination placed Egypt at a major disadvantage in anything approaching a major conflict. The torrid fighting of the Arab Israeli War, requiring tanks, personnel carriers, artillery and machine guns as well as aircraft was showing up these weaknesses mercilessly, most especially in contrast to the modern, cutting edge combat equipment deployed by the new and rapidly expanding Israeli Army.

The request by the Egyptians was the subject of a letter from British Ambassador in Egypt Sir Ronald Campbell to the Foreign Office in London on 29th December 1948, in which he recounted that the Egyptian Minister for War 'had sent a Staff Officer round with a message begging for war material in the shape of aircraft, guns, tanks, etc'[4]. The Ambassador revealed the true extent of the Egyptians' desperation: 'he went so far as to suggest the loan of British aircraft, tanks and guns with British crews but Egyptian markings if that would make it easier for us. He was told in reply that while I myself was not in a position to say what His Majesty's Government's attitude might be, I would consult you immediately.' The visit by the Staff Officer was shortly followed up by a phone call from Egyptian Minister of War Muhammad Haider Pasha who told the ambassador he was not concerned with the political side of things but 'only with the fact that the Egyptian army was in great difficulties and that British forces in the Canal Zone had it in their power to help'. Haider Pasha expressed the view that it would be a great tragedy for both Egypt and Britain if 'we stood idly by', and revealed that his approach had only been made after close consultation with

King Farouk but not with Egypt's Prime Minister.

But in this case Britain did stand by. Pressed on every side of its retreating Empire, with an independent India declared the year prior in 1947 followed by declaration of Israeli statehood on 14th May 1948, the British were not minded to place their hard pressed forces and military assets in harm's way in recently vacated Palestine. Whilst Britain, a traditional source of arms, armaments and expertise for Egypt had withdrawn its Military Mission to Cairo in 1948, it still possessed substantial military forces in bases along the 120 mile stretch of the Suez Canal, amounting to some 70,000 troops. The Canal Zone bases had everything the Egyptians needed, including air fields, modern fighter aircraft, tanks, ships, weapons systems, arms and equipment. In fact, the size of Britain's garrison in its Suez bases was very similar to Egypt's own armed forces. In July 1952, at the time of the military coup of the Free Officers these were judged to be some 80,000 strong, including one infantry division east of the Suez Canal, one infantry and one armoured division placed between Cairo and Alexandria and two infantry battalions in Upper Egypt and Sudan[5].

The refusal of the British to materially assist the Egyptian Military High Command in December 1948, notwithstanding the political implications, was a contributory factor in the collapse of Egypt's military effort in the first Arab Israeli war. This attempt to recover the land of Palestine for all Palestinians and for the wider Arab nation had the ideological underpinning, seal of approval and personal impetus of Haj Amin Al Husseini, aided amongst others by the growing Free Officers Movement in Egypt. Whilst Jordan secured limited objectives in east Jerusalem and the West Bank after the fighting was over, the military plan to defeat Israel was a general failure and the repercussions in Egypt were immediate. King Farouk sacked most of the Military High Command, including his Minister of War and Marine Muhammad Haider Pasha and it was not long afterwards that Afrikakorps General Artur Schmitt was invited to inspect the overall military situation and give his recommendations for a shake-up of the entire system, including arming and equipping Egypt's military forces.

At the same time, Farouk opened up lines of communication through European middlemen to reach out to German scientists and engineers who had been employed in the Nazi rocket and missile programmes up to the close of the war in 1945 in an effort to develop a home-grown Egyptian manufacturing capability in jet fighters, missiles and rocket technology. He saw these as modern weapons systems that would dominate the new military landscape and together tip the balance in future wars in Egypt's favour. The creation of a domestic arms and armaments industry was at the centre of Farouk's thinking and part of the terms of reference for the recruitment of German expertise to the Central Planning Board which was undertaken in 1951 and reached fruition the following year. At the same time as it sought to develop its own military manufacturing base, Egypt increasingly reached out through the 1950s to buy modern arms and armaments from foreign suppliers. This strategy turned out to be deeply controversial. Though partly successful in establishing Egypt's ability to act as an independent state in this regard, it became a defining factor in the shifting balance of power in the region, threatening an arms race in the Middle East and bringing the Cold War being played out between United States and Russia into the region's back yard.

Egypt goes it Alone on Arms

Dr Wilhelm Voss, leader of the Central Planning Board and Chief Technical Advisor to the Egyptian Government, had first appeared in Egypt in 1951. Over the next year, he was instrumental in recruiting German experts and advisers for both the military and for the arms and armaments business. Able to delegate much of the military and para-military aspects of the mission to artilleryman General Wilhelm Fahrmbacher and Panzer commander Oskar Munzel, Voss could focus on his specialism, arms and armaments research and production. In July 1952 when the Free Officers assumed power in Egypt, this process accelerated. Voss was himself an experienced and large scale player in the arms business, having spent the war in charge of the giant Skoda Werke factory in Czechoslovakia on behalf of the Third Reich. He had an extensive network of former colleagues and an in-depth knowledge of Germany's armaments production capacity and output. Voss also had access to the highest levels of Egypt's political leadership and military command structure and, at least in his early days on the job, the kind of authority that meant he could put decisions into action.

By May 1953 Voss had signed up a growing number of arms and armaments experts to Central Planning Board contracts, including Professor Dr Georg Romer, a chemist delegated to start up a high explosives factory in Cairo. He also contracted Dr H Andrea, a former heavy hitter with the German industrial giant IG Farben. Born in Gottingen in 1907, Andrea was a ballistics and munitions expert who had from 1937 been an employee of the German Ministry of War Production where he had spent his time developing tanks and a range of secret weapons. Voss handed out contracts to Engineer Hans Tokpfer, a chemist and explosives expert with the Dynamit AG company, Engineer G Zanke, born in 1902 in Posen and a member of the Board of Weapons and Ammunition during the war in charge of production and testing of small arms, Kurt Hanisch, a rocket scientist employed during the war at the rocket research centre at Peenemünde, chemist Dr F Frasoldati, born in the Austrian Tyrol in 1909 and an expert in nitro-cellulose, and weapons expert Herbert Borhmert [6].

The group of some 20 arms advisers between them represented almost every skill associated with large-scale arms production and assembly. The question was how effectively they could be put to work in planning and managing an arms production operation in Egypt that could satisfy the Government's ambition to attain rapid self-sufficiency. Initial evidence was that the money and resources required to design the tooling, machinery and assembly lines for this kind of industrial manufacturing was not instantly available and might itself take some time to put together.

From 1952, Voss had also been working in Cairo in parallel with the private CERVA organisation managed by rocket scientist Dr Rolf Engel, a former Hauptsturmführer in the Waffen SS and still an ardent Nazi. In 1944, Engel had been Head of the Skoda Research Centre at its arms factory in Prague. After the war he worked with his own team in Paris for the French Office National Des Études et Recherches Aeronautique (ONERA). And it was from here that he arrived in Cairo to work with the private CERVA company as leader of a team of 40 further German experts on rockets and rocket fuel development to establish a factory in Egypt[7]. Engel was to feature in the Egyptian domestic rocket programme from 1952 to 1957 when he left for Italy.

It was in arms manufacturing and production, as well as heavy industry, that Egypt looked to leverage economic and financial connections with German industrialists, some of whom had been intimately concerned in supporting the German war effort. One in particular was the banker Hjalmar Schacht, a Nazi Party member since 1932, personal advisor to Hitler and former Nazi German Economics Minister in the early 1930s. Schacht also happened to be the 'uncle' and protector of Otto Skorzeny's wife, Countess Ilse von Finkenstein who, along with her husband was a regular visitor to Cairo. The Daily Worker newspaper in the United States identified Schacht as assisting Egypt with finance in November of 1953. 'Having had all his property restored, he is now running three banks in Germany and has made trips to give advice to Iran, Egypt…and other countries', it reported [8].

In a piece entitled 'The Germans Dulles wants us to trust', the newspaper also identified Alfried Krupp von Bohlen and Halbach, 'the most notorious of the war criminal industrialists who subsidised Hitler and reaped huge profits from arms production' as having done deals in Egypt [9]. The Daily Worker, giving vent to its international socialist world view was deeply suspicious of a whole raft of German industrialists and bankers whose reputations and skills were being rehabilitated under West German Chancellor Konrad Adenauer and who were at the same time being endorsed by US Secretary of State John Foster Dulles. These included Dr Heinrich Kost, former director of Haniel Steel, Wilhelm Roelen of the Thyssen Company and Ludger Westrick, a former member of the Nazi Council of the aircraft armament industry which built the Luftwaffe.

In addition to experts in arms and armaments manufacturing, Voss recruited a number of arms dealers to the Central Planning Board, including some who had already set up partnerships and joint ventures in Egypt. The British named nine of these individuals on a list passed across to the Americans in 1955 [10]. Amongst them was Otto Skorzeny himself, who was thought to be acting as a go-between for the Egyptian Government with economist and resurrected banker Hjalmar Schacht, as well as representing commercial clients on his own behalf. The list named Albert Gay, arms dealer for the Cairo company Asiaca Ltd, Gunter Jackering, a dealer for the Egyptian Continental Trading Company and Heinrich Blum, a former Aide de Camp to Field Marshal Rommel and now representative of the Egyptian-German

Industrial & Trading Company which was heavily engaged in the arms trade. The list also picked out Rheinemetall Borsig AG representative in Egypt Walter Deter, Wilhelm Beisner who was a former SS officer captured by the Allies during the Italian campaign and now Middle East representative of the arms dealers Fabrica D'Armi Pietro Barata, former Nazi Party member Joachim Hertslet and Lt-Colonel M G Olbruk who had gone into partnership in Cairo with the Egyptian arms dealer Hasan Isnawi [11].

In their assessments of the German arms dealers who were central to Egypt's rearmament programme, the British did not appear to have realised the particular significance of Wilhelm Beisner and his business partner Joachim Hertslet. Beisner had been part of Einsatzkommando Egypt, a death squad assembled by SS officer Walter Rauff in Athens in 1941 tasked with eliminating the Jews in Palestine after Rommel's army had advanced through Egypt. The former intelligence officer was at the centre of a web of prominent Nazis in Cairo, and was directly connected to Otto Skorzeny, Otto Ernst Remer and the German Foreign Office deportation specialist Franz Rademacher. The CIA believed Beisner had arrived in Cairo in July 1951 where he, Hertslet and Jackering worked in the Egyptian Continental Trading Company, at one point negotiating a large order of machine guns for General Neguib. Beisner and Hertslet had unsuccessfully tried to pass themselves off as working for the West German government. It was also rumoured as late on as 1958 that Beisner had played a part in the training of Algerian freedom fighters in the struggle to liberate Algeria from French control, and that he sold arms to the Algerian National Liberation Front.

From 1950 up to the Suez crisis in November 1956, the Egyptian effort to build up a domestic arms and armaments industry gained momentum and achieved some initial success. The battle, however, was always to reconcile finance, resourcing and the expertise required to execute a sophisticated manufacturing process with the challenging conditions and logistics that prevailed in a country that was late to industrialise and financially underpowered. However in 1955, the year before the Suez crisis, the British acknowledged that the Egyptians had made progress in the arms programme, though they judged that the levels of success had probably been overstated. In January that year, the British Embassy in Cairo reported that Egypt had set up a factory for the production of small arms. A number of semi-automatic rifles had been assembled at the plant without production yet being fully sufficient to meet Egypt's needs.[12]

The British had identified the rifle in production as being either the Belgian NATO rifle, a Mauser pattern imported from Yugoslavia, or a Swedish model, the IABG Ljungman semi-automatic M42, with consensus on the latter. The Embassy also reported that Egypt had partially completed an assembly plant at Helwan for the production of Vampire jet aircraft, begun by British De Havilland technicians before they departed the country in 1952 [13]. However, installation of this plant was still incomplete and the Egyptian Air Force was negotiating with the De Havilland Company to dispose of as much of the equipment as they could. At the same time, German technicians were reported by the British to be working on the installation, without knowing details of precisely what this imported workforce was up to. The report from Cairo did, however, sound a note of concern: 'We have heard that the Egyptians have designed a jet engine which they are intending to have manufactured in Germany. Almost any engineer could, of course, design a jet engine of sorts today but manufacture calls for precise engineering practice, particularly where turbine blades are concerned, which is still beyond Egypt's capacity [14].

If after testing the Egyptian engine did not prove suitable, the Egyptians intended to purchase 200 engines from abroad, the Embassy sources revealed. At the same time, Egypt also had plans to begin assembly of an airframe, an initiative it was felt was within their capacity to do if they managed to import some components, and to install in the frame an engine either procured from abroad or manufactured to their own specifications. The finished product would then require testing so that the likelihood of Egypt being able to export fully operating jet fighters within a year was remote.

In giving only a partially complete picture, the Embassy report had flagged up a number of developments and trends that were now becoming clearer. First, Egyptian efforts to set up and manage its own jet propulsion industry were in play. Both jet engines and the airframes to carry them were now part of the plan, though not fully advanced. The element the British had missed was the parallel development of jet propelled ballistic missiles.

Research and arrangements for the secret production of these were also getting underway through the CERVA programme set up initially by King Farouk. The beginnings of a domestic arms production industry were now detectable, with the manufacture of rifles, mines and flame throwers amongst other weapons taking place in factories and assembly plants in or near Cairo. The report touched on a further trend which was the decision taken by Egypt to reach out increasingly to foreign sources beyond the British for either the components or finished products they wanted. It had taken the harsh lessons of the 1948/49 Arab Israeli war to show the Egyptian Government that reliance on one source of arms and armaments was not an effective or advisable strategy. They needed to look outwards. Increasingly through the 1950s and into the 1960s, Egypt militarised through combining domestic production with a series of foreign arms deals which were to shake up the balance of power in the region and usher in the realities of the Cold War era to the Middle East.

Arms Deals and the Cold War

Towards the end of January 1953, a mere six months after the Free Officers Movement took power in Egypt, a bombshell dropped on the British Foreign Office. A representative of the US Embassy called in person in London to pass on an important message from the US State Department. A decision at the highest level of Government in Washington had been taken confirming that the United States was to sell Egypt $US11 million of arms. In making the decision, consideration had been taken of British views in such a way that the offer had been made on a cash only basis, account had been taken of Britain's current ongoing negotiations over independence in Sudan and further consideration would be given to any items on the list which could potentially be used against the British in Egypt [15].

It was also true that the list of arms did not immediately include heavy weapons and their delivery was not only phased over two years but tied to Egyptian agreement to join the American backed Middle East Defence Organization (MEDO). This still-born alliance proposed by US President Harry Truman had been envisaged to guarantee the safety of the Suez Canal. Nevertheless, the list of American hardware that was dangled in front of the Egyptians to persuade them to join was impressive, including delivery within 45 days of 70 jeeps, 70 M8 armoured cars, 400 machine guns, 100 further jeeps with machine gun mounts and 70,000 helmets. Within a year, the Egyptians could expect to get a mountain of further hardware, including 1,700 rocket launchers, 100 tanks, 400 heavy calibre machine guns, tank loaders and mine detectors. Two years out, this would be supplemented with rockets, piles of ammunition, mobile guns and M71 tanks. The fact that the MEDO never happened made the deal naturally obsolete but this shock US offer turned out to be the tap that turned on the potential supply of foreign arms to the country over the coming years.

With US public opinion opposed to selling arms to Arab states that might be used against Israeli interests, the tripartite MEDO agreement signed between the US, France and Britain in 1950 had been designed to nip any Middle East Arms race in the bud. However, in 1955 Nasser broke the mold by signing a $US83 million arms deal with Czechoslovakia, seen as a proxy in the region for Russia. The deal included 100 T-34 tanks, 80 MIG-15 fighter jets, 30 Ilyushin bombers, ships for the navy, artillery and a wealth of small arms and munitions. This deal, which alone represented the greater part of all weapons shipped to the Middle East from 1951 to 1956, caused uproar in the West where it was perceived as marking the start of a decline in Western influence in the region. The reconstituted Egyptian Office for Military Procurement followed this up in late 1955 with a further deal in Prague for naval vessels and training worth LE £40 million. The deals between them ramped up British concern about the vulnerability of shipping passing through the Suez Canal and the potential increase in capability of Egyptian forces that might be deployed against them in any offensive in the Canal Zone.

After the Suez crisis in November 1956, Nasser continued to break the spirit of UN resolution 997 concerning the arms trade and pose difficult questions for the British and Americans by doing a deal directly with Russia for three submarines to supplement Egyptian naval forces. On 27th June 1957, the Foreign Office wrote to Washington: 'as a result of these Soviet deliveries it looks as if we shall be forced to take up a public position about the continued validity of the UN Resolution 997. Although the Resolution clearly remains in force until rescinded by the General Assembly, we doubt whether, in view of the changed circumstances, it can still be held to apply'[16]. The Jewish Telegraphic Agency Daily News Bulletin publicly broke the story on 31st December 1957 when it reported that the Chief of the Egyptian Naval Staff, Vice Admiral Suleiman Eizzat had made an announcement that Egypt would soon receive new warships from a foreign power. 'He did not name the foreign power but he made the announcement upon his return from a trip to Moscow' the paper reported [17].

Without naming sources, the newspaper revealed that the Egyptian Navy already included several submarines, along with two Russian destroyers, nine frigates and a dozen minesweepers. It suggested that Egypt's Red Sea flotilla had been 'rehabilitated' after the beating it had absorbed during the Sinai attack by the British and French and was now using a new naval base at Gardaka near Suez. After Suez the British did, however, make good on their promise of delivering outstanding equipment for two Israeli destroyers despite UN Resolution 997 still being in place, pointing out in a letter the same month: 'we have no intention of competing with the Soviet Union in the irresponsible delivery of arms to the Middle East and we are quite satisfied that Israel can defend herself adequately' [18].

Where the British and Americans had equivocated over UN Resolution 997 and balked at provoking an arms race in the region, it emerged that France had supplied Israel with quantities of arms. In correspondence from Amman in October 1955, the Foreign Office reported that the Jordanian military attaché in Paris had passed on details of an agreement by France to supply Israel with arms under a contract to be signed by the end of September.

'The precise details of equipment and cost are not known but equipment is thought to include King tanks, armoured personnel carriers, 105 millimetre guns and 'a large number' of Mystère Mk IV fighter jet aircraft. Delivery in some cases is certain to be scheduled for 1956 and 1957' [19]. Leaders of the Arab Legion, Jordan's professional army, considered the French arms shipments were primarily offensive in nature and that their supply to Israel would seriously increase the military threat to Jordan. Thus through the early 1950s the region was engaged in rearming and equipping for larger scale war and an arms race was already underway. From the Egyptian point of view, the edge in this accelerating race would be provided by the development of rockets and jet propulsion to fuel a generation of Arab fighter jets and ballistic missiles that could offer a strike capability across the region.

'Armed and Dangerous'

Dr Wilhelm Voss was at the heart of the Egyptian strategy to carry forward King Farouk's and latterly the Free Officers' vision of a next generation Egyptian military capability fuelled by rocket technology. With post-war operations like Paperclip and Osoaviakhim, they had watched the Americans and the Russians hijack the cream of German and Nazi expertise in these high-performance weapons of the future. So too had they observed Argentina, Spain and France in turn seek to harness for themselves some of the capabilities in advanced rocket and jet propulsion technology nurtured in the arms factories and research laboratories of the Third Reich. Even if many of the leading Nazi scientists and engineers had departed for the US and Russia, the talent pool was wide and deep and it did not take Egypt's appointed agents too long to find available options. Whilst Voss pursued the government backed recruitment programme for the Central Planning Board, other German specialists who had worked for the Third Reich in the research and manufacture of rockets and jet propulsion arrived in Cairo independently and signed their own deals to work alongside government programmes. Through the 1950s, this ecosystem of German scientists and engineers working on secret projects in Cairo grew into the hundreds and even thousands spread across multiple sites in and around the Egyptian capital.

A defining figure in this parallel wave was Dr Rolf Engel, reputed to be Germany's No2 specialist in V-weapons. A leading expert in solid-fuel rockets, satellites and space research, Engel had been in charge of research at the vast Skoda Werke factory in Prague during the war and thus well known to Voss. When Chief of Development and Technical Advisor at this vast facility from 1942-1944, he had also been a Member of the German Ministry of Armaments and was the nominated rocket expert for the Waffen SS with the rank of Hauptsturmführer. Captured by the French, Engel had gone to work in Paris in 1947 as head of the government ONERA Research Group. This sophisticated, accomplished scientist, engineer and ardent Nazi, born in Henz in 1912, was described in biographical sketches as personally attractive, suave and polished. But his good looks and charm masked significant character flaws. 'He has the definite air of being an opportunist and does not enjoy a good reputation among other German nationals, particularly older rocket men' his CIA file noted [20]. This attitude was reflected in the apparent refusal of the eminent space scientist Dr Eugen Sänger to work under him.

Resident in Cairo from 1952 with his wife Danielle, who worked as a secretary for CERVA, Engel was not part of the official German Military Mission but had a nonetheless critical role. He became director of the secret CERVA rocket factory at Almaza Airfield in Heliopolis with the remit of designing aeroplane rockets. Initially with a team of eight, Engel arrived in Egypt with two high-level colleagues, Dr Paul Goercke and a second scientist identified by the Americans as U T Bodewadt, a ballistics expert. The plan was for him to be followed by further personnel and his own group was to be expanded to 40 engineers. From the start CERVA was experiencing severe financial problems, unable to begin production of 80mm rockets because of lack of powder and propellants and foreign exchange with which to buy them. The complications were corroborated by multiple reports, including the CIA, which noted: 'a factory is believed to have been built in 1952 at Heliopolis to make 80mm and 100mm AT and AA rockets. However, it did not get far beyond designs and the Egyptian Government is reported to have abruptly cancelled its rocket order'. An informant speculated that once Engel had completed much of the technical work in copying a Swiss Oerlikon aircraft rocket, the Egyptians were deliberately imposing foreign exchange difficulties on his project [21].

This Egyptian equivocation had an effect on Engel's career planning and it seems he did not envisage a long stay in the country. In 1954, attending the International Conference of Rocket Experts in Innsbruck, Germany, Engel held a lengthy private conversation with the US air attaché in Egypt outlining Egypt's plans for continuing rocket development and offering to provide information for both Bonn and Washington that might impact political developments in the Middle East [22]. Increasingly falling out with one of CERVA's main funders, Stefan Czarnecki, it appears that by 1954 Engel was actively trying to get out of his Egyptian contract and into a job with NATO. Always a careerist, he was particularly anxious to ensure his library should leave Cairo with him when he went. It was reputed to be the world's largest technical library on rocket and guided missile development and Engel was shameless about using it as leverage with the Americans.

By the middle of 1955, Engel was telling the air attaché at the US Embassy in Cairo that he would be prepared to share extensive details about the activities of the Deuxième Bureau, the French Intelligence Service, in Egypt along with the large sums of money spent by its head Henri Picq in order to pursue French interests in the Middle East, often at the expense of other Western powers who the French were actively working against, according to Engel. His desperation to move on became more apparent as his problems at CERVA mounted. He listed these as low wages paid to workers, poor morale in the factory and the impending loss of more top grade people. By 1955, there were also severe problems in the Egyptian Government hierarchy, which he described as 'a three-way cleavage' between the Ministries of War, Production & Commerce, and Industry. In February 1956, Engel provided his own biographical details along with those of Kurt Hanisch and Bodewadt to the Americans in Cairo with the request that they be passed on to US aviation companies in the hope that one of the firms might hire the group as rocket specialists, with a start date not later than 1st January 1957.

Engel, equipped with special security pass and a side arm for self-defence, plied his trade from a converted British hospital complex in the desert beyond Heliopolis. This modern suburb of Cairo, designed at the turn of the century by the French architect Baron Louis Empain, was also home to many of the German military advisers and scientists living in Egypt. Designed as an integrated modern garden suburb with spacious villas, street lighting, modern drainage and wide boulevards, it lay just 10 miles north-east of the centre of bustling and noisy central Cairo. The enormous, white washed CERVA facility, heavily guarded and with access routes blocked to civilian traffic, was called Factory 333, known in Arabic as 'Thalathat'. Taken over in 1953 by CERVA, the factory and its four-square miles of facilities became the organisation's headquarters. The Israeli spy Paul Frank, in the course of executing a mission dubbed Operation Susannah for the Israeli Mossad organisation, was actually given a tour of the premises by Rolf Engel himself. In the Spring of 1954 Frank was invited to lunch at Engel's closely guarded villa at 10, Rue Qubbah in Heliopolis. Astonishingly he then took Frank on a tour of a plant where the rockets were being developed [23].

Engel's colleague who accompanied him from Paris to Cairo, Paul Goercke, went to work in a second secret facility south of Cairo in Helwan, a thriving and growing dormitory town of Cairo. Over the years this too gradually became absorbed into the capital but in the 1950s it was fast becoming a prime site for the newly industrialising Egypt, with much of the country's heavy industry, manufacturing plants and production facilities sited there. Goercke worked at a British built aircraft production facility called Site 36, a large, sprawling complex where German aircraft designer Willy Messerschmitt was at work on the wings and fuselage of an entirely new aircraft, the HA 300 supersonic fighter jet, as well as the HA 200 trainer. The HA300 Single-Seat, Single-Engine Jet-Powered Interceptor Prototype was to be revealed to the Egyptian people during a Revolution Day parade in 1960 when it was flown for the first time in public by a Spanish test pilot. The Egyptians had inherited the designs of the HA 300 from the Spanish, who had set out to build it immediately after the war but had abandoned the project as being too costly and impractical.

Paul Goercke would be engaged with one further major installation occupied by the rocket programme during his time in Cairo. Site 135, also at Helwan, was taken up by the rocket engine designer Ferdinand Brandner and his team of scientists. This heavily guarded and elaborately patrolled site accommodated a complex of hangers and wind tunnels for testing jet engines. It was here that Brandner successfully produced the E-300 turbojet engine which was to be incorporated into the Egyptian HA 300 jet fighter using the airframe and wings designed by Willy Messerschmitt for the Egyptian Government. This Egyptian conceived and built jet fighter was to encounter increasing problems and, whilst it remained in development both in Egypt and later in India, it was eventually abandoned as being unviable in 1969.

Test Firing Ballistic Missiles

On the morning of July 21, 1962 the combined Western military establishment's worst nightmares became a reality. Egyptian media reported that Egypt's first four surface-to-surface missiles had been successfully test fired. At the annual Revolution Day military parade in Cairo two days later, two of the missiles, the 17ft long Al-Zafar (The Victor) and its sister missile, the 25ft Al-Kahir (The Conqueror), were rolled out alongside other new military hardware, accompanied by precision drilled troops, cymbal clashing marching bands and cheering, ecstatic crowds. These missiles, dark harbingers of the nuclear age, pointed threateningly skywards on their wheeled launchers. They appeared to be a game changer in the Egyptian quest for dominance in the regional arms race. The 300 foreign diplomats summoned to watch the annual spectacle were impressed. In his speech, Nasser pointedly declared that the military was now capable of hitting any point 'south of Beirut'. The message could not have been clearer. Israel itself could now be successfully targeted and hit at any time. One immediate result of this development was for the Israeli secret service, the Mossad, to escalate its attempts to locate and take out some of the scientists and engineers behind the development, both to slow it down and create fear and panic amongst the team working on the programme. But who were they meant to target? And how had they been caught so far on the back foot?

The next day, The Voice of Thunder From Cairo, a Hebrew language radio station was more explicit still. 'These missiles are intended to open the gates of freedom for the Arabs, to retake the homeland that was stolen as part of imperialist and Zionist plots', thundered the news anchor [24]. It seemed that the years of planning and development, first by King Farouk and latterly the governments of General Neguib and Colonel Nasser had achieved the high water mark of their strategy to rebuild Egypt's military and security state. The rockets seemed to exemplify the image of a country that had achieved a new confidence and maturity as a regional power of equal status with its neighbours. These potent symbols of technical achievement and military aggression seemed to have put the seal on the Egyptian national renaissance and marked the end of the years of humiliation scarred by the 1948 Arab Israeli War and the Suez invasion of 1956.

But the status of the rockets and their true capabilities were more opaque than they seemed. In a restricted report called 'The United Arab Republic Missile Program', compiled by the Office of Scientific Intelligence of the CIA in February 1963 [25], both rockets were assessed as being meteorological sounding rockets, primarily to be used for atmospheric and space research. The Egyptians were still attempting to convert the larger of the two, The Conqueror, into a surface-to-surface missile, the report maintained. US analysts also confirmed that the smaller of the rockets, The Victor, was a copy of the French Veronique sounding rocket and that both had been designed by the same German scientist, Wolfgang Pilz. Whilst Nasser and other Egyptian officials had alluded to the use of the Conqueror as a military weapons system, it was in fact the first stage of a two-stage system whose original concept was for a sounding rocket that could lift a 20 pound payload to an altitude of 270 miles. The version of the rocket that was included in the military parade showed four jet vanes to the rear of the rocket motor similar to those utilised with the GermanV-2, the report concluded.

The Victor rocket was a single-stage liquid fuelled sounding rocket whose critical external dimensions corresponded closely to the French Veronique, developed in the late 1940s as an unguided surface-to-air rocket but adapted by Pilz as a sounding rocket to be wire guided during the first few seconds of flight. The CIA also confirmed in its report that the Soviet Union had in December 1962 supplied the Egyptian Navy with three KOMAR class patrol boats armed with short-range Cruise missiles, Type SS-N-2.

The scientists behind the rocket design and manufacture were in fact all part of the German and Nazi diaspora working in secret locations across Cairo during the 1950s and into the 1960s. This patchwork of experts who arrived and departed at regular intervals were in the main graduates of Nazi Germany's scientific establishment which had been responsible for the Third Reich's extraordinary output of next generation weaponry, including the V1 and V2 rockets. The hidden Cairo missile programme, which had successfully escaped too much attention, was headed by two formidable scientists, one of whom, Dr Eugen Sänger had refused to work with the opinionated Rolf Engel at CERVA in the 1950s. Sänger had worked during the war at the famous Nazi weapons research facility at Peenemünde on the Baltic coast, along with a second highly talented scientist, Wolfgang Pilz. In 1954, both joined the Research Institute of Jet Propulsion Physics in Stuttgart. From here, in 1959, they offered their services to the Egyptian Government with a view to helping Egypt develop its capability in long range surface-to-surface missiles. Their offer was accepted at a time when most Germans on the Central Planning Board under Voss had more or less packed up and gone home. A combination of domestic arms and armaments production and a number of productive arms deals with third countries had set Egypt on the path to modernisation of its military and thus set a new tone of confidence and self-reliance in the country.

Nasser readily agreed to the appointments and arrangements were made to accommodate a new team of experts to supplement the existing groups engaged on other areas of Egypt's military programme. Sänger, the 54 year old director of the Jet Propulsion Study Institute, had the perfect credentials with which to become a star contributor to Nasser's rocket programme. His track record included extensive work on engines and the enhanced performance of rocket fuels. A member of the German Society for Space Travel from the 1930s, his talents were greeted with enthusiasm by the Nazi Party and Sänger made his reputation as a pioneer of designs for a high-speed projectile that would be capable of travelling vast distances beyond the hemisphere at supersonic speed. In particular he perfected a liquid-fuelled rocket engine that was 'regeneratively cooled' by its own fuel and moved at a speed that was, by contemporary standards, 'quite astonishing' [26]. In Egypt, Sänger, Pilz and Goercke worked alongside a carefully selected team of highly experienced German scientists and technicians. One of these, and the last man to formally take charge of the Egyptian rocket guidance programme was Karl Knupfer, who arrived in Cairo in the Spring of 1964. Knupfer and his wife were courted by Wolfgang Pilz and his wife Waltraud, who also got to know some of Knupfer's assistants on the programme, among them the electronic engineer Erich Traumm, as part of their brief to monitor the progress of the scheme.

The high-water mark of the Egyptian rocket and missile programme was certainly reached by the mid-1960s, when technical problems on assembly, procurement of parts, lack of money and manpower, and a debilitating programme of intimidation and assassination carried out by the Mossad agency brought developments to a halt. Secret operations such as Susannah and Damocles succeeded in intimidating German employees on the programme in Cairo and even in Germany, where the Israelis were able to reach individuals connected to the project. A campaign of intimidation, including warnings, letter bombs, unscheduled personal visits and newspaper articles was highly successful in causing many of the German scientists to go home early, or fail to renew their contracts.

Life in Cairo, with military escorts, armed protection, security passes, special uniforms and endless alarms and anxiety for themselves and their families, proved too much for many who simply wanted to pursue post-war careers for good money and a life in the sun. Consequently, by the time of the six-day war against Israel in June 1967 most of the rocket scientists and engineers, along with the Central Planning Board employees, had left Egypt for good. Some remained, but they had their own and often darker and more complex reasons. The era of the German military advisers was primarily over.

Whilst the Americans, and to some extent the British, had never thought that Egypt had the financial or other resources to successfully develop a domestic rocket and jet propulsion industry which would produce viable jet fighters and missiles, the Egyptians had succeeded at least in making them pause for thought. The Israelis in particular, in the midst of producing their own first generation arsenal of nuclear weapons aided by the United States, were rattled enough for a time to take their closest Arab neighbour seriously. The Israeli Government and their intelligence agencies felt forced to respond to the Egyptian programme with its German specialists. The systematic planning and execution of the secret Susannah and Damocles operations confirmed this seriousness, costing them agents, reputation, resources and countless operational hours. In the same breath, Egypt regained temporary status and credibility as a regional force that was at least serious in intent. To some extent it was successful in changing the thinking amongst Arab states as to the potential and role of a domestic arms industry in affecting the regional balance of power. From 1970, Egypt was to pursue a strategy of purchasing jet fighters rather than making them. To do this, it turned to Russia.

As Dr Rolf Engel and his wife Danielle packed up to leave

Cairo for the last time on 25th May 1957, to be followed in due course by his beloved library, he was already looking ahead to the next stage of his career. Engel took up a position in Italy as co-ordinator for a new French-Italian-German research project in rocketry called SIMPRE. His parting shot to the Egyptians was a recommendation that attempts to produce rockets at the CERVA factory should be held in abeyance. Instead he recommended that the plant should continue to operate for the training of personnel in research and development. The question of whether the army or air force should oversee this switch was not yet decided. In some respects, this lack of decision making was indicative of the wider malaise that had characterised much of the management and development of the Egyptian rocket programme during its troubled lifetime. For Engel at least the prevarication and endless frustrations posed by the project had proved too much and new, more fertile pastures now beckoned.

A model WW1 German General: Otto Liman von Sanders commanded Turkish forces during the Palestine campaign, 1918.

King Farouk 1 of Egypt *(above, centre)* and King Ibn Saud, inspecting Egyptian troops in 1946.

General Artur Schmitt *(left)*: his appraisal of the Egyptian military after its defeat in the first Arab-Israeli war in 1949 triggered reforms in the army.

Panzer commander and tank warfare expert General Oskar Munzel *(below)* despaired of Egypt's tank capabilities. Here at war on the eastern front in 1943.

Nazi fugitive Walter Rauff *(above)*, appointed head of Einsatzkommando Egypt in 1941, passed through post-war Cairo and Damascus

German Special Forces chief Otto Skorzeny *(right)*, considered using frogmen to sink ships and blockade the Suez Canal in 1944.

Identity card *(below)* of German spymaster General Reinhard Gehlen, architect of West Germany's new intelligence service and head of 'The Spider'.

General Wilhelm Fahrmbacher *(above left)* took over training of Egypt's soldiers in 1952. He told reporters: 'now the Egyptian army is fit'. General Muhammad Neguib and Cairo Chief Rabbi Nahum Effendi meeting in 1952 *(above right)*. Relations with the Jewish community temporarily improved. 5th May 1953: West German Chancellor Konrad Adenauer *(below, left)* meets Winston Churchill in London to discuss the German military advisers in Egypt. Hjalmar Schacht *(left)*, Nazi Economics Minister in the 1930s became a trusted adviser and regular visitor to Cairo during the 1950s.

General Otto-Ernst Remer *(above left)* helped train Egyptian guerrillas for Canal Zone fighting, 1954. Nazi racial theorist and propagandist Johann 'Omar Amin' von Leers *(above right)*, arrived in Cairo from Buenos Aires with his family in April 1956.

The Czech arms deal *(below)*: hardware on display at Almaza in Cairo, September 1956

A group of Palestinian Fedayeen *(above)* during a raid into Gaza in 1956.

A Jewish family emerging from their sl after the British attack on Port Said November 1956.

Popular support for Nasser was overwhel after Suez *(below)*, pictured here in late 19

A residential street in Maadi, Cairo *(above)*. The German cemetery in Old Cairo *(right)*, first burial place of Nazi fugitive Dr Hans Eisele.

The Russians in Egypt: President Nikita Kruschev with Nasser *(above)* during a Cairo ceremony in 1964.

Chapter Eight
THE MASTER SPINNER

'Nasser is a moderate man. He is a Muslim and he understands to let time take its course. He knows the Egyptian horse is a strong horse but a slow one.'

Johann von Leers,
in an interview with Bill Stevenson,
Toronto Star, August 1956

'You are Professor Leers. May I speak to you?' The question startled the small, balding and blue eyed little man with the apple cheeks seated behind his desk in an anonymous office on the fourth floor of Egypt's Ministry of National Guidance. The blue eyes widened and he stroked his balding head nervously before asking the questioner's identity. Bill Stevenson, foreign correspondent of Canadian daily newspaper the Toronto Star revealed himself as a reporter. 'I am a newspaperman too', Leers twittered. 'I was a correspondent in economics in Argentina. I have come here in April.' Recovering his composure he went on to explain why his office was next to that of the propaganda chief directing Egypt's State propaganda programme against Israel: 'Yes, Israel', he said hurriedly: 'Well, I am a translator, they speak many languages in Israel and I translate. I am a man of peace. A peaceful man. Yes.' Von Leers stood up, sat down again and mopped his brow. At which point a messenger brought in a fat file with documents on the Suez Canal. The professor opened and closed the file, then let loose a torrent of words[1].

When he caught up with von Leers Bill Stevenson had been Nazi hunting in Cairo for a week or so. Whilst he had heard endless rumours of hundreds of Germans in town working for Nasser, he had found it tough to actually locate one in the flesh. 'Germans are everywhere and everything in Egypt today but they are the hardest people to find or to interview,' he wrote. Whilst Stevenson wrapped his subsequent interview with von Leers in a blanket of hyperbole – 'the shadow Egyptian general staff is composed of Germans whose jackboots crunched across Europe' – he nonetheless scored an important first. A mere four months after von Leers' arrival in Cairo, he had engaged with the notorious Nazi ideologue and propagandist who was widely known to Western intelligence agencies and whose movements and work were of significant interest in the context of the looming Suez crisis and the formalising of Egypt's state narrative and communications policy within its first Information Department.

Whilst the interview did not really reveal much detail as to the nature of von Leers' work in Cairo, which he tried to pass off as inconsequential, it was more illuminating about some of his missing backstory and also of his personal views. Complaining that he had been held in concentration camps run by American Jews and then a Russian prison for a year and half after the war, von Leers let slip that his little castle in Mecklenburg was occupied by the Communists, 'swine, thieves and bandits' who would have to return it when they were booted out. He cautioned Stevenson: 'do not believe in humanity, mercy or kindness. I tell you this. You must escape always.' Neither was Leers, unlike the British or Americans, of the view that Communism had any future in Egypt: 'No, it is impossible. These are very religious people. The West should realise that the Egyptian song is a modest song.' He also gave vent to his feelings about the State of Israel and in the process perhaps a clue to the true nature of the work he was undertaking. 'Israel is abnormal. It is not big enough or fertile enough to supply millions of Jews for the homeland. It must go. It causes trouble. You ask why Nasser spends so much time and money rallying Arabs outside Egypt against Israel when so much has to be done at home. Well, there is Israel. Zionists are responsible for most of the world's press attacks on Nasser and Egypt.'

In fact, the Stevenson interview was deeply unhelpful for von Leers, coming as it did so soon after his arrival in Cairo and proving an embarrassment to his Egyptian employers who had been anxious to keep his appointment low key. His recruiter, Abd Al Majid Amin, told a CIA informant in September 1956 that Leers was not working out too well as an adviser and might not last more than a few months in this capacity. The CIA did not necessarily swallow this story, although they acknowledged that the publicity caused by the Stevenson interview might have been unwelcome[2]. In the process of telling the CIA informant 'Kitteridge' that he thought Stevenson deserved to be kicked out of Egypt for overlooking, like most Westerners, the really serious side of the turmoil in the Arab world, Majid also revealed that the Egyptian Government was serious about using Leers' anti-Semitic background and experience as an adviser. The informant stressed that Egypt's first Information Department, set up by Dr Abdul Kader Hatem, Deputy Premier and Egypt's first Information Minister, was charged with 'the undertaking of a worldwide propaganda scheme to further the Arab cause'.

The knowledge and skills possessed by von Leers and flexed in Berlin and Argentina were meant to be part of the realisation of this game plan, acknowledged by Western intelligence agencies and diplomats as the first systematic attempt by Egypt to organise its propaganda machinery. Leers, though not a fluent Arabic speaker, quickly became a Muslim convert in Cairo, using the name Omar Amin von Leers. He possessed a deep and wide level of experience in planning and managing anti-Semitic propaganda campaigns forged in wartime Berlin from 1941 with Haj Amin Al Husseini and continued in Argentina as an active Nazi in exile. He would be a major asset in the new and expanding information set-up as it extended its reach and amplified its message.

Stevenson was not the only Western journalist to track von Leers down in Cairo during his early days there. Somehow, the cherubic and goblin-like propagandist with his uncompromising views and gaffe-prone pronouncements had become something of a macabre magnet for unwelcome foreign press interest. The same year, a mere two months before the Suez invasion, a piece appeared in the Washington Daily News by correspondent Anne Sharpley under the blaring headline: 'He threw me out…I knew too much about his regime'. Sharpley told readers that she had arrived in Cairo with the intention of seeking out and interviewing General Neguib, the leader of the Free Officers Movement and figurehead President of Egypt before being removed from office by Nasser in November 1954. In the course of her trip, Sharpley failed to catch up with the imprisoned Neguib and was instead accused by the Egyptian Government of plotting to rescue him from political exile. 'Nothing could convince the Egyptian Intelligence officers who questioned me that news curiosity had impelled me to take the road to Al Marg (a suburb of Cairo) where Neguib is held under house arrest,' she wrote[3].

However, in the course of her time in Cairo Sharpley did manage to find and interview von Leers, 'the propagandist he keeps hidden in his dictator's Ministry of Information, pouring out practised anti-Semitic hatred against Israel. That was the last straw and I was asked to leave within 24 hours,' she told readers breathlessly. Though sometimes descending into caricature, Sharpley's information was accurate enough to include a mention of General Fahrmbacher's activities in training the Egyptian army, claiming he was leading a mission of 300 German officers. Like Stevenson, Sharpley tracked von Leers down to his office in the Ministry of National Guidance where 'brushing aside the numbers of sleepy guards-cum- office boys that clutter every corridor of Colonel Nasser's Ministries, I happened to glance inside an office just as a door was opening'. The surprised propagandist, caught entirely on the hop, at first refused to register her dramatic greeting of: 'Professor von Leers!', then responded to Sharpley's unasked for intrusion with a 'half-hysterical flood of confession, reminiscence, excuse and fear'.

These explosive news exposés were to an extent inconvenient both for von Leers and his employers. But in some other respects the Stevenson and Sharpley interviews played into Hatem's and Egypt's hands. Unwittingly both journalists fell into the trap of portraying the Egyptian people as poor, uneducated fellahin exploited mercilessly by a militaristic government set on achieving its own narrow ambitions, aided and supported by fugitive Nazi war criminals. In fact, the revolution of the Free Officers in Egypt and the abdication of King Farouk was generally a source of inspiration and hope to much of the Arab world, Egyptians most of all. Nasser was widely seen by the 'Arab street', tired of corrupt and ineffectual domestic politics, as the saviour of his country from its long colonial past of economic exploitation, social marginalisation and political disenfranchisement. Sharpley's portrayal of Egypt 'as a country where misery, filth and poverty are apparent in a degree probably unequalled in the rest of the world' could be seen as representing wider Western prejudices and spoke of ignorance of both the heritage and modernising agenda of a country clearly in transition.

Egypt was not only industrialising but on the way to becoming the major source of educated professionals in fields such as medicine, engineering and teaching across the Arab world. In fact the export of teachers and educational resources was increasingly one of the pillars of Egyptian soft power in the region and a growing source of worry for the British who were themselves pursuing a similar strategy of extending their sphere of influence by ramping up the funding and reach of state backed institutions such as the British Council and British Broadcasting Corporation (BBC). Egypt through the 1950s and 1960s became a cultural power house, exporting mass consumer entertainment products such as films and books for the world's growing Arabic speaking market. By the early 1950s, 'Egypt's Hollywood' was producing over 70 films a year feeding 226 film theatres in the country, with a total domestic audience of more than 40 million film lovers and many more around the region. Cairo was the film capital and publishing centre of the Middle East, with Egyptian Arabic dubbed 'the language of film' (al lughat al aflām). Cairo's 40 film companies were operating 15 separate sound stages across the city, turning out every genre of movie from musicals to Westerns[4]. The portrayal by Sharpley of 'a regime exercising an increasingly merciless hold on a people too weak and ignorant to protect themselves' increasingly did not chime with the actions of an Arab government that fewer than two months later at Suez would see off Britain for good and close the door on its time as a global power.

The von Leers Network

In truth, von Leers had a varied work portfolio in Egypt and, whilst his role to an extent was always opaque, he was certainly engaged in a number of simultaneous tasks which together made him a formidable and productive operator. Those who dismissed him immediately as simply an eccentric or a crank were somewhat wide of the mark, a fact supported by his supposed secret recruitment by the West German intelligence service shortly after his arrival. Whilst he may not have had Nasser himself on speed dial, Leers was connected at the highest levels of the Egyptian Government.

Since moving to Egypt in 1956, he had become widely known and 'apparently considered the first-ranking German there in terms of confidence', a CIA analysis revealed [5]. Amongst his personal high level contacts were Ali Sabri, Minister of State for Presidential Affairs, Anwar Sadat, then President of the Afro-Asian Security Council and destined to be a future President of Egypt and Muhammad Abd-Al Khaliq Hassuna, Secretary-General of the Arab League. Leers was closely concerned with the Algerian resistance movement in its war against the French and his active hatred of the West German Government and its politicians was increasing all the time.

The official position of von Leers in the Egyptian Government was as political and propaganda adviser in the Information Department of the Ministry of National Guidance. To do this, he operated under the cover of a second position as a Professor of Language at Cairo's King Fuad University. Von Leers held German language classes for students at the university and his job there helped swing the alternative narrative he pedalled of himself as a simple translator and sometime academic.

Nonetheless, Leers was actively engaged in the affairs of the Arab League and in 1956 was described as 'the current Arab League representative for Germany in Cairo'. In addition to writing propaganda articles for the Arab League in German newspapers, he continued to write for 'Der Weg' as he had in Argentina and in the mid 1950s was engaged in writing a lengthy book, scheduled to appear in 1959 under the title 'The World Fight Against Imperialism and Colonialism', having obtained a publishing deal for it with the firm of Karl Heinz Priester in Wiesbaden, Germany. Together with H Kurkut, Secretary to Haj Amin Al Husseini, Leers was in the process of translating the Grand Mufti's book 'The Truth About The Palestine Question', also scheduled to be published in Wiesbaden by the Priester publishing house [6]. US sources claimed Leers had proposed that Karl Heinz Priester, who was Head of the German Social Movement, move to Cairo and publish a newspaper for German residents of the Arab states. Leers indicated to Priester that the funds and suitable housing for this venture would be provided by the Information Office of the Arab League. Priester declined the offer.

Other parts of the industrious von Leers' portfolio career in Cairo included a radio show to which he was a regular contributor and the construction of a language course at a government school. Less clear, but a reasonable supposition in the circumstances is the part Leers may also have played at the end of 1956 in the scripting and production of a major Egyptian propaganda film. At the beginning of December 1956, only weeks after the British and French were forced into humiliating withdrawal of all their forces from Port Said after the failed invasion of Suez, a masterful atrocity propaganda film 'The Anglo-French Aggression Against Egypt' was produced in Cairo for distribution in the cinemas of Egypt's friends across the Middle East and Africa. Produced by Egypt Today, a mysterious company set up solely for the purpose of making the English language film, it sold a version of the events of Suez focusing on extensive civilian atrocities, damage to residential neighbourhoods, the deaths of heroic resistance fighters in the streets of Port Said and hospitals spilling over with the wounded and dying, victims of indiscriminate British bombing.

The film portrayed the Suez attack on Egypt as a colonial and imperialist assault on the people of Africa and the Middle East that was heinous, unwarranted and cast as a foreign policy failure and disaster for British Prime Minister Anthony Eden and French Prime Minister Guy Mollet[7]. The film was a consummate piece of atrocity propaganda in the grand style, portraying a high-impact, distorted version of events but with enough facts to persuade many observers of the justice of Egypt's case and explaining its outrage at the invasion. Most unwelcome and surprising to the British was the core of truth at the heart of the film, that the invasion had been a secret conspiracy cooked up by the British and French, with the connivance of their 'catspaw' Israel to create an entirely false premise for the British case that the Canal needed external protection in order to guarantee the unhindered progress of international shipping.

This collusion was not in fact officially admitted until 1967. The film's impact beyond Egypt caused the British hastily to produce three films themselves in early 1957 to put their side of the case, the longest and most comprehensive being 'Suez In Perspective' commissioned from the newsreel company British Movietone [8]. It was noteworthy that the film, which focused on the care and attention that British military planners gave to preserving and safeguarding civilian life and residential neighbourhoods during the invasion singularly failed to give the same truthful account of the hidden series of agreements between the British, French and Israelis.

Any analysis of von Leers' career for the decade in which he resided and plied his trade in Egypt must acknowledge that for at least the early years this former SS Sturmbannführer, member of the German Foreign Office in the 1920s and Professor of Law at Jena University was an important component in Egypt's plans to inject organisation and method into its new information infrastructure. The plan to export Egypt's state propaganda beyond its borders and cleverly stitch it into foreign policy and intelligence gathering required experienced operators like Leers to give it traction and provenance. In the propaganda business since 1941 in Berlin, Leers was familiar with the personalities and issues that determined how public opinion in the 'Arab Street' might be best captured and harnessed. The evidence that this energetic, determined and prolific propagandist was central to the Egyptian State effort lies everywhere across the path he carved through his Cairo years. He acted as a switchboard and lightning rod for the continued propagation of anti-Semitic and race based hate that constituted a seam of Egyptian information policy. This accelerated most especially after the Israeli invasion of Sinai in October 1956 that triggered the Suez crisis. It may be in the final analysis that Leers was not destined to play the leading role envisaged for him when first recruited. Accounts of his mental deterioration in Cairo pepper his later years. The German secret service recruit, tagged by the codename 'Nazi Emi' was dismissed in 1958 'because he was both inefficient and insane' according to one account [9]. A former student of von Leers in Cairo, Magda Al Kadi, learned Latin from him. Known in Cairo as 'Goebbels' right hand', he claimed to be Nasser's personal teacher, according to Kadi. She remembered: 'he used to eat sugar cubes. When the bus arrived at Ramses Square he would stand up and shout 'Ramses, Ramses!' [10].

One of the last descriptions of Leers and his wife Gesine at their elegant two-storey villa in Maadi was recorded by Wolfgang Lotz who portrayed him as 'a wizened infirm old man with sparse white hair and watery, pale blue, expressionless eyes'. According to the Israeli spy, he said to Lotz: 'come in my dear Lotz, come in. Heil Hitler.' During the visit, Leers' wife revealed that the old man was homesick and would have dearly loved to visit Germany. He was, however, afraid to do so, fearing that 'the Jews would throw him into prison'.

Despite the mystery that surrounded von Leers in Cairo, his role at the heart of the Egyptian propaganda effort leading up to and just after the Suez crisis was of sufficient worry to the British to prompt a question in Parliament as to the extent of his activities. On 25th February 1957 Barnett Janner, the Labour MP for Leicester North West asked Junior Foreign Office Minister Ian Harvey whether the government was aware that a number of Nazi propagandists were currently in the public service of Egypt. 'Amongst these are such persons as Johannes Von Leers, Otto Ernst Remer and Leopold Gleim. Will he ask the United Nations organisation to enquire into this propaganda so that it may have information of the violation of the United Nations organisation Charter and the Declaration of Human Rights by Egypt before coming to a decision in respect of what guarantees will be available to Israel for her security against Fedayeen and others who are trained and indoctrinated by Egypt?' Harvey batted the question away, confirming that the reports were authentic and that 'there is no reason to doubt them'. However, he told Janner that the Government 'does not consider that any useful purpose would be served by a special enquiry by the United Nations or any other body. I am sure that the considerations advanced by the Honorable Member are in the minds of all those now engaged in the debates in the United Nations', he responded.

Nasser's Propaganda War

In 1962, six years beyond the Suez crisis Nasser was approaching the zenith of his power and influence across the Arab world and the continent of Africa, with which his vision of Egypt closely identified. Through the global non-aligned movement that connected powerful independent countries, Nasser was becoming a prime mover and increasingly influential voice. He was listening closely to Yugoslavia's independent Communist leader Marshal Josip Tito, who he considered was an exemplar and who became something of a mentor to the Egyptian President, visiting Cairo frequently from the mid 1950s onwards. Besides Egypt's increasing political and cultural reach, Nasser himself was becoming something of a cult figure with a following that at times moved beyond fascination and admiration into hero worship and even adoration. His identification with the world's revolutionary elite, as evidenced in photo-opportunities with Che Guevarra, Fidel Castro and Algerian FLN leader Ben Bella amongst others, offered a strong clue as to the roots of his self-image and positioning as a global statesman.

In February that year, the secret Information Research Department (IRD) of the British Foreign Office wrote a major report addressing Egypt and Nasser's progress, likely strategic goals and general prospects. It was a detailed attempt to analyse the reasons behind the rise of Nasser's Egypt, learn from them and at the same time clarify a political and diplomatic way forward for Britain in its future bilateral relations. The report, 'Propaganda Attitudes Towards Nasser and the UAR' stated upfront that Egypt was currently harming Britain: 'the conclusion seems inescapable that Nasser damages British interests, insofar as they are served by British policy' [11]. Seeking out the roots of the Nasser regime's hostility to Britain, the authors singled out the Egyptian President's upbringing, which was 'conditioned by a sense of inferiority and humiliation inflicted by Britain, both indirectly by the establishment of Israel and directly by the paternalistic or patronising manner of many British officials in Egypt, shading off to unveiled contempt by the British Army for 'the Wogs' [12].

This institutional racism in British behaviour towards the Egyptians had created a hard wired hatred for Britain which was the fuel on which the young Nasser was brought up. 'It is for him a deep and abiding emotion, not susceptible to change by any intellectual approach', the report stated. British failure to appreciate this deep-seated loathing was a principal reason why the legitimate meeting of Egypt's national aspirations with the withdrawal of British troops had not cleared the path for the development of a new and fruitful association between the two countries. Many in Britain continued to blame the events of Suez in 1956 for Nasser's continuing hostility whilst failing to appreciate that the Suez invasion in itself was its excuse, rather than its cause. In some respects, the report suggested, the reverse was actually true. Nasser and Egypt owed much to the events of Suez: 'the fact that two great powers had paid them the compliment of treating them as dangerous enemies enabled Nasser to give the Egyptian people and, through them, the Arab world what they most craved – a measure of self-respect' [13].

The British analysis suggested that Nasser's search for political justification led him first to Fascism, whose single-party nature, anti-Jewish fanaticism and hostility to Britain must jointly have exerted a powerful appeal. However, this changed in 1955 when Soviet propaganda ceased to attack Nasser as a fascist dictator and switched to praising him as a patriot and national leader. 'Russia thus presented herself to Nasser as an ally who would be against Israel, implacably opposed to Britain and provide ideological justification for a single party system and the persecution of his wealthy political enemies' [14]. This ideological alignment with the Soviet Union had in turn caused Nasser's propaganda in the field of foreign relations to make common cause with Russia. The output of Egypt's propaganda machine had become indistinguishable from Moscow's on issues such as 'imperialism', 'colonialism', 'capitalist monopolies', 'economic imperialism' and in its wide vilification of Western democracies. Egypt, wittingly or unwittingly, had become an ally of the Soviet bloc in furthering its Cold War aims, the report suggested.

Nasser was a man of his time, stuck with an inferiority complex instilled by the contempt of powerful Christian nations for Muslims as backward people incapable of governing themselves, the official analysis went, exposing in the process one of the principles underpinning the Orientalist mind set and associated administrative system. To this sense of inferiority must be added the final humiliation of defeat by the Jews in 1948. Thus no act or policy that ignored this inferiority complex would stand a chance of being fruitful. Arab inefficiency, sense of inferiority and the continual frustration of their hopes of Pan-Arabism required a scapegoat – Britain. The report finally recommended that Britain's own propaganda approach going forward be developed on the principle of active intervention by continuing to tell the truth rather than lie, binding allies in the region more tightly to British objectives and focusing on those countries where most converts might be found. Specific tactics should include offering British citizenship to Palestinians, preventing Israeli expansion, exploiting friendships and building relationships with students and keeping up the war against communism as the agent of Russian expansionism.

Egypt's use of Subversion in Foreign Policy

This way forward for British projection in the region took some time and considerable argument to formulate. In April 1962, a full six years out from von Leers' arrival in Cairo, the British were still waging an internal war to decide how best to address the undoubted success of Nasser's propaganda strategy. One school of thought suggested that the most effective response was for Britain to keep its head down and not give Nasser a target to aim at. In a memo entitled 'Egyptian Propaganda and Subversion' British official R S Crawford wrote: 'by reacting too directly and too vigorously we are only likely to provide Nasser with the sounding board he needs to attack us. It is in general better to treat him gently rather than aggressively and thereby avoid setting up a target for him to attack' [15]. This approach which was echoed amongst many administrators, was passionately rejected by top civil servant B L Strachan who believed the passive path of least resistance recommended by colleagues was a recipe doomed to failure. 'The weakness is...they accept as irreversible the present lamentable decline of Western prestige in the region and the concurrent growth of that of the Communist bloc', he wrote.

The argument that raged on amongst the upper layers of Britain's Foreign Office had been fuelled by a further report from IRD which offered the first detailed analysis of Egypt's overseas propaganda programme, one that von Leers had in part been engaged to prosecute. Called 'Egyptian Propaganda and Subversion in the Middle East and Africa', the IRD report found that in the years since the Suez crisis in 1956 Egypt had devoted 'much money and energy' to a campaign of propaganda and subversion in the Middle East and parts of Africa exploiting Arab nationalism, anti-colonialism, neutralism, anti-Zionism and lower-class discontent. It was spending millions to combat European and Zionist influence in pursuit of a goal to become the leading Arab country in the Middle East and Africa. A vital cog in this campaign was the use of Nasser's own larger than life image which had become one of the most popular pin-up subjects in the Middle East, his portrait used on consumer products from stamps and flags to matchboxes and magazine covers. The image projected to the Arab masses was that of 'the infallible pan-Arab leader'. Unsurprisingly, Nasser exercised 'great emotional influence' over the mass of the people in the Middle East and North Africa.

The report contained a startling revelation which confirmed the far-reaching influence of the German military advisers who had been active in Egypt under Dr Voss' Central Planning Board. 'Only since 1952 with the building up of a military intelligence service using methods copied from Nazi Germany, and with the use of modern radio and propaganda techniques, has subversion become a recognised weapon of Egypt's foreign policy', it stated. It was Dr Joachim Deumling, a former SS Obersturmbannführer and officer in the Reichssicherheitshauptamt (RHSA), the Nazi Party security establishment which operated the Gestapo who had been in part responsible for this strategy. Recruited by Voss in 1954 to replace the abrasive and unpopular Ernst Zolling, Deumling had been working highly successfully for the Egyptian Ministry of the Interior under Colonel Zakaria Mohieddin, the head of Egypt's first intelligence agency, the Egyptian General Intelligence Directorate.

Nasser had first started using subversion as a tactic in those Middle Eastern countries whose policies he disliked, especially those like Iraq, Jordan, Iran and Lebanon which had friendly relations with the West [16]. The way the Egyptians influenced opinion in these target countries was to exploit local subversive movements by using intelligence agents operating from Egyptian embassies and consulates. 'The extent to which diplomatic privileges were misused may be judged by the frequency with which UAR staff were expelled from such countries as Lebanon, Jordan, Iraq the Yemen, Ethiopia and Libya', the IRD claimed.

Methods of indirect subversion used by Egypt included the encouragement of revolutionary factions in target countries, subsidies to Press outlets, politicians and army officers; the supply of arms, funds and equipment and any other form of aid barring open armed intervention. However, with the success of these initiatives proving limited, the tide had turned towards methods of more peaceful cultural indoctrination including the export of teachers. Into the 1960s, propaganda, cultural missions and the secondment of teaching staff had become the new less aggressive, more effective methods of indoctrination for spreading the Egyptian world view and encouraging pro-Egyptian attitudes.

By 1962, nearly 4,000 Egyptian teachers were employed in schools across the Middle East and North Africa. Cultural institutes, schools and mosques had been established in centres as far apart as Mogadishu, Beirut, Rabat and Accra. Creating a two-way street, large numbers of Arab and African students were being offered scholarships at Al-Azhar University and other universities in Cairo. In addition, Egyptian radio which had taken its cue from the Arab language radio stations set up in Berlin during the Second World War by Von Leers and Amin Al- Husseini and the station Sawt Al Arab (Voice of the Arabs) set up in Cairo in 1953, was pumping out a continuous flow of broadcasts in Arabic, Farsi, Kurdish and African languages.

Overall, the IRD analysis of Egypt's propaganda activities post Suez painted a detailed picture of a country that was ambitious in its objectives of dominating the Middle East and the Arabic speaking world by using a combination of overt and subversive techniques to move into the ideological territory vacated by the departing colonial powers. It was a methodology in part enabled by techniques introduced by German intelligence in Egypt under Nasser and in part using propaganda expertise deployed by Nazi Germany across the Arab world in the 1940s, with radio broadcasting at its heart. The campaign was increasingly successful, as suggested by the evidence of British uncertainty as to whether a response should be mounted at all and, if so, what might prove effective. Either way, the Foreign Office admitted that whatever Nasser's limitations, he had become a world figure and unquestionably the most formidable leader in the Middle East [17].

In refuting an approach of appeasement and passivity, B L Strachan wrote in a Minute that the picture of Britain as a neutral and mildly benevolent onlooker was unhappily one shared neither by the Arabs nor by the Soviet Bloc. 'Such an approach, I submit, betrays a complete lack of understanding of the psychology of the Middle East peoples- for it is where British diplomacy has been most successful in projecting itself as the bored rather cynical man of the world keeping a contemptuously paternal eye on 'the

Wogs' at play, that it has been most successful in diminishing the considerable fund of goodwill that still remains to us,' he wrote.

Not one to give in to lack of action, Strachan did not himself see the decline of Western prestige in the region as inevitable. 'I make the current Middle East score 49 million allies, 15 million friends, 18 million fairly hostile and 32 million enemies. I believe we should aim by vigorous and skilful handling to improve on these proportions,' he wrote, along with his suggestions for a more positive propaganda manifesto which was in due course to be adopted by the British.

The Mythology of *Mein Kampf*

There is no doubt that von Leers stuck out in Cairo. Wearing European dress, usually a suit and tie and determinedly and distinctively himself, he made no secret of his presence there. His behaviour was generally guided by a sense of self-importance, recklessness and even a flamboyance that made him a high-profile, sometimes eccentric personality who people tended to notice and often engage with. He used his expansive villa in Maadi, in the south of Cairo, with its large rooms and high ceilings as a party destination for other Allemanni in the capital and to entertain his extensive network of Egyptian and Arab contacts, including Amin Al Husseini. Working between the Ministry of National Guidance and King Fuad University, he was happy to take the public bus and conduct a conversation with anyone who happened to be on board at the time. His behaviour, to some extent, spoke of a man who was enjoying a certain protection from the Egyptian authorities and was happy to integrate both as a Muslim convert and as a hired hand in Egypt's ministries, untroubled by the social and financial precariousness of life as an emigré. It was as if his years as an exile first in Italy and then in Argentina had prepared him well for a further transplantation to this bustling Arab city at the crossroads of the Mediterranean, Middle East and Africa.

But there were other Allemanni said to be employed in the Department of Information whose identities and roles were altogether more shadowy. The London Daily Telegraph in January 1960 ran a piece under the headline 'Ex-Nazi Officials in Cairo Named' in which it outed a number of former Nazis working for Nasser's administration in the city [18]. Amongst these were two little known Nazi propagandists, one of them allegedly Louis Heiden, a senior official of the German Press Agency during the war and the other Hans Appler, known in Egypt by his Muslim name of Saleh Shafar. Appler, a former collaborator of Nazi Propaganda Minister Josef Goebbels escaped to Spain in 1945 and arrived in Cairo in 1955, the year before von Leers, who was to become both his boss and mentor. Their presence, though lower profile, proved that von Leers was not acting alone in delivering the anti-Semitic strain of Egypt's propaganda programme but was part of a more collegiate and well supported effort.

In fact he was part of an altogether larger team. The Institute for the Study of Zionism, set up in Cairo in 1955 as a leader in 'the struggle against Zionism and International Jewry', acted as an independent spearhead of this programme and was headed up by a Maadi neighbour of von Leers called Alfred Zingler, himself an escaped Nazi known by his Muslim name of Mahmoud Saleh [19]. The Institute, about which little was publicly known or remains on record, employed a number of further German expatriates including Dr Werner Witschale, another former employee of Goebbels' Propaganda Ministry. The Institute was allegedly responsible for publishing two seminal Nazi texts in the Arabic language. The first of these, 'The Protocols of the Elders of Zion' was a spurious book originating in Russia in the early 20th century which had been used to create an ideological underpinning for the pogroms of Russian Jewish communities in the early 1900s and subsequently by the Nazi Party in its school curriculum in Germany in the 1930s. The book, a source of conspiracy theories about Jewish global ambitions ascribed to the exiled writer Matvei Golovinski, was allegedly recommended by some in the Egyptian hierarchy including Nasser himself in the 1950s.

Though debunked, it still offered some ideological traction for anti-Semitic and race hate based sentiment. The second work said to be translated by the Institute was Adolf Hitler's manifesto and memoir, *Mein Kampf* or My Struggle (Arabic, Kifāhi), written across the years 1925 and 1926 when the author was imprisoned. This lengthy, bestselling German language treatise offered a rationale for Hitler's racist ideology and in particular his rabid anti-Semitism which in time was brought into play as a platform to justify the events of the Holocaust enacted against the Jews during the Second World War. The translation of this discredited, racist book into Arabic and its dissemination in Cairo was contentious and spawned its own mythology that has remained long after the physical presence of any Nazis in the city became a distant memory. The book was first translated into Arabic in 1934, the year after Hitler came to power in Germany, by Kamel Mrowa, then a young editor of the noted Arab newspaper An-Nida. He published parts of the book in daily instalments and allegedly wrote to Nazi Foreign Minister Joachim von Ribbentrop that all Arab youths were enthusiastically pro-Hitler[20].

The first full version of *Mein Kampf* in Arabic is thought to have been translated by Ahmad Mahmoud Al-Sadati in 1937 and published through the German bookshop Overhamm in Cairo [21]. This was done without German approval, as parts of the text were not consistent with the original. A further translation, though not of the full text, was carried out in 1963. This work was often wrongly ascribed to the fugitive German Nazi journalist Louis Heiden. Over time Heiden's identity became confused and conflated with that of Louis Al-Hajj, the Lebanese editor-in-chief of the Beirut newspaper An Nahar, who died in 1994 but who was the author of the 1963 edition.

Somewhere in the accruing mythology of the Arabic language version of *Mein Kampf*, the story spread that specially produced pocket versions of the book had been found in the knapsacks of Egyptian soldiers captured during the Israeli invasion of Sinai in 1956. This rumour was proliferated by many, amongst them Israeli Foreign Minister Golda Meir in a speech at the UN in New York in 1956. However, definitive corroboration of the episode has never followed. Instead, the Arabic version of *Mein Kampf* has become a propaganda trope which is used as part of a wider effort to illustrate anti-Semitic strains in contemporary Egyptian and Arab thinking. In this way, the book has continued to exert a debilitating though tangential effect on Egypt's reputation.

When Hitler was writing the book in his prison cell in 1925, he was already thinking of Arabs and Muslims as reliable allies, according to the historians Rubin & Schwanitz. In the draft of his book, though this did not make it into the final version, Hitler counted the people of ancient Egypt and India as examples of Aryan cultures. 'I am prevented' Hitler explained, 'by mere knowledge of the racial inferiority of the so-called oppressed nations from linking the destiny of my own people with theirs.'[22].

With the enforced departure of all foreign military forces from Egyptian territory after the events of Suez in November 1956, the colonial era in Egypt came to a definitive close. Egypt was strengthened by the Suez crisis, with Nasser's personal authority and grip on power greatly enhanced by the oxygen and credibility it provided. One effect of the invasion was a reinforcing of the state intelligence and internal security apparatus in the country and its more aggressive use to monitor and prosecute dissent. Amongst those on the downside of the Suez episode were the remaining British and French citizens in Egypt, many of whom chose to finally leave the country rather than endure the strength of feeling unleashed by the surging tide of populism and nationalism that gripped the country.

The collusion of Israel in the invasion and the ensuing deaths of large numbers of Egyptian soldiers at the hands of the Israeli army in the Sinai campaign leading up to Suez was especially intolerable for Egyptians already humiliated by the defeat of the 1948 Arab Israeli war. For the large minority Jewish population in Egypt, their future prospects as citizens in a less tolerant, more polarised society were not promising. In November 1956, at the defining moment of the Suez crisis, it seemed that the internal security forces within Egypt already had the country's Jewish minority population in its sights.

Chapter Nine

A QUESTION OF STATE SECURITY

'I always imagine that in this region in which we live there is a role wandering aimlessly about in search of an actor to play it.'

Gamal Abd Al-Nasser,
The Philosophy of the Revolution,
Ministry of National Guidance, 1954

After Nasser wrested full control of Egypt from fellow Free Officer General Muhammad Neguib in late 1954 he was able to widen his horizon to encompass a more grandiose vision of Egypt and its place on the global stage. This ambition included a future role for the country as the rightful leader of the Arab, Muslim and African worlds, inheritor of a unique status bestowed by geography and history and now further propelled as the region's ascendant ideological and political force. But Nasser's most immediate concern was the Middle East. He did not necessarily view the Jewish State of Israel, surrounded by four Arab neighbours, as a special threat 'but rather as an artificial outpost of Western imperialism, an illegitimate entity, albeit one not worth provoking into a war' [1].

The first Arab-Israeli War had been a cathartic event for Nasser and Egypt, one whose outcome the British Foreign Office's Information Research Department had characterised as 'the humiliation of defeat by the Jews'. But in late October 1956, in collusion with France and Britain, Israeli forces invaded the Sinai Peninsula to provoke the intricately planned international Suez crisis. The Israelis only discontinued their advance westwards deeper into Egypt just short of the eastern side of the Suez Canal, thus paving the way for the British led and French supported invasion of Port Said. Though not fully disclosed until almost a decade later, this secret agreement between Israel and the two major colonial powers in the Middle East resulted in estimated losses of Egyptian forces of up to 3,000 dead and 4,000 wounded, quite aside from delivering a second hammer blow to Egypt's national pride by violating its territorial integrity.

In a lengthy and candid interview with the British Labour politician Richard Crossman in December 1953 Nasser had announced that he had no desire to destroy Israel and that the idea of throwing the Jews into the sea was pure propaganda [2]. However two military defeats by Israel within a decade contrived in time to chip away at this sense of magnanimity and laissez faire to fundamentally shift Nasser's view about his newest neighbour. Loss on the battlefield was to harden his growing opposition to Zionist expansionism and alignment with the West and accelerate his efforts to arm Egypt with its own modern arsenal of offensive weapons and better trained fighting forces. At the same time defeat caused Nasser to look internally for scapegoats on whom he might hand off some of the blame. This exercise in introspection and national soul searching resulted in profound downstream implications for the long established Jewish population of Egypt.

It was therefore inevitable that between the 1948/49 Palestine war and the invasion of Suez eight years later the State of Israel would increasingly move into Egypt's crosshairs. In 1948, Israel had exerted an unexpected military superiority to increase its percentage share of Palestinian land, a position that was fundamentally unacceptable to Arab public opinion. At Suez in 1956 Israeli forces had moved in a co-ordinated campaign to 'force' the British and French to trigger their option of military invasion to protect shipping using the international waterway. In both cases, Israel had stamped its military authority on Egypt's affairs through aggressive action which demanded a response. When planning and prosecuting these two military campaigns, did the Israeli Government give any consideration to repercussions for the Jewish population of Egypt? Or had they already accepted that Egyptian Jews would have to pay a price for Israel's alliances and military choices and considered such a sacrifice justifiable? It is unlikely that the subject was high on the agenda but Israeli politicians certainly knew from reports within Egypt from 1948 onwards that the country's Jewish population was increasingly vulnerable to sanction by the Egyptian State. After the Suez invasion and the withdrawal of British and French forces and civilians from Egypt, the negative impact on Egypt's Jews worsened significantly and conditions finally became urgent enough to trigger alarm bells in both Tel Aviv and Washington.

Detecting a German Hand

From an early stage, the hands of German advisers could be detected in the organisation and deployment of internal security forces tasked with managing the response to the Jewish question in Egypt. On 13th December 1952, Dr Wilhelm Voss had told Associated Press in Cairo: 'certain sections of the internal security forces have been placed under my mission's care' [3]. A year later in December 1953 the Israeli spy Avi Seidenwerg, posing as former German officer Paul Frank, was in Egypt gathering as much information as he could about the activities of the German experts. He was successfully building a social life that included meeting significant numbers of German military advisers including naval specialist Baron Theodor Von Bechtolsheim, senior tank advisor General Oskar Munzel, army commander General Wilhelm Fahrmbacher and various arms manufacturers and scientists working on weapons programmes. At this time, the influence of the German advisers contracted to Dr Voss' Central Planning Board and acting independently through the CERVA company and other organisations was growing. It would continue to expand for the next two or three years as the Egyptian Ministry of War and Marine ramped up its military development and arms manufacturing programmes. Seidenwerg, who continued to put himself about socially until his capture by Egyptian Intelligence during the exposure of Operation Susannah in late 1954 was also increasingly invited to functions held at the German embassy in Cairo. It did not take him long to build up a big picture of just what was going on and in due course he reported back up the line that some of his worst fears were being confirmed.

One area of concern was the shape and direction of the newly formed State security forces that were being organised under the Interior Ministry in order to manage the response to all perceived political or ideological enemies of the State. This included at various times in the 1950s and 1960s the Egyptian Communist Party, the Muslim Brotherhood, socialist workers' rights activists, religious communities such as the Copts and minority populations such as the Greeks and in particular the Jews.

'The recently established Staff (sic) Security Cadre seemed to be structured like Hitler's SS, shock troops and secret police. The Economic Department was a true replica of the SS Wirtschaftsamt, with a special Jewish section that had worked at full speed to register all Jewish property,' he reported. Such similarities chilled Seidenwerg for 'as a child in Austria I had grown up during the beginnings of a nightmare. Now history was repeating itself.' [4]

One of the first names to surface in connection with the internal security initiative was particularly disturbing. Leadership of the newly created State Security Cadre (SSC) was being credited to former Nazi Leopold Gleim, an SS Standartenführer during the Second World War when he had been stationed in Warsaw in charge of Jewish affairs in Poland. Having arrived in Cairo in the mid 1950s he had converted to Islam, taking the name Ali Al-Nashar and enrolled as an employee of the Egyptian Ministry of the Interior with responsibility for Jewish affairs. He was accompanied by another former SS officer, Willi Brenner, who had allegedly helped set up and run the Mauthausen concentration camp in upper Austria where nearly 200,000 enemies of the Third Reich had died. Could these rumours really be true? And to what extent was the information that was now trickling out of Egypt to be relied on? There were many who were inclined to believe that such a thing was impossible. Others thought this was exactly the kind of disinformation that had been fabricated and used as a tactic by Egypt's enemies to discredit Nasser and Egypt, his regime and his methods. However in time a more comprehensive picture was to be established, some of it contested, that cast a longer and darker shadow over the Nasser Government's reputation.

The Jewish Backstory in Egypt

Since the early 1800s Egypt had always had a significant population of Jews. By 1947, a national census showed around

46,000 Jews living in the country, active in all aspects of national life from agriculture to industry and banking to finance. Under Egypt's first nationality law, introduced in 1929 some seven years after Egyptian independence, it became more complicated for all minority groups living in Egypt to obtain Egyptian citizenship. Consequently, by the time of the Suez crisis in 1956, only about 10,000 Egyptian Jews were formally Egyptian citizens. A further 15,000 were still foreign nationals with their own passports and many Jews in Egypt remained technically stateless [5].

After the first Arab-Israeli war in 1948 several hundred Jews were arrested and their properties sequestered. On September 15th 1948, the Director of the US Federal Bureau of Investigation (FBI), John Edgar Hoover, wrote a letter to his counterpart at the CIA attaching a press release which claimed that the pogrom against the Jews had been instigated by the Nazi war criminal Adolf Eichmann who was in Cairo at the time. The American weekly German language magazine Aufbau, published in New York, claimed that Eichmann was responsible for the murder of up to 250 Jews in Cairo along with 'quite a lot' of foreigners, among them an American citizen called Haas. 'The infamous Gestapo agent Adolf Eichmann, who escaped from a prison camp at Regensberg in Bavaria is now in Egypt, apparently working underground', the magazine claimed. 'Eichmann's relatives, living at Linz in Upper Austria, received news which gives the impression that Eichmann found asylum in Cairo', the press release said. The magazine tried to put Haj Amin Al Husseini into the frame for the murders as well, as 'he was in Cairo at the present time and the pogroms which were staged in the Egyptian capital showed all the signs of an expert hand'. It claimed too that Adolf Eichmann had introduced Haj Amin to Hitler [6].

The situation of the entire Jewish community was precarious, although there were some improvements in relations after King Farouk was deposed in 1952 and General Neguib came to power. He held a meeting with Cairo's Chief Rabbi Nahum Effendi which promised a more positive approach. The atmosphere in the country was made more volatile, though, by the arrest of 13 Jews working for the 'Operation Susannah' spy ring in Egypt during 1954, two of whom committed suicide and two of whom were eventually executed in a blaze of international publicity. Operation Susannah had been set up by the Israeli secret service to destabilise Egypt and thereby ultimately encourage Britain not to withdraw its forces from the Suez Canal Zone. The subsequent exposure and trial of the conspirators raised feelings in the country against the Jews and helped to cast them as subversive. Between 1947 and 1956 a sense of increasing unease caused many Jews to emigrate. The Jewish population at the end of 1956 could not be precisely determined but estimates ranged from 35,000 to 55,000, according to the American Jewish Committee [7].

But it was immediately following the Suez invasion that the situation in the country immeasurably worsened. The foreign media, both American and French, working with Jewish sources inside the country were quick to alert the world to a new phase of the problem. William Richardson wrote in the New York Post: 'The second flight from Egypt is now in full swing. I have just seen it. The apologists for the Nasser regime say there is no persecution of Jews in Egypt but I would bear witness that I have seen it and felt it and heard it in the past few days...Egyptian officials claim they hold only 131 Jews there but every Jew in Cairo knows there are hundreds and some reliable sources believe the figure may run to 3,000' [8]. This was backed up by an editorial in the New York Times: 'Despite an Egyptian denial there is enough evidence now that Jews are being deported from Egypt – because they are Jews – to require United Nations intervention. The methods used are so similar to what Hitler did before the war as to be frightening [9].

In the media war on the issue that was in full swing by the end of 1956, senior figures in the Egyptian Government continued to downplay or deny the problem. Head of Egypt's Ministry of the Interior and intelligence chief Zakaria Mohieddin gave an interview to the Journal d'Égypte in which he claimed: 'Egyptian Jews are treated without any discrimination whatsoever, and if we have detained a certain number of Egyptian Jews, their number is no more than 120'[10]. Egypt's Foreign Minister Dr Mahmoud Fawzi used the same number when he was quoted in the New York Times: 'out of 66,000 Jews in Egypt, only 120 have been interned for valid reasons of public security' [11]. Even Dr Hatem, boss of Johann von Leers at the Department of Information added his voice to the debate, terming reports of Egypt's persecution and expulsion of Jews as 'completely false'.

There was, however, solid evidence that on 1st November 1956, only a few days before the invasion of Port Said by the British, the Egyptian Government moved to initiate a series of measures against the Jewish community. On the night of 1st November, Egyptian police had stormed without warrants into Jewish homes in Cairo, Alexandria and other leading cities and taken away one family member from each home, typically the breadwinner. These detainees were shunted around a series of common-law jails, including the Citadel in Cairo and the Prison des Barrages, about 25 miles outside the city. British and French Jews were accommodated in two French and British school buildings in Cairo; stateless Jews sent to the Abassiah Jewish School in Cairo; and the Barrages Prison held Jews from a variety of countries including Greece, Italy, Spain, Portugal and Iran. Conditions in these prisons varied from tolerable to bordering on inhumane. Some incidences of torture were reported and things did not improve until a visit by the Red Cross. As of 7th December 1956, at least 900 Jews had been arrested and interned but, with more arrests every day, these figures were thought to be conservative [12].

Mass expulsions began on 15th November when the Ministry of the Interior ordered a number of Jews, mostly stateless, to report to the Ministry where they were told they had between three and seven days to leave the country. The alternative was to be placed in camps. Many agreed to go and, with their families boarded planes or International Red Cross transports that plied their way between Alexandria and European ports. The departure of one such group of 967 Jews was observed by foreign correspondent of the New York Post, William Richardson: 'For the last 100 yards they were marched through the streets where Arabs shouted at them. At the station they were left handcuffed and under guard for more than an hour. A mob gathered, began cursing and spitting and then threw stones. The guards and their officers taunted the Jews: 'You're going to die' [13].

Expulsion orders were increasingly issued to Egypt's Jews of all backgrounds. In an effort to minimise records, written expulsion orders were soon abandoned in favour of verbal instructions. As little trace as possible of the expulsions was to be left. Even Jews with Egyptian passports were persuaded to leave by Egyptian police and within three months some 10,000 Jews had left the country. By February 10th, 1957 ships leaving Egypt had carried over 8,500 Jewish refugees to Europe: 2,092 to Greece, 3,855 to

France and 2,600 to Italy. Many others left Egypt by air, going directly to Switzerland, Belgium and elsewhere [14]. Departing Jews were allowed to take very few possessions or money with them. At first the cash limit was 20 Egyptian pounds, which was increased to 100 Egyptian pounds along with two suitcases of personal items.

On top of imprisonment and expulsion, the 1st November 1956 also ushered in a series of measures designed to provoke economic strangulation in the remaining Jewish communities. Under Military Proclamation No 4 regarding the 'Regime of Sequestrations' a self-styled official referred to as 'the director-general of the management of properties of persons interned or placed under surveillance' assumed the management of properties of all those placed on a watch list or interned, or who it was felt posed a threat to the security of the State.

Henry Mourad was a student at Cairo University. He wrote later: 'at the beginning of my third year in college, the family business was nationalised without, of course, any possible reparation or compensation. My father was given a meagre salary, and thus, we had no choice but to get ready to leave Egypt. This was economic strangulation. Worse yet, the government boasted in the newspapers the seizure of the family's business and thus exposed our religion. I was finally discovered as being a Jew. A difficult confrontation with my friends arose at the (Cairo) University. And as soon as we applied to leave Egypt, we were stripped of our Egyptian nationality, which we had through five generations. Our personal assets — bank accounts, homes, etc. — were also confiscated, and we were told never to return [15].

Whilst Proclamation No 4 effectively struck at the economic means of survival for Egyptian Jews the parallel Proclamation No 5 was introduced for British and French nationals, both Jewish and non-Jewish. This programme of sequestrations, aimed ultimately at shutting down the economic means of survival for the British, French and the Jews in Egypt might be framed as direct retaliation for the Israeli invasion of Sinai, already underway on 29th October and the impending invasion of Port Said by the British, itself just a few days off on 5th November. It now became increasingly difficult for Jews to hold on to their jobs in firms that had been subject to sequestration. In addition, bank transfers and funds became difficult for Jews to access and they, along with all Westerners became marginalised by the introduction of new, deliberately divisive and labyrinthine business processes. The Egyptian Cotton Exchange, for example, made it compulsory for all transactions to be carried out in the Arabic language, an imposition that made it impossible for the majority of non-Muslim brokers to continue doing business.

In the final part of the legislative onslaught, the Egyptian Government modified its citizenship and nationality laws in order to prevent further Jews becoming Egyptian citizens and to provide a means of rescinding Egyptian citizenship for those Jews who had already attained it. Article 1 of the new Nationality Law of 22nd November 1956 stipulated that 'Zionists shall not be eligible for citizenship'. And Article 18 of the same law stipulated that 'Egyptian nationality may be declared forfeited by order of the Ministry of the Interior in the case of persons classified as Zionists'.

Under the new laws, only those who were established on Egyptian territory prior to 1st January 1900 and who had maintained their residence until the new laws were introduced were eligible for citizenship. Of course no such documents that might have proved this longevity existed in the Egyptian civil administrative system. Thus amidst an Orwellian bureaucratic blitzkrieg ended all realistic prospects of any remaining Jews in Egypt obtaining their legitimate rights or claims to Egyptian citizenship.

The Worsening Situation

Jewish organisations and NGOs lobbied the US Government to do more to help the thousands of stateless Jews now in transit from Egypt, some of them to Europe, some to Israel and others with no obvious onward destination. Like the refugees from the Hungarian uprisings of November 1956 in flight from the invading Russians, the Jews fleeing Egypt had limited choices. But many felt the US could have extended a hand of friendship by organising a mercy airlift or easing the provisions of the McCarran-Walter Act to trigger parole provisions which had been amended to accommodate some of the fleeing Hungarians. A common response around the world was to urge the United Nations to look into Egypt's treatment of its Jews on the basis of a potential violation of the UN's Universal Declaration of Human

Rights which outlawed arbitrary arrest, detention or exile or the stripping of a person's nationality.

In the US, Jewish lobby groups and representative bodies worked hard to gather and publish evidence that could be used to engage and mobilise domestic public opinion. They felt that public awareness and support of the plight of Egypt's Jews might in turn generate political leverage to influence the course of events on the ground. Besides, as a prime sponsor and enabler of the State of Israel, the United States with its powerful Jewish lobby was the natural advocate for the new country which had stood alone against the combined power of its Arab neighbours in 1948. By this time, Israel was well on the way to becoming an anchor alliance for the US in the post-colonial Middle East and the relationship between the two states was increasingly central to US interests in the region.

One New York based Jewish pressure group, calling itself The Society for the Prevention of World War 111 Inc. was successful in getting a report it had assembled of alleged events in Cairo admitted as testimony on the floor of the US House of Representatives in July 1957, the year following the Suez crisis. Representative James Roosevelt managed to get the text of an article printed in the Summer 1957 issue of the Society's magazine 'Prevent World War 111' under the headline 'From Dachau To Cairo ' admitted in its entirety on the basis that it was vital information which US lawmakers should be aware of. In his introduction he said: 'Mr Speaker, under leave to extend my remarks in the Record, I include the following article…this article contains many bits of information which I believe will be of interest to the Members of the House, as it is a situation that would appear to require consideration' [16]. The article gave a lurid and detailed account of the progress of the Jewish persecution in Egypt during and after the first wave of expulsions. It largely chronicled the state of affairs that had engulfed many of the Jews who had been unable to get out of the country. Whilst some attempt at justification of policy and events by Egyptian government ministers and officials was included, these senior spokesmen between them could not offer a convincing defence of the State's treatment of its Jewish population. Though the article, along with many others printed by Prevent World War 111 could be described as polemic or propagandist in intent, the central proposition it advanced of illegal detention and sequestration appeared authentic and there remain few other contemporary accounts of the Egyptian Jewish experience at this time that successfully challenge its central thesis.

The account offered a considerable insight into the organisation and methodology which the State adopted in its treatment of Egypt's Jewish population. Perhaps the greatest charge levelled at the SSC, of the setting up and use of dedicated internment camps for Jewish prisoners inside Egypt, was consistent with the treatment meted out to other dissidents active against the Egyptian State at the time, most particularly Communists and trade unionists. 'From Cairo to Dachau' is carefully calibrated so as to portray an essential reconstruction of the Nazi model used to dispossess, disenfranchise and demonise the Jews in Germany during the 1930s, policies which together resulted in the wide scale dispersion of the German Jewish population and which led during the Second World War to the events of the genocide perpetrated during the Holocaust. This Egyptian model was alleged to include the same use of oppressive legislation, dispossession and economic marginalisation, banishment, internment and denial of human and civil rights though it stopped far short of any kind of extermination strategy, systematic or otherwise. The convenience of this explanation fitted a more general anti-Nasser narrative at the time, one that might best be summed up by British Prime Minister Sir Anthony Eden's use of the terms 'the new Mussolini' or 'Hitler of the Nile' when referring in Parliamentary speeches and media interviews to Egypt's revolutionary leader.

The Nazi parallels were constructed around a trinity of people, processes and precedents. At the heart of the Jewish accusations of individual complicity in the process was the person of Leopold Gleim, Commander-in-Chief of the State Security Cadre which was judged to be 'as precise a copy of the Nazi Sicherheitsdienst as Egyptian inexactitude permits'. The organisation comprised a public relations department, an economic department and the secret state police, each with their own area of expertise, operations and personnel. 'From Dachau to Cairo' even included an insider account of a lengthy address given by Gleim at a meeting of the League for German Arab Brotherhood (al-ikhwan al-almaniya al-arabiya) in Cairo on 17th December 1956 [17]. During the meeting, Gleim pointed out the significance of the

SSC as 'the backbone of Egypt's protective apparatus against the aggressive elements of Zionism and Imperialism'.

In a more private, select post-lunch conversation, Gleim gave further details. 'The plan for the SSC was drawn up by several technical advisors of German origin and approved by the Ministry of the Interior', he stated. The SSC headquarters was set up in Cairo and its administration handed over to precisely 6,249 'arabised' Nazis presently in Egypt, aided by perhaps 70,000 Egyptians, he told his audience. These numbers used by Gleim, almost certainly inflated, have never been accurately sourced or independently verified.

Of the three SSC branches, the PR Department was entirely managed by Germans holding Arab passports. Gleim revealed that one of these was SS Gruppenführer Alois Moser, a Sudetenland German wanted in the USSR for crimes against Jews. He had assumed the Muslim name Hussa Nalisman. Moser was supported by ex-Gestapo officer SS Gruppenführer Friedriche Buble, now known as Ben Amman who was also a consultant to the police force. The PR office operated 'with German precision' said Gleim, targeting Jews for attack from a network of offices spanning Cairo and Berlin to Vienna, Milan and Bordeaux. The propaganda output was highly successful in reaching Egyptian youth, using roaming vans with loudspeakers combined with targeted literature, wall posters, a live introduction to the concept of militarism held in a tent outside SSC headquarters in Cairo's Liberty Square and youth clubs, set up under the brand 'the Youth Club of the Arabischer Bruderschaftsverband'.

The Economic Department of the SSC was founded on 2nd February 1954 to replicate the working of Germany's SS-Wirtschaftsamt, controlling the SSC Treasury which was entirely independent of the Government Exchequer. Following the Jewish expulsions, the Jewish Section of the Economic Department had collected 14 million Egyptian pounds in currency, policies and securities, along with 27 million Egyptian pounds worth of properties and assets abandoned by the deported Jews. In addition to generating revenue from prison workshops, the Economic Department also made money from operating a Public Sales Centre in Cairo where property which departing Jews had 'voluntarily' assigned to its administration, such as furniture, clothes and paintings were auctioned. The head of this Department, Colonel Abd-Al Qadir Al-Hatem was offering assurances that nothing had been confiscated from the departing Jews, saying all property was given up without coercion [18].

The Secret State Police, the third branch of the SSC, was centred on the Egyptian Intelligence Service with an add-on section headed by a Yiddish speaking former SS Sturmbannführer called Bernhardt Bender, now known as Lt Colonel Bashir Ben Salem. Bender, it was alleged, had during the war served as Chief of the Gestapo Special Branch in charge of exposing Jewish underground movements in Poland and Russia. He was now acting as liaison between the Secret State Police and the Economic Department. In addition, Bender was in charge of the SSC Interrogation Centre. This was based in an old disused 12,000 tonne Italian cargo vessel called the Marinajo Rosso. Known by Egyptian Jews as 'The Floating Hell' the ship had 80 cells which were all wired for sound and reserved for cases of special interest, generally thought to be the very wealthy. Two White Russians were said to be operating the recording equipment, Sergei Klinikin from Odessa and Alexei Morganoff, 'a true Muscovite with an enchanting smile, huge feet and a Swiss watch'. Prevent World War 111 alleged that the Egyptian Jewish banker Elie Politi had been held in the Floating Hell where he had succumbed to the interrogation methods and handed over 112,000 Egyptian pounds, all he possessed.

Politi was a prominent Egyptian businessman and entrepreneur who was active in Jewish and Zionist causes in the first half of the twentieth century. Born in Chio, Greece in 1900, Politi arrived in Egypt with his family in 1906. He attended the Menasce High School in Alexandria and then studied law at the French School of Law in Cairo. Politi became one of Egypt's most successful businessmen, an important figure in the stock market, and an entrepreneur in the fields of real estate, insurance and banking [19].

It was Bernhardt Bender's 'solution of the Jewish-Zionist Problem' which had rolled into effect on 1st November, with the SSC police units, plain-clothes men and army squads deployed to round up Jewish men, women and children throughout Cairo. As a result they seized 1,711 people earmarked for deportation. These Category A (Alif) detainees were placed in a variety of prisons in Cairo where they were treated to a harsh regime of little fresh air, limited food and almost no opportunity for communication. The 18,000 Alexandria Jews, mainly classified as Category B (Ba), were subject to home imprisonment, strict dusk to dawn and 11.00am to 3.00pm curfews, blocked bank accounts and no opportunity to work. It was felt that the Alexandria Jews were known to have strong connections with Israel but these links were not yet developed enough to be formally exposed and therefore proved. The regime of house arrest was supplemented by the closure of all Jewish shops and the forbidding of all Jewish professionals, with the exception of a few dentists, to practice. Jewish schools were closed and all community activities paralysed. Under this first phase, 500 Cairo Jewish men were interned indefinitely in the English Grammar School; their wives and children were interned in the Hadrah Prison. A further 830 Cairo Jews were held in the ruins of the Qalat Al-Qahira, outside the City. This first phase of the SSC operation, which involved identifying, rounding up and then containing Egyptian, foreign and stateless Jews was intended to persuade as many as possible to leave the country, taking as few possessions as possible with them. The second phase of the SSC programme was to be based on internment in camps that were less visible to the outside world and thus more sinister and reminiscent in their approach.

Evidence of Life in the Camps

Amongst the most startling and concerning revelations to emerge was the allegation that five new camps for Jews were being deployed as the flagship element of Bernhardt Bender's second phase of a programme now known as 'The Solution of the Jewish-Zionist problem within territories of sovereign Egypt'. The first four of these camps were listed as: the Heliopolis Fortress, destined to absorb 2,000 detainees; the Gizeb Barracks, which served during World War 11 as a POW camp that could accommodate 10,000 men; and two former army training centres, the Mustafa Hanun-Pasha Barracks near Almaza City, originally built for 16,000 men and the Burg Al Arab Barracks near Alexandria which once sheltered two divisions of recruits [20].

Most shocking were the alleged details of the fifth camp, described as the Samara Barracks in the Suheillah desert region 200 miles west of Cairo. This camp had only recently been vacated by the 3rd regiment of the Egyptian Liberation Army, the unit which Nasser commanded in 1948 and which had withstood the

Israeli attack on the Faluja Pocket. It was being converted at a cost of 17,000 Egyptian pounds and patterned on photocopies of the original plan of the infamous Nazi 'Medizinisches Versuchlager Mannerheime bei Dachau' otherwise known as Dachau's 'Block 10' where hundreds of Jewish girls were sterilised, according to the authors. The photocopies of the original plan of this camp were supplied to the SSC by SS-Hauptstabszart Heinrich Willermann, presently 'arabized' as Lt Col Naam Fahum and now in charge of converting the Samara Barracks, the article stated [21].

This allegation was not a one-off, so could not be simply dismissed as atrocity propaganda. There were numerous media reports at the time alleging that former Gestapo and SS members augmented the secret police and helped build internment camps for opponents of the Nasser regime. The Wisconsin Jewish Chronicle was amongst the US newspapers reporting the allegations in detail: 'the issuing of yellow-coloured cards for Jews born in Egypt, the mass arrests carried out at night on the lines of the infamous 'Nacht Und Nebel (Night & Fog),' the classification of those arrested into categories 'A,' 'B' and 'C,' their detention on no charges whatsoever, the engagement of Jewish brokers on a non-remunerative basis for the SSC-Purchase section and the seizure of hostages in order to secure loyalty in the performance of their duty, the confiscation of all property of persons interned and deported and the methods by which they were forced to sign the forms confirming that they have no claim on their property, all these are the reasons…' [22].

Further allegations were made again a decade later in testimony to the US House of Representatives in 1967 by the Hon Theodore Kupferman who based his information on extracts from the article 'The Grand Mufti and his friends' by Sid Goldberg, in the September 1967 issue of the bulletin of the Anti-Defamation League. 'Colonel Fahum, formerly Dr Heinrich Willermann, wanted by West Germany for sterilisation experiments to be conducted in several Nazi concentration camps…now runs the Egyptian political prison at Samara. Ibrahim Mustafa, formerly Joachim Deumling, wanted by West Germany for crimes committed in Dusseldorf while a storm trooper there… is an adviser to the Cairo police on concentration camps [23]. The physician Heinrich Willermann, a former SS official in Poland and Ukraine, both supervised jails in Alexandria and ran the

Samara Concentration camp in the Western Desert, according to the two contemporary historians Rubin and Schwanitz [24].

For those who were inclined to write off the existence of such camps as Samara as mere anti-Nasser propaganda, there was growing evidence that the policy of arbitrary arrest and internment for dissidents and political opponents of the Nasser regime was being used more widely. One group which was also increasingly reporting detention and abuse of human and civil rights was the Egyptian Communist Party, a large and powerful grouping of Egyptian workers encompassing trade union members and workers groups who had been lobbying and striking systematically for some years for fairer employment practices and decent wages. Many of these workers were to fall victim to the same hidden persecution in detention camps whose conditions were as brutal as those faced by the Jews.

A wave of post-revolutionary repression against the communist movement was in full motion after the Revolutionary Command Council passed legislation to dissolve all political parties in January 1953. At the same time, the RCC also passed legislation abolishing the right to strike just months after a large dispute had paralysed the major industrial city of Kafr al-Dawwar in the Nile Delta. The Egyptian Government was intent on fostering stronger relations with the United States and believed its cause would be helped by stamping down on trade unions and especially communist elements involved in promoting workers' rights. Thus the property of all parties, especially offices and printing presses, was confiscated and leaders of political parties were arrested and put under house arrest pending trial [25]. Their personal situations would shortly get more extreme and more desperate.

In September 1954, Ahmed Taha was one of 21 communists sentenced to five years hard labour. Taha was a member of the Progressive Liberation Front (Al-Jabhat al-Tahrir al-Taqadamiyah), had been Chairman of the Committee of the Preparatory Congress of Unions of Middle Eastern Countries and the Egyptian delegate to the World Trade Union Federation. In early June 1955 Ahmed Taha and some 500 other prisoners were deported to a prison camp 'in the middle of the desert,' roughly 20 km from Kharga Oasis in Egypt's western desert. At least 60 of these prisoners were communists. The Daily Worker newspaper referred to it as 'Desert Hell Camp', giving an indication of the analysis by the international communist movement of the Nasser government's treatment of communists during this period [26].

The conditions described at Kharga were tough by any standards, even for the most resilient and physically robust inmates. The prison was administered by the Egyptian Army as most prisoners had been convicted by military tribunals and were sentenced to hard labour. One report suggested that the conditions put prisoners' lives in danger, with 20 prisoners to a tent which did 'not protect them either from the burning sun or from the sand storms', one bucket of water per day for every 20 prisoners, low quality and insufficient food, a camp area infested with snakes and scorpions and little to no medical care. Prisoner testimony included one inmate who went by the initials A.A. explaining that 'mosquitos buzz and sting in daytime; scorpions and rats make a nightmarish ballet at night… food is scarce and disgusting enough to keep the prisoners alive until the next day. No visitors are allowed and no parcels may be sent by families. The result of such horrendous living conditions is 'chronic dysentery, violent headaches, widespread Asiatic flu and severe undernourishment' [27].

A letter from Taha dated June 21st, 1955 stated: 'I am alright, but my health is deteriorating… You know well that the medical treatment is insufficient and even bad, but what to do?' Taha remained resilient, however, declaring: 'Don't worry about me, you know me well my friend, I will pass this crisis physically and morally successfully, because I love so many things, wider than our narrow world' [28]. A second wave of repression of Egyptian Communists got underway at the start of 1959 and lasted until 1967. It reportedly resulted in over 2,000 new prisoners in Egypt's internment camps, many of them still in a state of shock that all the political advances they thought they had made in the intervening years were being rolled back.

By June 1967, only an estimated 4,000 Egyptian Jews remained in the country and they were in due course punished for Israel's third military victory in the ensuing six-day war. Eight hundred Egyptian Jews were detained on conspiracy charges and had their property seized. On 11th June, the day after the war was lost, 54 Egyptian Jews sought refuge in Naples, Italy. The refugees said that they were motivated to flee Egypt after the war began on 5th June, when shortly afterwards they were imprisoned, beaten, and deprived of food and water for long periods of time. Historically under the Ottoman Empire, many Egyptian Jews had been granted dual citizenship in European nations, and their asylum was made possible due to their possession of Italian passports. After the war, an estimated 300 Jews remained in Egypt, mainly in Cairo and Alexandria. On 20th June, the Associated Press reported that Egyptian and Libyan Jews were planning to emigrate out of fear of Arab retribution [29].

The account of the Jewish population of Egypt and the events determining the fate of many Egyptian Jews spanning the first Arab-Israeli war in 1948, the invasion of Suez in 1956 and the six-day war in 1967 to some extent remains contested history. Although much evidence exists from Jewish and American witnesses and media accounts, and the paths of many of the individual Jewish families fleeing from their homes in Cairo and Alexandria have now been retraced and brought to the light by the families of those who walked them, there is little official Egyptian recognition of events, either through witness accounts or written records. The switch of expulsion orders from written forms to verbal instructions is one example of how, at the time, Egyptian bureaucracy showed some awareness of the need to cover its tracks and leave little evidence to be raked over by future generations. It must also be true to a degree that polemic and propaganda were driving the contemporary Jewish narrative enough to embellish the facts and sway public opinion in the United States in order to provoke political action. At least one contemporary scholar, Joel Beinin, claims that so soon after the Holocaust's full horror had become apparent, Jewish organisations such as the American Jewish Committee were projecting their paranoia and obsession with Nazi antisemitism on the Egyptians. Beinin lays the blame for the flight of Egypt's Jews at Zionism's door by dwelling at length on Operation Susannah in 1954 and its negative impact amongst Egyptians on attitudes to the Jews [30].

However, the violent repression and expulsion of Iraq's Jews from Baghdad in 1941 in the violent and destructive pogrom that came to be known as the Farhud was in part inspired by the Nazi supporting Iraqi government of Rashid Ali Al Gaylani. It establishes a precedent in some respects for the later Egyptian expulsions, which were on a much larger scale but in no way carried out against as violent a backdrop. The involvement of the

SSC in planning and managing the programme of detentions, sequestrations and internments in Egypt has been contested by Egyptian sources who remain tight-lipped about the episode and certainly any systematic part played in it by German advisers. To a great degree certain aspects and details of this dark Chapter have always been and are destined to remain opaque.

The Last Jews in Cairo…

Cairo, September 2014. Magda Haroun, elected head of the Jewish community in the city, unlocks the doors to an ancient, ornate synagogue in the heart of Cairo's old Jewish district. The building echoes with the ghosts of a congregation that no longer gathers here and the silence of absent prayers that are never spoken. Magda considers herself the guardian of the Jewish legacy in Egypt. But now she oversees a total population of 12 remaining Jews in a country where once 100,000 Jews enjoyed a flourishing culture and community full of schools, businesses, synagogues and traditional homes. 'We are dying, we are drowning, we are finished' she says in despair. Later, she goes to see one of the 12 Jews still hanging on to their precarious existence in the Egyptian capital. Lucy Shaoul is living in a home for the elderly in the city. No-one except Magda goes to see her. All her relatives and family members are dead. 'I had friends here, I had a nice life, it was my home', Lucy remembers with strong emotion. In Cairo's Jewish headquarters, Magda sorts through some memories of happier times, photographs of football matches, school classes and family and social gatherings. She goes to the cemetery to show where her father is buried, a tomb amongst many neglected tombs now surrounded by vanishing memories and the accumulating rubbish and discarded packaging of the relentlessly encroaching slums. Here she breaks down in tears, lost for further words to describe the sadness of her past and the uncertainty of her future[31].

Chapter Ten
HUNTING THE BIG BEASTS

Personal description of Nazi fugitive Adolf Eichmann from 1947: 'age about 40 years; height 1.75m; very small, bony face; big nose; big ears; sunken cheeks; short, dark; sparse hair with bald temples; slender build; does not speak with an Austrian accent and can easily be taken for a North German. Has an unpleasant, exaggerated laugh. When talking, his cheekbones move constantly. Has a nervous twitch. Constantly under alcohol. Always carries a poison ampoule on his person. Desperate type who, if cornered, will try to shoot it out. Resourceful Alpinist. Present whereabouts, probably Austrian Alps. Unlikely that he can be found in an Alp Hut. Presumably frequently changing his location [1].

Report from Berlin
June 17, 1946.

On 30th April 1945, a residential neighbourhood of Milan only 10 minutes' walk from the city's Cathedral was crowded with furious and vengeful locals intent on lynching the uniformed Gestapo officers huddled in a staff car outside the Regina Hotel. The group had been holed up in the hotel, barricading themselves inside since retreating there the day before after leaving the city's Gestapo HQ and signalling to the occupying Allies that they were ready to give themselves up. As the car moved away from the hotel entrance and into the crowded street, the Italians reached in to administer a punch or slap to the leather coated and peak capped passengers, occasionally lobbing a missile into the open topped vehicle. The cowed and frightened occupants ducked or held up their arms to evade the blows, looking anxious and in fear for their lives [2]. Their undignified exit from the Regina Hotel, captured on film by a news team somehow symbolised the defeat of Nazi Germany's garrison in Italy, a former ally now turned bitter opponent and determined to hold some of those responsible to account for their many crimes during the toxic and often vicious occupation. The collapse of the German effort to hold back the incoming tide of Allied troops sweeping up through the country was complete. One of the occupants of the car was of particular interest and had his captors at the time been aware of his overall war record, they would in no way have left his fate to chance at the hands of an angry mob.

SS Standartenführer Walter Rauff, head of the Gestapo in Milan, was even in 1945 notorious as the ruthless overlord of the three great northern Italian cities of Milan, Turin and Genoa. Rauff, who always denied having ever killed anyone personally, was a deputy to Heinrich Himmler. Little is known about his early life. He had risen without trace from obscure beginnings in turn of the century Germany, serving separate unremarkable terms as policeman, naval officer and Intelligence operative in the Third Reich. Rauff's route to the list of the world's most wanted Nazi war criminals had come through his role in the development of commercial vans specially adapted as gas chambers. By 1941 Rauff was an SS officer personally responsible for developing and directing the use of these 'Black Raven' vans in which victims were sealed and then asphyxiated with exhaust fumes. The vans, disguised with Red Cross emblems, were widely used in eastern Europe in 1941 and 1942 before Hitler's network of concentration camps was completed. Captured Nazi documents claimed the vans killed 50 people at a time in 15 to 20 minutes and were used in the Soviet Union, Poland, Yugoslavia, Lithuania, Estonia and Latvia. In a secret report dated July 5th, 1942, Rauff, then a section chief in the Reich security office in Berlin which was in charge of the mass killing of Jews, said that since December 1941, 97,000 people had been 'processed' in the vans. However, Nazi hunters and European Governments that sought his extradition estimated that as many as 250,000 people, most of them East

European Jews, died in the vans [3].

It was the success of Rauff's mobile gassing programme that led him to North Africa and then Syria and Egypt, firstly as an officer of the Third Reich and latterly as a civilian touting his skills on the open market. In 1942, Rauff was put at the head of a dedicated killing squad called Einsatzkommando Egypt, which was assembled and despatched to Athens in the summer of that year, where it waited to cross into North Africa. The group, which included the SS officer Franz Hoth, was under orders to take 'executive measures' against civilians on its own authority.

Contingent on the victory of Erwin Rommel's Afrikakorps in its campaign to sweep across North Africa and wrest Egypt from British control, Rauff's orders were to take the Einsatzkommando into Egypt, begin the process of eliminating Egypt's Jews and then follow the Wehrmacht into Palestine where he would repeat the process. In June 1942, Rauff and his killing squad did in fact begin this project, setting up internment camps for Jewish citizens in Vichy controlled Tunisia and killing 2,500 of the estimated 550,000 Jews in North Africa [4].

At the end of the war Rauff was moved to an internment camp in Rimini on the north-east coast of Italy, but he didn't stay there long. Bored and under employed he decided to walk out and did so on 29th December 1946. Arriving incognito in Rome, Rauff at first found work as a gardener in a cloister of one of the Catholic convents there, then as a German language tutor to one of the many groups of orphaned children in the city. Perhaps inadvertently, Rauff became a beneficiary of Pope Pius 12th and the Vatican's policy of reconciliation. The Catholic Church was anxious to mount a concerted front against a resurgent Communism sweeping across post-war Europe. In 1948, when Rauff was working in the Santa Maria del Anima monastery in the Vatican, a Syrian agent from the country's Deuxième Bureau travelled to Rome to seek him out to lead a search for military and intelligence advisers for the country's security services. The Deuxième Bureau's office in Rome was recruiting German candidates for well paid jobs in Damascus. Within months a number of Nazis and former Wehrmacht officers made their way to Damascus, amongst them former Austrian policeman Franz Stangl who had commanded the Sobibor death camp in Poland [5]. After being reunited with his wife and two sons, Rauff too went to Damascus to work under contract for the Syrian Government. Arriving in the city in early 1949, Rauff obtained a job as adviser to Syria's Deuxième Bureau, then being expanded under Husni Al-Za'im, President of Syria and its first military ruler having seized power in a coup d'état in March that year.

On the day of the counter coup against Za'im in August Rauff was arrested along with Ibrahim Husayni, Chief of Syria's MPs and Abdullah Raslan, of the Deuxième Bureau. They were all charged with terrorism. Rauff, according to his accusers, had set up the torture devices which had been used on the persons suspected of being connected with a Jewish bombing incident in Damascus. 'The idea of trying Rauff for these offences was pushed on by the fact that, as one of Za'im's foreign friends whom Za'im trusted more than his own Syrian officer supporters, he was very unpopular with the army', according to a contemporary CIA report on Rauff's time in Syria [6].

After Rauff convinced the military authorities that he, as a mere hired adviser, had no command responsibilities and had simply given his advice to Husayni when he asked for it, he was released and told to leave the country. 'Accordingly, he is proceeding this week to Egypt where, he…hopes to get a job as adviser to the Egyptian services. If he has no luck there he hopes to go to Italy. He is accompanied by one Otto Gruber, a young German who had been employed by the Deuxième Bureau as a Soviet and Communist expert. There was no charge against Gruber. He was fired simply because the new Bureau does not think it worthwhile to pay a Communist expert', the report noted [7].

Whether Rauff ever physically appeared in Cairo after the war to offer his services to King Farouk and the Egyptian intelligence service remains open to question as the evidence for his presence there is scant and uncorroborated. However, in late 1949 Rauff travelled to Ecuador via Italy and nearly a decade after that turned up in Chile which had a large German community and where he was to live for the rest of his life despite several attempts to extradite him. Rauff was yet another high-ranking Nazi who was allegedly recruited by the Mossad when he was in Syria and Egypt and was feeding information to the Israelis throughout his time working for the Syrian intelligence services. Rauff was to die in Chile on 14th May, 1984. One of the last Nazi fugitives never brought to justice for major war crimes, the 77-year-old German had long been ill with lung cancer, but he died of a heart attack at his home in Santiago's affluent Las Condes section, first reported on by Chilean radio [8]. His death prompted the comment from famous Nazi hunter Beata Klarsfeld: 'it was God that made justice'.

Walter Rauff was one of the most hunted and high profile Nazi war criminals who somehow managed to successfully negotiate the Allied post-war internment, prosecution and denazification process to live out his days as a free man. His experience, briefly, included applying his specialist skills in the service of at least one post-war Arab regime seeking to develop its intelligence capabilities. As the war years receded and the ensuing hiatus evolved into the Cold War of the 1950s and 1960s, the polarisation of western liberal democracy and Russian state-directed communism changed the calculus of foreign policy in the former colonial Middle East. This shifted to accommodate a new generation of economic and political alliances between Egypt and the global powers, most particularly the United States and Russia, which reflected the new realities of the Cold War. It was Nasser's awareness of Egypt's strategic importance and the potential of its post-colonial reincarnation that shaped his vision for the country, a transformation he saw as being enabled by renewed military force and hard power alongside large scale industrialisation and full employment in an economy boosted by more job opportunities, higher wages and a better standard of living for the working class. The creation of the Central Planning Board, the setting up of the CERVA organisation and the systematic import of German military expertise and know-how all played a part in delivering the altered psychology and practical tools to enable Egypt to make this major step change. No longer able to accept the persona of the ancient, exploited, colonial culture of subservience, it reached towards reinvention as a modern, influential non-aligned state at the forefront of the Arab and Muslim world. German efficiency in military and security affairs, manufacturing industry, finance, armaments production, propaganda and internal security structures were all seen as means of enabling major change in national infrastructure, bureaucracy, administration and attitudes.

In their analysis of the impact of the German military advisers in Egypt, the British Chiefs of Staff had voiced their worry about the authoritarian nature of the German character and its mobilising potential in Egypt. They believed that the German presence and the introduction of West Germany's new military operating procedures into the Egyptian army enabled by Dr Wilhelm Voss could trigger a different Egyptian mind set and more professional modus operandi. This way of thinking was potentially dangerous to British interests as it opened up a new, bolder set of possibilities which Egypt's leadership might exploit.

British, West German and US Government thinking supported the thesis that the German advisers in Egypt during the 1950s and 1960s were for the main part representatives of the professional German officer class. Most were identified in time as *bona fide* experts with the experience to deliver specific military ojectives, whether rocket engines, explosives factories or guerrilla fighting techniques that, whilst unwelcome were in themselves relatively narrow and contained. By and large, they were not worried that the German recruits were hard core, proselytizing Nazis with an agenda of extending the reach of the vanquished Third Reich directly into the Egyptian political sphere. The only ideological strand that stood outside this definition was the rabid anti-Semitism espoused by die-hard propagandist Johann von Leers and some of his colleagues at the Egyptian Department of Information and within the State Security Cadre. This overall evaluation was confirmed during the London meeting on 5th May 1953 between British Prime Minister Winston Churchill and West German Chancellor Konrad Adenauer, who stressed that in the main the German advisers should be considered as private contractors plying their legitimate trade and thus beyond the sanction of the West German Government.

However, the problem for Egypt was increasingly one of public perception and international reputation when it became apparent over the course of the 1950s that there were indeed a number of Nazis both sheltering and operating in Egypt and neighbouring Syria, the two countries temporarily joined in a political union as the United Arab Republic (UAR) from 1958 to 1961. Whilst the main thrust of German activity in Egypt during the first half of the 1950s was that of the advisers attached to the Central Planning Board, public perception was also shaped by a much smaller number of unrepentant Nazis who were present and active in the country. Most of these individuals were officially employed either fully or in part by the government. The practical issue for both the Egyptian and Syrian governments was that a small group of these high profile Nazis were wanted by the international criminal courts and thus sought for extradition in order to stand trial for war crimes. Egypt's laws provided a shield that made extradition next to impossible and thus played a part in constructing the narrative of Egypt as a safe haven for exiled Nazis, their dark pasts and their polluting ideas. Something of this narrative in time generated a corrosive mythology around the subject.

Two Doctors Too Many

On 30th May 1958, the Munich Police in West Germany received a sworn statement from a local businessman Wilhelm Jellinek that Dr Hans Eisele, a physician living comfortably in the suburb of Passing had personally killed at least 200 concentration camp inmates as an SS doctor. Jellinek said he witnessed Dr Eisele commit the murders 'with injections of Evipan-Natrium'. Eisele defended himself vigorously, even writing a letter to the editor of the Munich Evening News which had published the accusations against him. Then a sympathetic individual in the government warned Eisele that his arrest was imminent. The man who had beaten two death sentences vanished from Germany and quickly resurfaced in Egypt. The West Germans tried to have him extradited but Egyptian law dictated that the murders and attempted murders he was accused of committing had already passed their statute of limitations. Thus like tank officer Gerhartz before him, Dr Eisele was allowed to build a new life in the Middle East [9].

Later in 1958, instead of doing time in a West German prison for crimes committed against the Jews during the war, Eisele was staying in the comfortable Maadi villa of Dr Johann von Leers and his family in Cairo. It is believed though not confirmed that his invitation to live in Cairo actually came from von Leers himself. Not only did Eisele make himself useful by organising familiarisation tours of Cairo for incoming fellow German exiles, but he was well on the way to receiving from the Egyptian authorities a license to operate in the city as a medical doctor. In due course he received the go-ahead, setting up his practice under the name Carl Debouche in a discreet building in a comfortable, leafy and shaded middle-class suburban street. Patients reported being somewhat taken aback by the gaunt, heavily lined and stooped figure of Eisele with his immaculate old-style German manners practising medicine with both experience and skill. Some time in the early 1960s when von Leers fell ill and suffered a debilitating stroke Eisele played a major part in helping restore him to health, to the great surprise and astonishment of many who thought von Leers was finished.

Hauptsturmführer Dr Hans Eisele's career in the concentration camps of the Third Reich was long and infamous, perhaps as bad as any and certainly worse than most. Eisele began working in the Sachsenhausen concentration camp at Oranienburg north of Berlin after he was wounded at the front. There he was known as 'the Angel' and the former prisoners later endorsed his good conduct. He was transferred to Dachau where his treatment of the prisoners changed, according to Lt. Col. William D. Denson who prosecuted Dr Eisele twice, once for crimes at Dachau and again for crimes committed at Buchenwald. According to Harold Marcuse, author of 'Legacies of Dachau', Eisele had served as an SS camp doctor successively at Natzweiler, Buchenwald, Mauthausen and Dachau from August 1941 until the liberation of Dachau in April 1945. He was first brought before an American Military Tribunal as one of the 40 accused war criminals at Dachau and was sentenced to death for participating in the common plan to commit war crimes there. His sentence was commuted to life in prison because he had only been at Dachau for two and a half months. At Buchenwald, however, which was a Class II camp for hard-core Communist political prisoners, Dr Eisele became known as 'the Butcher' for the offence of murdering prisoners by injection and of doing improper surgery. He was sentenced to death again for his crimes there. In time Eisele's prison sentences were significantly reduced. He opened a licensed family medical practice in Munich where he lived untroubled by his past until 1958 when he was outed and subsequently fled in the face of new and highly damaging allegations.

Hans Eisele died in Egypt on 3rd May 1967 at the age of 55 after self-administering a lethal dose of morphine. He was buried in the small German Cemetery in Al Kafour, Old Cairo in Grave 99 a mere two years after von Leers himself died in the city. His body was later disinterred and moved back to Germany by his son. Whilst in Cairo, his shadowy presence unquestionably contributed to the tarnishing of Egypt's reputation, helping frame it as a refuge for Nazi war criminals escaping justice. Living in Maadi and practising medicine with freedom under the protection of the Egyptian authorities, Eisele was able to enjoy a comfortable existence, to socialise with some of his former comrades and make a new life for himself in a city where some of the more awkward questions surrounding his past could be sidestepped.

Eisele, for all the horror of his war crimes was never reliably accused of taking any official role on behalf of the Egyptian Government or any other government. During his years in the Egyptian capital, he initially helped out at a military hospital for a short time after his arrival. Then alongside his private practice, he became physician to the German workforce in Egypt's aircraft factories, looking after the German experts, according to the Israeli spy Wolfgang Lotz. Meeting him at a party at von Leers' villa, Lotz recalled that he and his wife Waltraud took measures to avoid shaking the sinister doctor's hand, too appalled by his record of mass murder even to go through the social motions.

The Mystery of Dr Death

A coincidence, though perhaps not totally surprising in the conditions peculiar to Nazi exiles in Cairo, was the meeting between Eisele and another Nazi doctor resident in the city from 1962. Dr Aribert Heim, like Eisele, had served as a camp doctor in Mauthausen concentration camp in Austria where he had become known by prisoners as 'Dr Death'. The two met briefly at von Leers' house in Maadi which served as a switchboard for fugitive Nazis in the city. But they did not go on to develop a close relationship as Heim deemed it too risky to see German former colleagues or acquaintances and steered away from any kind of regular contact with the German exile community. He preferred to mix with Egyptian friends, of whom he had a number, in his own lower key and more anonymous working class neighbourhood of Al-Azhar on Port Said Street.

Heim's backstory as a doctor practising for the Waffen SS was dark and terrible, but it did not come out fully until some time after the war. On 15 March 1945, Heim was captured by US soldiers and sent to a POW camp. This was the only occasion he served jail time after the war. The military released him, apparently unaware that investigators in Austria were building a case against him.

There, on 18th January 1946 less than a year after the German surrender a United States war crimes team took testimony about his crimes from Josef Kohl, a former inmate at Mauthausen: 'Dr Heim had a habit of looking into inmates' mouths to determine whether their teeth were in impeccable condition,' Mr. Kohl said according to a transcript of the interview. 'If this were the case, he would kill the prisoner with an injection, cut his head off, leave it to cook in the crematorium for hours, until all the flesh was stripped from the naked skull, and prepare the skull for himself and his friends as a decoration for their desks' [10].

Heim, like Eisele, achieved the rank of Untersturmführer in the Waffen SS, which he joined in 1941. After release from detention he went home to Baden-Baden in Austria where he lived in grand style in a spectacular Palladian manor house surrounded by large, manicured grounds, together with his heiress wife and two sons. He went back to work in his own medical practice in the town as a respected gynaecologist. However, Heim was always aware that his past might catch up with him. A highly accomplished, athletic and experienced ice hockey player, at one time on the fringes of the Austrian national squad, Heim continued to play games for a local club. But he made sure he never appeared in team photographs, always hanging about on the periphery or finding the right moment to duck away from the camera. Suddenly, in 1962, Heim dropped out of view entirely. It transpired that an international police warrant issued in West Germany was responsible for his flight and subsequent disappearance. Despite following up family, social and professional contacts the West German police could not locate Heim and he became the subject of intense international scrutiny.

In due course, after the scale of his crimes at Mauthausen was revealed and in the public domain, he became the third most high profile Nazi on the run. Only Alois Brunner, Adolf Eichmann's number two and Josef Mengele, thought to be still alive and living in South America, preceded him on the list of infamy. According to his son Rüdiger, when Heim fled Baden-Baden he drove through France and Spain, took a boat from Algeciras to the Spanish enclave of Ceuta on the north coast of Morocco and proceeded eastwards through the Maghreb, finally arriving in Egypt via Libya.

'It was only sheer coincidence that the police could not arrest me because I was not at home at the time,' Heim wrote in a letter to the German magazine Der Spiegel after it published a report about his war-crimes case in 1979. It is unclear whether he ever sent the letter, which was found in his files, many of which were written equally fluently in English and German. In the letter he also accused Nazi hunter Simon Wiesenthal, who was interned at Mauthausen of being 'the one who invented these atrocities.'

Despite rumour and counter-rumour, false sightings and the occasional news reports, Aribert Heim had effectively vanished off the face of the earth. Clandestine investigations by the West German police, monitoring of his family's movements and oversight of their bank accounts offered no reasonable leads that might have resulted in his arrest, let alone knowledge of his whereabouts. Like many other fugitive Nazis, Walter Rauff amongst them, Heim was rumoured to be in South America where it eventually emerged that his illegitimate daughter Waltraud was living in Chile. No report of Heim's presence in Egypt filtered out and Heim built a life in Cairo that lasted successfully for the best part of three decades. Converting to Islam at the city's famous Al Azhar Mosque and living under the Muslim name Tariq Hussein Farid, he became a property developer in partnership with an Egyptian friend, building a small block of apartments in Alexandria. He grew to know Cairo intimately in the process of his daily walks which often extended to 15 miles or more. Heim lived on the top floor of the Kasr Al Madina, a modest and nondescript hotel mainly used by Egyptian salesmen and commercial travellers. There he befriended the family of the hotel's owners, erecting a tennis net on the hotel roof and handing out sweets and pastries bought at Groppi's to the children who came to know him as 'Uncle Tariq'.

The full story of Heim's life in Cairo, his network of Egyptian friends, his daily habits, the secret visits of his son Rüdiger over a number of years and the circumstances of his slow and painful death from rectal cancer in a shabby room on the top floor of the Kasr Al Madina only emerged after his death in 1992. His son recounted how he and a member of the Doma family who owned the hotel had taken Heim's body out of the hotel wrapped in a sheet and placed in a coffin, put his father's remains in a car and tried to get it accepted at one of Cairo's hospitals. Heim's wish was that his body be donated to science. However, no hospital was willing to take a corpse without formal arrangements and official documentation so the body was eventually dropped off with an undertaker for commital in an unmarked, common grave in one of Cairo's many cemeteries. This fact alone has caused the controversy of Aribert Heim and his eventual fate to be the subject of contentious debate as no DNA or teeth that might offer proof of death have ever been recovered.

The lead that eventually exposed Heim's flight to Egypt and his life there as a Nazi exile came through arrangements he had made with his lawyers in Germany to receive the rents paid by tenants of a residential block of 40 apartments that he owned in Berlin. It was eventually discovered that the beneficial owner of the block was Heim and the payments were sequestered and frozen by the West German authorities. The entire sum of Heim's personal possessions and assets were contained in a small, dusty briefcase that was recovered by the New York Times and the German television station ZDF from the Doma family who had kept them after Heim's death. The files in the briefcase offer the only official record of Heim's life in the Egyptian capital including his driving licence, bank account statements, payment records and bills. The various documents showed that Heim had taken a close interest in the international search for him over the years. They also offered an outlet for his sometimes eccentric views on race and geopolitics.

Some documents were in the name Heim, others Farid, but many of the latter, like an application for Egyptian residency under the name Tarek Hussein Farid, had the same birthday, June 28, 1914, and the same place of birth, Radkersburg, Austria as Heim. A certified copy of a death certificate obtained from Egyptian authorities confirmed witness accounts that the man called Tariq Hussein Farid died in 1992. 'Tarek Hussein Farid is the name my father took when he converted to Islam,' said his son Rüdiger. In an interview in the family's villa in Baden-Baden, Mr. Heim admitted publicly for the first time that he was with his father in Egypt at the time of his death from rectal cancer. 'It was during the Olympics. There was a television in the room, and he was watching the Olympics. It distracted him. He must have been suffering from serious pain,' he said. The fugitive died the day after the Games ended on 10th August, 1992, according to both his son and the death certificate [11].

Playing The Numbers Game

Whilst post-war South America was long known and acknowledged in the public mind as a destination for fugitive Nazis, scientists and other miscellaneous servants and ideologues of the Third Reich, the Middle East only entered the picture tangentially and as something of an afterthought. The appointments to the Central Planning Board of Dr Wilhelm Voss, tried after the war at Nuremburg in his capacity as an arms manufacturer and of artillery general Wilhelm Fahrmbacher raised some eyebrows and generated limited news coverage in 1952. But only the activities of die-hard Nazi Johann von Leers as propaganda adviser at the Department of Information from early 1956 garnered much specific outrage. Otherwise, most coverage of the German advisers in Egypt was the subject of vague interest, rumour and speculation.

However, all that changed in May 1960 when Adolf Eichmann, one of the principal architects of Nazi Germany's plan to annihilate Europe's Jews, was found in Argentina and flown back against his will to Israel. Eichmann, who had made a speculative pre-war trip to Palestine in 1934 to determine the Jewish situation for himself had been reported by FBI Director J Edgar Hoover as being in Cairo in 1948 where he was suspected of leading a pogrom against Egyptian Jews during the first Arab Israeli war. Beyond that, it was a source of embarrassment to US intelligence agencies that they had lost sight of Eichmann, who it was thought at the time of his capture might even have been living in Kuwait. In fact, Eichmann had been in Argentina for some years. Living with his family on Garibaldi Street in the San Fernando district of the city, Eichmann was going by the name Ricardo Klement. In 1957, the Mossad first located him in the city. It took until 11th May 1960 for a beefed up snatch squad to pick him up on leaving his house one morning for the bus. He was kept under cover in the city for a week and then smuggled out of the country on an El Al flight, disguised as an injured airline worker.

Eichmann's extrajudicial rendition to Tel Aviv caused a

ripple of angst to spread through the Nazi exile community in Cairo and other destinations in the Middle East. It brought the uncomfortable reality of unmasking and eventual accountability a step nearer. In Egypt, German scientists and engineers working on the country's rocket and missile programmes at factories in Heliopolis and Helwan had already been targeted by Israeli agents eager to discourage and slow down production. Apart from at least one assassination attempt in Germany, on rocket scientist Heinz Krug, the Operation Damocles campaign launched by Israeli intelligence included a series of personally targeted mailshots, 'chance' threatening encounters on the street and exploding letter bombs which had caused some of the Germans to abandon their government contracts and leave the country early.

The trial of Eichmann and his sentencing to death in a bullet proof glass cage in a Jerusalem court room caused a global sensation. His execution at Ramleh Prison outside Tel Aviv on 1st June 1962 was the first in the Jewish State since Israel was established 14 years earlier. The thirst for detail about his case was as insatiable as it was macabre. Eichmann went to his death on the gallows watched by a number of observers including the Canadian evangelist missionary the Reverend William Hull and Reuters News Agency's Israel correspondent Arye Wallenstein. Wallenstein described the unforgettable midnight scene of Eichmann's last moments, when the ashen faced but quietly determined German had spoken his last defiant words: 'long live Germany, long live Argentina, long live Austria. …I had to obey the law of the war and my flag'[12]. The execution of Eichmann was a major moment in the healing of the Jewish national soul right across the world. It held a symbolic meaning and importance that transcended the events of the trial and hanging, sending out a message that no individual war criminal could now sleep safely in their bed, and that the darkest crimes brought final consequences.

The death of Eichmann once again focused the world's attention on the Nazi fugitives. It has never been authoritatively established just how many German experts and military advisers were either working or living in Cairo and Egypt between 1949 and 1967 when the Six-Day War to all intents and purposes drew the episode to a close. By dictionary definition, the number could certainly qualify as a colony, to the extent that the Germans constituted a sizeable group of people of one nationality or race living in a foreign place, often assembled in the same neighbourhoods, speaking their native language and observing their own customs. The Cairo colony of German advisers and their families was even to some extent conspicuous, in that a succession of journalists including the American magazine writer Sanche de Gramont had described the 'blond Afrika Corps giants' loafing by the pool of the Heliopolis Sporting Club, openly drinking their beer and eating specially imported German sausages. The unrepentant Johann von Leers and his wife had thrown parties at their home in the exclusive enclave of Maadi where the Israeli 'champagne spy' Wolfgang Lotz had described the carousing Germans singing the Nazi anthem 'Horst Wessel' late into the night.

Between them the senior advisers of the Central Planning Board and the scientists and engineers working on the secret rocket programmes had more or less moved in wholesale to populate the modern garden suburb mansions and villas of Heliopolis, Maadi and parts of Helwan. They had spread outwards to Zamalek Island and Gizeh and inwards into the city itself. There was no collective attempt by the Germans as a group to maintain a low profile in greater Cairo until Operation Damocles and then the execution of Adolf Eichmann radically changed the mood music and altered some of their more extravagant behaviours in the process. Only Aribert Heim stuck throughout to a survival strategy of anonymity, trying to blend in with traditional working class Cairo.

Whilst never definitive, various estimates of the numbers have nonetheless been attempted. In December 1956, the head of Egypt's new State Security Cadre Leopold Gleim gave his audience the precise figure of 6,249 'Arabised Nazis' working for the SSC aided by some 70,000 Egyptians. Both numbers seem inflated and random and were unsupported by evidence. Likewise in his 1965 exchange with the US embassy in Lima Cesar Ugarte Jr offered the figure of 3,087 Nazi members in the Odessa organisation 'under the payroll of the Egyptian government since the fall of Perón's regime'. Estimates of Nazis in Egypt over the period ran as high as 20,000 but this number was never justified or formally corroborated. None of the various estimates offered have subsequently been converted to the status of a sure thing. The Mauthausen survivor and assiduous

Nazi hunter Simon Wiesenthal believed the likely operating number and ceiling was probably some 6,000 to 7,000 men at the height of activity and it is perhaps this estimate that serves best as a benchmark. The German advisers and specialists were spread widely across the Central Planning Board, responsible for Egypt's armed forces, the rocket and missile programmes including employees of the CERVA company, the State Security Cadre, the foreign office, intelligence service and Department of Information at the Ministry of National Guidance. There were almost certainly others in various undocumented government support roles, along with freelance military trainers, especially of Egyptian paramilitaries and Fedayeen. As a group these were much harder to categorise and may never have been formally catalogued whilst entering and leaving the country.

British and West German government estimates of the advisers on Central Planning Board contracts varied from 40 at the lowest end up to about 80 at the top end, largely calculated and borne out by the salaries bill at the time. It seems unlikely that there were ever more than 100 German military specialists, arms manufacturers and arms dealers in the country at any one time working on Central Planning Board contracts alone.

All of these individuals were named and their passport numbers and entry details into the country logged by Western intelligence agencies. Their presence ran broadly from 1952 to 1958 although many had gone by the time of the Suez crisis in late 1956. Scientists, engineers and technicians working on the jet aircraft HA300 and HA200 and the missile programmes in the Thalathat factory and other manufacturing plants in Helwan and Heliopolis numbered many hundreds, almost certainly rising into the low thousands at the height of the programmes. These efforts ran well into the 1960s and beyond in some cases although commercial production of Egypt's own jet aircraft and missiles never became a reality. In addition to a wide variance in the numbers, many names of former Nazis who signed up to work in an individual capacity at Egypt's ministries have also surfaced over the years, among them Franz Bartel, a Gestapo boss in Poland and Oskar Dirlewanger, head of the 36th Waffen SS Division in Russia. However, hard corroborative evidence of most of these names has never been forthcoming and Egyptian records still remain inaccessible.

The Beast in the Basement

'He was very tired, very ill. He suffered and he screamed a lot. Everyone heard him. The chief guard gave him food, a soldier's ration of one egg or one potato. . . he also laughed very loudly. He banged his head on the walls. . . he had a skin disease because of the lack of sunlight and fresh air. . . he couldn't even wash himself. You wouldn't keep an animal in such a place,' [13].

These were the words of one of the 22-strong detachment of Syrian guards detailed to watch over hunted Nazi war criminal Alois Brunner in the last decade of his life. Kept in a basement cell in a building near the Presidential Palace in Damascus up to his death at the age of 89 in 2001, Brunner 'suffered and cried a lot in his final years and everyone heard him', according to one of the guards, identified only as Omar [14].

Thus ended one of the final and most abiding mysteries of the hunt in the Middle East for the last of the remaining Nazis on the run. Alois Brunner, living in Syria for the best part of 30 years under the alias Dr Georg Fischer, had become something of an embarrassment to the Syrian regime which had offered him both employment and protection over the years. Like Walter Rauff and Franz Stangl before him, Brunner fled to Syria from Europe where he was being hunted for war crimes including deporting 136,000 European Jews, many of them children, to concentration camps. Brunner had personally been in charge of the French internment camp at Drancy and responsible for rounding up and deporting Jews living in the Vichy controlled parts of southern France. He arrived in Damascus in 1956, around the time of the Suez crisis and set up a number of import/export businesses in the Syrian capital, including dealing in arms.

In 1961 a West German security service informant code named Glueckrath told CIA officials in Munich that Brunner was part of a grand council of the Egyptian SS Group, which met several times in late 1960 and January 1961. Brunner attended these meetings along with the former SS Police Chief of Galicia, Fritz Katzmann, the propagandist Johann von Leers and a number of Egyptians in the intelligence and information departments. At the January meeting Brunner claimed to have a list of Jews who had collaborated with the Nazis during the Final Solution and who could thus now be blackmailed to help finance the SS group, according to Glueckrath. Von Leers was enthusiastic about publishing the names in any case, even if the blackmail failed.

After Hafez al-Assad came to power in 1971, Brunner allegedly helped the new ruler of Syria reconstitute the country's secret state police organisation (al mukhabarāt), modelling the compartmentalised structures and processes of the service and even designing individual pieces of torture apparatus such as 'the German Chair', a notorious hinged device which slowly broke the backs of detainees. Brunner was also said to have put in place individual training programmes for some of Syria's intelligence chiefs. Adolf Eichmann had allegedly turned to Brunner when he wanted things done if he thought progress in the elimination programme of Europe's Jews was too slow, referring to Brunner as his 'best man'.

At times, it seemed as if Brunner was taunting those seeking his trial and detention. On 1st November 1987, the Chicago-Sun Times ran a story titled: 'Nazi War Criminal Alois Brunner's Presence in Damascus Hits the Papers Again'. Seventy-five year old Brunner, it was reported, was living quietly at 7, Rue Haddad in the city protected by round-the-clock bodyguards provided by the Syrian Government in exchange for his recent service to Syria in security matters. In a brief conversation in front of a telephone witness Brunner said: 'all of them deserved to die because they were the devil's agents and human garbage. I have no regrets and I would do it again'. After confirming he had been living under the name of Georg Fischer, he hung up' [15]. The paper revealed that German prosecutors working with Israeli agents and representatives of the Anti-Defamation League's anti-Nazi taskforce had pieced together Brunner's travels after World War 2. He first fled to Cairo and tried to hide his identity by relying on the confusion surrounding the execution of another man named Brunner from the same Nazi unit. The two were unrelated, but it enabled him to move freely while the Allies were rounding up Nazi war criminals. Only after spending some time in Cairo did he move to Damascus [16].

The CIA tracked Brunner's whereabouts and activities for years. The American embassy in Damascus was in regular touch with the Agency, picking up on press reports, rumours and chance encounters that might deliver more definitive information about his status and whereabouts. In January 1993, the Embassy followed up French and German sourced reports, quoting a Western diplomat in Damascus, that Brunner had died. The French contacted the Americans in the Syrian capital for confirmation that they might have been the source. The report was eventually tracked down to an interview given in France by the Nazi hunter Serge Klarsfeld [17].

On 27th June 1991 the US ambassador in Damascus received a letter from Democrat Senator Edward Kennedy requesting information on the US Government's efforts to seek the extradition of Brunner. Officials at the embassy wrote to their bosses asking for advice on how to respond. 'While I welcome Syria's support during the Gulf crisis, I remain concerned about Syria's unwillingness to co-operate on other matters of concern such as the extradition of Mr Brunner, a chief aide to Adolf Eichmann who was responsible for sending thousands of people to death camps. I would be grateful for any information you can provide regarding our government's efforts to seek Mr Brunner's extradition as well as the response of the Syrian Government,' Kennedy wrote [18].

With the death of Alois Brunner, the hunt for fugitive Nazis who had sought post-war refuge in the ancient, immersive cities of the Arabic speaking eastern Mediterranean came to an end. Some of them had learned Arabic, converted to Islam and become absorbed into a life which unfolded against a backdrop of teeming, dusty streets in unfamiliar neighbourhoods. Despite their best efforts, most were doomed to bear the label of 'farangi', marked out as foreigners and thus perpetual outsiders. They had mostly toiled in carefully guarded obscurity, inhabiting anonymous, nondescript ministry buildings and isolated military camps, factories and secretive industrial zones. Here they had developed lives of renewed purpose in the service of demanding, often capricious foreign masters who were prepared to pay good money for the specialist expertise and skills required to shape the fledgling military and security states they were fostering. Assiduous and methodical, determined and persistent, the Germans had tried hard to succeed in their new incarnations, encountering technically complex and culturally challenging conditions that in the end took more energy, focus and staying power than they could muster over the long haul. It was despite these efforts that time was to show much of their advice and influence was destined to be transitory. In the end they were seen to have endured, but for what ultimate purpose history has found harder to determine.

Chapter Eleven

LIVING THE CAIRO LIFE

'There's nothing more difficult than making decisions in Cairo, since it's Cairo that usually makes decisions for you. How to live your life. Where you can have relationships and when they can end. When you can eat, how many years of your life will be wasted stuck in traffic. Your chance of getting cancer, the precise timing in your getting hit by a car, the amount of filth in the food you're forced to eat from the street.... You are a slave to this city. The only way to win her over is to sell her soul in a contract written with blood fresh from your veins.

Ahmed Naji,
Egyptian novelist
The Use of Life, 2014

Straddling the Nile, at the meeting point of Africa, Asia, the Eastern Mediterranean and the Middle East, Cairo (Al-Qāhira) has always been a cornerstone for empire builders with aspirations of regional dominance. This great Islamic metropolis has over centuries fused cultures and traditions, married architectural styles, outlasted invasions and blended ethnic ingredients from Arab, African and European roots into a heady national stew. A vast, sprawling, vivid city often juxtaposing conspicuous wealth with unspeakable poverty, Cairo has been bounced from ancient civilisation through successive centuries of conquest, colonial subjugation, political disenfranchisement, cultural ascendancy, war, revolution, poverty and bread riots. By the time the first German advisers arrived in Cairo at the end of the 1940s, the city of two and a half million inhabitants was on the cusp of one of its regular transformations, about to drop some of the exuberant European traits and freedoms of the Farouk years and begin instead to adopt a more sober, austere face that reflected the resurgence of Islam and its renewed prominence at the centre of national life. In July 1952, with the revolution of the Free Officers, this trend accelerated and reached maximum velocity when many Europeans and Jews left the city after the xenophobia and violence that led up to and followed the Suez invasion in November 1956.

The Germans thus found themselves in a city in transition, poised between two opposing poles of excess and austerity, licence and limit, the national psyche traumatised by the defeat of the 1948 war with Israel over Palestine. Used to a military culture in which political power and the threat of force marched in lock step, they were nonetheless entirely unprepared for a state that was run on a financial shoe string and a labyrinthine, largely antiquated bureaucracy which creaked at the seams and worked at snail's pace. Most soon found that their jobs often required negotiating poor infrastructure, primitive logistics, inefficient communications and lower professional standards than they were used to. Whilst the process of post-war denazification had revealed the realities of a more marginal life for many of these former high flyers, it had done nothing to prepare them for the arms-length, precarious status of the hired hand in foreign employ.

Some of the Germans had engaged directly with Arab and Muslim society through the North African campaign fought in Libya and Tunisia by the Afrikakorps during the war, but many had no idea of what to expect from a city such as Cairo with its potent blend of east and west, ancient and modern, aspiration and prejudice. To experience the fullness of Cairo was to embrace the mythology of the pharaohs, numberless antiquities and sacred sites, iconic mosques and palaces, the cupolas of Coptic churches, architectural echoes of imperial Britain and Ottoman Turkey, bustling markets, noise, heat, dust, slums and the enduring toil of the fellahin in the fields and reed beds alongside the life-giving Nile.

In the main well paid and highly valued, the Allemanni nonetheless needed to be adaptable, imaginative and pragmatic, setting out to make their tenure at the heart of the Egyptian military renaissance as familiar and tolerable as possible. Uncomfortable with the more primitive facilities and poor security of working class neighbourhoods of Cairo they were to find their way to the more conspicuously European parts of the city which offered them privacy, a certain luxury and more easily afforded protection. For, integral to the experience of the German advisers in Cairo was the angst of living with a permanent glance over the shoulder, always guarded by the Egyptian military and alert for the unwanted attentions of Israeli Mossad agents, scalp hunters and ambitious reputation seekers.

Besides coping with the stresses and difficulties of building up the Egyptian rocket programme or munitions factories from scratch, the Germans had other issues to deal with. Many found the intense summer heat to be a serious distraction, while others succumbed to tropical illnesses such as malaria or fell prey to environmental hazards that included a toxic cocktail of mosquitoes, flies, poor hygiene and dirty water. All knew they could never afford to wholly drop their guard. On arrival all of them were automatically issued with pistols and special identification passes, and all were constantly accompanied by bodyguards. [1]

Thus the fast growing, modern and sometimes grandiose suburbs and dormitories of Cairo were to become home to this rapidly expanding band of military and intelligence specialists, rocket scientists, arms manufacturers and propagandists. It was in the incongruous, elaborate and very European style ghettoes that they were able to construct lifestyles in the image to which they were more accustomed. Here down the leafy and cool avenues, in expansive gardens with their murmuring fountains set behind the high walls of formidable ornate mansions they could network, socialise and exchange confidences and plans far from prying eyes and ears.

Many of the Germans were concentrated in the upscale districts of Helwan, Heliopolis and Maadi. They could eat German food at a number of restaurants or watch foreign movies at one of Cairo's western style cinemas. 'It was a golden era', recalled one German woman who lived in Cairo at the time and said there was little or no difference from home in the life-style or the treatment of women. In cosmopolitan Cairo, women dressed in skirts and few wore headscarves. In the capital there were trattorias and bars where Greek waiters served alcohol to young military officers.' [2]

'City of the Sun'

In his dazzling description of 12th century Cairo, the British historian Justin Marozzi depicts a city at the heart of the 'Dar Al Islam', in its time the most important and distinctive expression of Islamic civilisation on the march away from its seventh century roots in the Arabian Peninsula. 'For the most commanding view over Cairo in all its sprawling, steaming, stinking, minaret-studded magnificence, there is only one place to go. Set on a spur of the 200 metre Muqattam hill, the great Qalaa or Citadel of Saladin has lorded it loftily over the city for eight centuries.... it has become one of the defining symbols of the Egyptian capital.'[3]

By 1949 when former Afrikakorps general Artur Schmitt, in the thinly veiled persona of Mr Goldstein, arrived in Cairo to begin his appraisal of the state of the Egyptian military, the north-east of the city had experienced an early 20th century metamorphosis more akin to the construction of a very grand garden suburb, a development beyond the existing conurbation, later to be absorbed into it, that had reimagined the idea of an entire upper class neighbourhood with its own vision, style and infrastructure. Heliopolis, in the Sahara desert some 10 kilometres north-east of the centre of Cairo, embodied the skyward ambition and vision of Baron Edouard Louis Empain, a Belgian entrepreneur who bought this 600 acre parcel of land on the cheap from the British authorities. There, in 1907 he built an entirely new city 'of luxury and leisure', one which coined its own Heliopolis style of architecture. In these unlikely circumstances now mimicked all over the modern Middle East from Dubai and Doha to Casablanca and Marrakesh, Empain built a large collection of conspicuously opulent houses and villas, some for rent, spaced around a breath taking landscape of broad avenues equipped with modern infrastructure including water, drains and electricity. Luxurious hotels like the Heliopolis Palace and Heliopolis House were part of the vision. The suburb boasted extensive recreational facilities too, among them a golf course, racetrack, park and the

Heliopolis sporting club, one of the most luxurious sporting clubs in Egypt, established in 1905. Amongst the development's long list of firsts was Africa's inaugural amusement attraction, the famous Luna Park.

In keeping with the mood of monumental thinking that had resulted in the construction of the Suez Canal 40 years earlier in 1869, Empain commissioned a French architect, Alexander Marcel, to construct his own residence, a Hindu style palace modelled on Angkor Wat in Cambodia and the Hindu temples of Orissa. This exuberant building, which embraced all of the most manifest and unfettered contradictions of colonial thinking, took three years to construct and was completed in 1910. Still in place today, now restored and finally open to visitors, it remains one of the finest examples of the early architectural use of concrete, of which it was entirely built. Empain's neighbours included Pashas and Sultans, drawn to the seductive mix of extravagance, originality, peace and exclusivity. After the 1952 revolution led by Nasser, many of Cairo's educated middle class built their lives in this imaginative new realisation of urban possibility.

It was in Heliopolis that former Wehrmacht artillery General Wilhelm Fahrmbacher, hero of the siege of Lorient, set up his office in the infantry training school of the army headquarters based there in 1950. And Rolf Engel, head of Egypt's secret CERVA rocket programme lived in the garden suburb in a closely guarded villa on a quiet street, visited in the Spring of 1954 by Israeli spy Paul Frank who was taken on a tour of a plant where the rockets were being developed [4]. The military importance and role of Heliopolis was reinforced by the presence of both the Egyptian military and air force headquarters. The Military Airbase is close by in the Almaza district along with the Military Air Force Highschool; and it was here that former Air Chief Marshal and Egyptian President Husni Mubarak lived[5]. In a nod to the British colonial past in Egypt, over 4,000 soldiers of the British Indian army are buried in the War Cemetery on Nabil Al Wakkad Street. As Cairo has expanded, the once large distance between Heliopolis and the original city limits has vanished and it is now well inside the extended cityscape, many of the spectacular original gardens subsumed beneath buildings that have been erected to take up the slack of Cairo's growing population.

Ironically perhaps in a city so connected to Islam and its vibrant past, Baron Empain was not the only Christian foreigner at work on a plan to leave his own footprint on Cairo. His contemporary, retired Canadian army officer Captain Alexander Adams was also intent on realising his own modern vision of a city within a city. Town planner Adams set out the specifications for the southern Cairo suburb of Maadi in 1905 and it was entirely his vision which led to the spacious boulevards and luxurious villas which characterised the new development. In a foretaste of the strict planning regulations and guidelines that were to be a feature of similar contemporary garden suburbs such as Hampstead in London, designed in 1906, precise rules set out how big houses could be, how much of the property could be occupied by the house and how much had to be left for the garden, and the size of the sidewalks. Even window shutters had prescribed colours and regulations were said to cover wireless radio noise control after 10 o'clock at night and fines for not maintaining gardens properly.

Maadi occupies an ancient Egyptian archaeological site, founded in 3500 BC, but its modern significance lies in its position on the railway line intersecting north and south Cairo and its Second World War past as a military base for the New Zealand Expeditionary Force which occupied it between 1940 and 1946. It is claimed that the British army set up an interrogation centre there in 1942 at the height of the Western Desert Campaign. In step with other European populated areas of Cairo, Maadi witnessed an exodus of Europeans and foreigners after the 1952 revolution of the Free Officers when the tide of Egyptian public opinion turned against them. However, this merely opened the door for a number of German advisers to walk through.

Perhaps the most conspicuous, and at times even flamboyant of them, was the prolific and subversive propagandist Johann von Leers. Having taken a house in the district at 21, Rue 83 Maadi in April 1956 when he first arrived in the city, he moved with his wife Gesine and daughter on 1st October 1958 to a larger, two-storey villa at 52, Rue 11, Cairo-Maadi, partly in order to get a direct telephone line. His move, paid for by the Arab League which was giving von Leers a salary of up to 100 Egyptian pounds per month, was documented closely by the watching CIA who were told of the upgrade by 'a well-informed West German rightist in touch with von Leers'[6]. The CIA was also interested in the fact that von Leers was housing Dr Hans Eisele, wanted in a number of countries for mass murder. During the war he had been a physician at several concentration camps, notably Dachau and Buchenwald, where he had conducted lethal scientific experiments on inmates and had subsequently been condemned to death by two separate post-war tribunals.

In its report, the CIA noted with some interest that 'the UAR government (United Arab Republic, signifying the political union of Egypt and Syria) promised to give officially to Dr Eisele the right of political asylum, and he will receive the opportunity to practice as a physician'. Somewhat counter intuitively to his immediate and well documented past, Eisele had played a major part in bringing von Leers back to health when he had fallen dangerously ill with a stroke in Cairo, and was also helping to familiarise some of the scientists on Egypt's rocket programme with their new surroundings.

Von Leers held numerous parties at his Maadi spread, sometimes breaking into song and drinking late into the night. The Israeli 'champagne spy' Wolfgang Lotz remembered the occasion in 1961 when he and his wife Waltraud attended a party hosted by von Leers, whose inebriated guests sang the Nazi anthem known as the Horst Wessel Lied. According to Lotz, von Leers ushered the couple into his spacious living room where there were close to 30 guests drinking cocktails and conversing in a cosmopolitan mix of German, English, and Arabic.

Soon Lotz realised that he was enjoying a remarkable stroke of good fortune. During a private conversation on the veranda, Leers took Lotz aside. 'I have an excellent memory for faces. I happen to remember yours very well', smiled the former propaganda chief. 'We met only once, at some conference in Wannsee…I remember you distinctly, looking very smart in the black uniform of an Obersturmbannführer. Don't deny it my dear boy. I am happy you are one of us and I will keep your secret. None but a chosen few shall know about it. I promise you'[7]. Trying to win his confidence further, Leers argued: 'Goebbels trusted me, and also the Führer. I did not betray either.' [8] Lotz denied the claim, which was erroneous, and by doing so became more convincingly part of the expatriate elite.

Dr Hans Eisele was also amongst the guests. Eisele, whose escape from Europe was reportedly facilitated by von Leers, was not the only Nazi concentration camp doctor with whom the propagandist got acquainted at his Maadi home. Fugitive Mauthausen physician Dr Aribert Heim, in hiding for many years at the Kasr Al Madina Hotel in Port Said Street, a more working class neighbourhood in Old Cairo, and active in Egypt as a property developer also met him several times but chose not to cultivate a friendship. He found the prospect of such an openly Nazi association far too risky [9]. Leers was, however, close to long-time contact Mahmoud Saleh aka Alfred Zingler, leader of the anti-Zionist Movement in Cairo, who had his offices at 14 Street, 26 July, Maadi [10]. Among the denizens of Maadi alongside Johann von Leers were arms adviser Dr Fritz Schultz and his wife Margarete and chemist and explosives expert Professor Georg Romer, who was planning the construction of a new high explosives factory in Cairo, along with his wife and children who all lived at Villa 72, Rue 16, Maadi.

Through the early 1950s, as more German military advisers took up temporary residence in the city with their two-year renewable contracts, the upmarket suburbs of Cairo took on a positively German expatriate feel. In a list of German military advisers in Egypt that the British released to the Americans in 1955, the precise whereabouts in Cairo of many of the 'Allemanni' were explicitly identified [11]. Like birds of a feather they had tended to flock together. Head of the Central Planning Board Dr Wilhelm Voss and his wife were based at 17, Iskandar Al Akbar (Alexander the Great) Street in Heliopolis. General Fahrmbacher, head of the military arm of the Central Planning Board shared a house at 9, Ashgar Street in Heliopolis with former tank commander General Oskar Munzel. Just down the road at Number 13 was his ordnance adviser Colonel Karl de Bouche. His assistant, and suspected agent for the Soviets, staff officer Colonel Kurt Ferchl lived at 13 Al Kubbah Street in Heliopolis in the same road as desert navigation expert Colonel Ernst Zolling and his wife Elisabeth, who were at number 21.

The paratroop advisor Major Gerhard Mertins, also under suspicion as a Soviet spy was at 11, Abd Al Wahid Pasha Street in the same suburb, along with former diplomat Major Rudolf Rosser, who had been military attaché in the German Embassy in Ankara during the Cicero spy scandal, and staff officer Colonel Hans Richert. The German residents of Heliopolis were numerous, if sometimes fickle, and their situation was replicated to some degree in both Maadi and Helwan as well as other upmarket districts such as Gizeh and Zamalek Island where expansive villas, modern apartments and lush gardens offered an inviting ambience. It might be said that in the first half of the 1950s when the German presence of military advisers in Cairo was at its height, they created the collective conditions to constitute a *bona fide* colony which, by its ethnic, professional, commercial and social distinctions constituted a Little Germany by the Pyramids.

To some extent, the tendency of the German advisers to head for these exclusive areas of Cairo were not entirely fortuitous but had actually been set by precedent before the Second World War. On the morning of 6th April 1939, Nazi Propaganda Minister Dr Josef Goebbels had landed at Almaza Airport in a Focke-Wulf 200 plane branded with the name of Nazi air ace Max von Muller and bearing the German swastika, for a private visit to Egypt. Whilst he had no official meetings with Egyptian or British Government representatives, he was primarily in the Egyptian capital to connect with the German community and senior expatriate residents of the city. Amongst the welcoming committee for the two-day visit were three highly significant and prominent residents of Maadi. First amongst them was President of the German Chamber of Commerce in Egypt and director of the Dresdner Bank, Baron Leonard Von Richter. Alongside him in the welcoming committee stood fellow Maadi neighbour Wilhelm Von Meeteren, the local director of Siemens. Third in line was Hans Pilger, the German Consul in Cairo who lived at the sumptuous Villa Basque in Maadi. Local gossip claimed that the Van Meeteren-Von Richter-Pilger threesome were closet Nazi agents, and even if these innuendoes were never actually proven, 'the fact that subversive elements were promoting Nazi propaganda all over the globe was no secret' [12]. In at very least a curious coincidence the Journal d'Égypte published an article on the day of the Goebbels visit claiming that 25,000 Germans had converted to Islam and were en route to various countries in the 'Muslim Orient' in an attempt to destabilise Franco-British influence.

There can be no doubt that Goebbels, in his discussions with the most influential representatives of the German community in Cairo, was preparing the way for German military intentions in North Africa. Egypt, with its British garrisons and extensive facilities across the country providing a tight grip on the Suez Canal and air routes eastwards, along with the naval bases of Alexandria and Port Said, was a prime target for the Wehrmacht. It saw Egypt as a springboard from which to drive on into Palestine and thence to Syria, opening a land bridge to the fertile oil fields and wells of Kirkuk. At the same time occupation of Egypt offered control of the sea lanes of the eastern Mediterranean, traffic through the Suez Canal and oversight of Russian or Turkish naval movement through the Black Sea and Dardanelles.

One of the excuses for the visit was to flag up the declining state of German trade with Egypt, set out the Reich's intentions to import more Egyptian cotton and, as its third largest user, to establish formal representation on the Board of the Suez Canal Company where it had been prevented from exerting any influence. The Egyptian Government, in any event, was wary of engaging with the Reichminister during his Cairo visit, preferring to keep him at arm's length so as not to offend the British. Apart from signing the Visitors Register at Abdin Palace, Goebbels made no formal gestures in his capacity as a visiting senior politician representing a foreign state. He confined himself to a largely cultural itinerary which included a moonlit ride around the Gizeh pyramids and a meal at the nearby Mena House Hotel where he subsequently stayed, ironically perhaps in the same suite as was to be occupied four years later by British General Bernard Montgomery ('Monty'). By the time Goebbels' Focke Wulfe took off from Almaza airfield to begin his trip back to Rhodes, with the smiling Reichminister clutching a farewell bouquet of flowers proffered by his German hosts, it could be assumed that the main threads of Nazi Germany's plan for North Africa had been safely communicated and that senior figures in the German community in Cairo were now on side.

Military-industrial Complex at Helwan

In Maadi and Heliopolis life at home could to some degree be recreated in a somewhat exotic setting where nothing completely worked in the same way or with the same efficiency. The German advisers could find a semblance of home in which to relax and embrace the emigré lifestyle. At the centre of both Empain and Anderson's visions for the new 20th century Cairo was the injection of grand design into the planning of urban space, the introduction of trees to provide shade, and wide boulevards and streets to instil a sense of order and calm. These purpose-built neighbourhoods created the feel of an oasis amidst the heat, dust and chaos of densely populated downtown Cairo and provided a suitable setting for architectural flamboyance and social exclusivity.

Some 15 miles south of Maadi, just beyond Cairo and in a line narrowly south-west from Heliopolis lies the city of Helwan, a destination that was also to be of major significance to the German advisers and their work. Site of Egypt's Khedivial Astronomical Observatory and home to the country's most famous psychiatric facility, the Behman Hospital constructed in 1939, Helwan had also housed a major British Royal Air Force base, RAF Helwan, up to the Second World War. From here, the RAF could mount operations eastwards to service its main Iraqi airbases at RAF Habbaniya, 60 miles west of Baghdad and at Shaiba, near Basra in southern Iraq. RAF Habbaniya was also an important staging post for onwards flights to India, and civilian flying boats refuelled there using the waters of nearby Lake Habbaniya as a landing strip.

This military association was to be preserved and massively extended under Nasser's rule, but at the same time his plan to industrialise Egypt and thereby develop it into the Arab world's first manufacturing powerhouse was also focused here. He was aware that Egypt's economy lacked the industrial and manufacturing base to power the armed services and armaments production that he deemed necessary for the country to become the predominant Arab regional force. Central to this plan and key to Egypt's future economic security and full employment was the construction of the Aswan High Dam. The refusal of the United States to fund the dam was the match that set the fuse of the Suez crisis burning in 1956. But prior to that, after Nasser and the Free Officers came to power in 1952, the process of industrialisation at Helwan was well underway.

Ironically, both post-war liberal democratic West Germany and newly Communist East Germany were competing to partner Egypt and make money from its industrial regeneration. East Germany had participated in a major industrial exhibition in Cairo in 1954 and both countries held further directly competing industrial exhibitions to showcase their wares and skills in the capital in 1957 [13]. Throughout the 1960s, Helwan developed into a massive steelworks zone, with numerous car factories also being built.

The West German firm Hoch-Tief began constructing the first iron and steel plant there, partnered by industrial giant Krupp. Mercedes and BMW started automobile manufacturing plants. The Helwan motor vehicle factory for trucks and buses was started by Magirus in partnership with Kloeckner-Humboldt-Deutz and a railroad car factory and concrete production plant were both established. In the midst of this industrial renaissance powered by resurgent German industry, first King Farouk and then Nasser had Helwan in their sights as the logical spot on which to base Egypt's secret rocket and ballistic missile programmes.

Far enough from the centre of Cairo yet easy to reach, near to industrial facilities and logistics hubs, better placed for a security cordon and with a military footprint including aerodrome and air support facilities already in place, Helwan became home for many of the Germans who had signed on to help Egypt realise its dream of a new generation of military hardware. In a no-holds barred exclusive in Spring 1963, the German newspaper Der Spiegel revealed to the world the extent to which the hidden arms and rocket programmes in Egypt had become a magnet for German expertise. 'Where thousands of years ago a nameless army of slaves built pyramids to the glory of the first pharaoh, roughly 500 highly paid German armourers manufacture the weapons of the new pharaoh of the coloured world: jet aircraft and rockets for Gamal Abd Al Nasser' the magazine wrote. It went on to describe a world of: 'professors who carry pistols, engineers whose telephone numbers are listed in no phone books, and skilled technicians who each morning must show their gray-green photo identity cards from the Egyptian Ministry of War to the khaki patrols with machine guns checking them, to enter the secret armament center of the United Arab Republic'.[14]

At the hub of this ant hill of industry were two vast, secret sites at Helwan which contained extensive research, manufacturing and test facilities. Site 36 was a hidden aircraft factory that had been originally built by the British. It was here that Willy Messerschmitt could be found working on the wings and fuselage for his new supersonic jet plane, the HA-300, and developing his trainer aircraft, the HA-200. The other was Site 135. This was the home of huge hangars and wind tunnels that scientists such as Ferdinand Brandner could use to test prototypes of his aircraft engine. Both sites were inaccessible and heavily guarded by the Egyptian military. The third of the secret rocket sites was near to Heliopolis. Called Factory 333, it was known by its Arabic name of 'Thalathat' (The Threes) and was a huge white-painted construction in the desert beyond the suburb. Here in 1953 Rolf Engel, head of the CERVA Project rocket programme, took over the four-square mile site to use as his headquarters. The nature of the work underway at the Helwan sites meant that apartment blocks and houses had to be hastily put up in order to accommodate the many workers being hired to provide labour. In due course Helwan began to reflect this new status as an industrial and residential hub by expanding its physical footprint and morphing into a mass suburb of Cairo for the working class.

Between these three increasingly inter-connected suburbs and dormitories of Cairo, the German advisers were able to construct a reasonable facsimile of domestic and social life. Work might have been in the main Ministry buildings and government offices of central Cairo or in the hidden manufacturing facilities and labs of Helwan and Heliopolis but the city itself and its surroundings remained a magnet for many of the Germans seeking diversion and amusement and their presence did not go unnoticed by the Cairenes, who remarked on their boisterousness and drinking habits in a number of regular watering holes. Astonishingly, even here, they were able to engineer some echoes of a more familiar life.

In a piece titled 'Nasser's Hired Germans', the international correspondent of the Saturday Evening Post, Sanche de Gramont, wrote in 1963: 'The German scientists, engineers and technicians who work for Nasser today live in an atmosphere of luxury. After hours, they live a carefree fun-loving life… at carnival time they nostalgically caroused at a 'River Carnival' party in the Nile Hilton Hotel. The blond giants loafing in the sun or diving off the high board at the Heliopolis Sporting Club look like incongruous leftovers from the Afrikakorps days. With their air-conditioned penthouses, their sports cars and their special imports of sausages and other delicacies from Hamburg, they are the inheritors of the opulence of King Farouk's days……'[15].

Alcohol was not in short in supply and the Allemanni even had access to Dutch licensed beer, a variation on Egypt's favourite drink. In 1937, Heineken International became a major shareholder in the Pyramid Brewery in Cairo, later turning it into the brand 'Al Ahram', (Arabic for 'the pyramids' and also the name of the capital's most famous daily newspaper). Many of the German exiles organised for their favourite foods to be imported and at least one German food and drink festival was held at the Nile Hilton Hotel in central Cairo. A landmark destination for the Germans and Cairenes alike was Groppi's, on Talaat Harb Square, an old style European café and cosmopolitan crossroads famous for its delicious sweets and pastries, chocolates and potent cups of coffee.

This ornate stage set created a permanently buzzing switchboard for political news, social gossip and the comings and goings of Cairo life. Founded in 1909 by Swiss pastry chef and chocolate maker Giacomo Groppi with the help of his son Achille, the Art Deco café with its secluded and leafy sunken garden became an integral part of the Cairo scene and a destination for many of the advisers seeking a taste of home. Groppi's was also to become something of a bell weather for the change in sentiment towards Europeans when the 1952 revolution sparked deadly street violence between British occupation forces and Cairo's police force. On 'Black Saturday', 26th January 1952, anti-colonial protesters torched hundreds of downtown establishments and shops; estimates put the damage to British and foreign property in Cairo, including the Cairo Opera House, at some £3 million.

On Talaat Harb, the damage to Groppi's was extensive. An anonymous eyewitness account published in the Egyptian Chronicle reported wild mobs on the rampage: 'some climbed for the Groppi's sign and dismantled the royal emblem 'Confiserie de la Maison Royale' from it. ..the mob proceeded to attack a paint shop next door and set fire to it,' the eyewitness wrote. 'The fire quickly spread to engulf both Groppi's and a small ammunition store...then, the mob proceeded to attack any building that looked foreign."[16].

For Protestant worshippers, the German Evangelical Church in Bulaq catered for spiritual needs and the Deutsche Evangelische Oberschule, an international school founded in 1873 to cater for the Protestant population of Cairo, reopened after the war in Dokki, just north of Cairo's famous zoological gardens. The school had been a stopover on Goebbels' visit to the city in 1939. Whilst there he had observed to the boys: 'the Reich recognises your valiant services and believes you should be rewarded. When I saw young British soldiers walking the Cairo streets I asked myself, wouldn't it be wonderful if they had been our schmucksoldaten marching out there?' [17]. A month before the Suez invasion, in October 1956, a course on Islam was added to the school curriculum and in 1957 the study of Arabic was made compulsory.

Some of the most important and high profile German scientists and advisers hankered after a more central Cairo lifestyle rather than being shunted off to the suburbs and, for them, almost any domestic extravagance seemed possible. The jet aircraft designer and former Nazi Party member Willy Messerschmitt and his entourage occupied an entire floor of the luxurious Shepeard Hotel in Cairo, also burnt down on Black Saturday, to be re-erected half a mile from the original site in 1957. Scientist Ferdinand Brandner chose to live on the exclusive Zamalek Island where he was given three apartments knocked together into one, an arrangement which occupied an entire floor of a residential building. The V2 rocket scientist Hans Kleinwachter could sometimes be found riding a horse in the desert around the Pyramids at Gizeh or fishing in the Red Sea. Many of the Germans went to Alexandria, on the Mediterranean coast at weekends to enjoy the beaches and the palm-lined sea front corniche and café nightlife.

In truth, life in Cairo for the German advisers was something of a patchwork, and numbers of them left early as soon as their contracts were up or a break clause could be negotiated. For some the security situation was too tense and living with the permanent threat of disablement or assassination all too real. In November 1956 a spate of Israeli driven parcel bomb attacks on scientists working on the rocket programme caused some physical damage to property and personal injuries, but the negative psychological impact was in some respects even more corrosive and enduring. Other emigrés were simply unable to cope with the climate, the cultural landscape, social and family deprivation and health issues. For the bulk, though, the Egyptian military reconstruction was simply a much needed source of work and income where their professional expertise still had a value, a career staging post from which they would return to Germany or go on to work on other ambitious arms programmes around the world with greater experience under their belts. For a significant cohort of fugitive Nazis with less technical or specialist skills, Cairo provided a port in a storm, a cloak of anonymity and temporary refuge from a former life which always threatened to catch up with them. For all of the advisers, however, the very particular challenges of the city and the toll it took on their reserves of energy, health, perseverance and purpose became a major factor as they toiled on the reconstruction of Egypt and Nasser's new military state.

Chapter Twelve
THE GERMAN FOOTPRINT

'Scores of people have been crushed or battered to death in Cairo as millions of people crowded onto the streets for President Abdel Nasser's funeral. The funeral cortège should have been a sombre state ceremony attended by 40 major-generals and 5,000 troops. But as the president's bier passed through the capital towards its final resting place, the sheer weight of numbers of grief-stricken Egyptians threatened to disrupt the procession. As the coffin crossed Qasr El-Nil bridge soldiers were simply overwhelmed...in a surge of spontaneity hysterical mourners attempted to bear their beloved leader's coffin themselves. Soldiers used rifle butts and batons to repel the crowd in the ensuing pandemonium. The march was abandoned and the coffin transferred to a military vehicle.'

BBC News, 1st October 1970.

The scale of the outpouring of national grief amongst Egyptians over the death of Gamal Abdel Nasser, from the fellahin to the middle classes, the military to the students, the shopkeepers and beggars in the street to the slick tourist guides in the Valley of the Kings was as monumental as the Pyramids themselves. An estimated five million Egyptians attended, or tried to attend, his funeral in Cairo on 1st October 1970. The event remains one of the largest of its kind in human history and the death of no other Arab leader has ever generated a populist response on such a scale. His death from a heart attack came as a devastating blow and plunged the nation into an immediate crisis of leadership. For Nasser was not in any sense a typical post-war Arab leader. He was a change making visionary, iconoclast, autocrat, revolutionary, 'saviour', above all things a patriot and nation builder. In the 16 years Nasser held absolute power in Egypt, from late 1954 to 1970, he had also become a cult figure, his charismatic image dominating billboards, his speeches charged with impassioned rhetoric consuming television air time, radio waves and news print, his likeness reproduced on consumer products and public spaces from t-shirts to banners and murals to flags. The Information Research Department of the British Foreign Office had early on identified 'the Nasser factor' as a prominent element in Egypt's propaganda strategy and one of the keys to the successful projection of its agenda across the Arab, African and Muslim world. His stellar PR persona and profile had proved a bridge too far for the traditionalist, patrician British Prime Minister Sir Anthony Eden in 1956.

The first to coin the phrase 'the Arab street' to describe Egypt's working class and fellahin as a political constituency and the bell weather of public opinion in the country, Nasser understood his audience and spoke directly to them without formalities or intermediaries. As a result, he was adored in return and greeted for the most part as the saviour of Egypt. For Nasser had done what no other had done before him. He had faced down the global powers of Britain and France at Suez, given the country and the wider Arab nation back its pride and dignity and helped bring Egypt into the modern post-colonial era through his grand scheme of industrialising, militarising, professionalising, employing, educating and empowering. It was Nasser's vision to build the Aswan High Dam and industrialise Egypt, to convert the workforce from farmers to makers, to create concrete and cotton industries, start factories and assembly plants to churn out entirely new lines of products from fridges to motor cars and fighter jets to flame throwers; nothing less than to enable an economic revolution that would in turn make Egypt the trading powerhouse and professional wellspring of the post-war Arab world.

The political ambitions of the Free Officers had been to rid Egypt of foreign influence, unite the Arabic speaking people

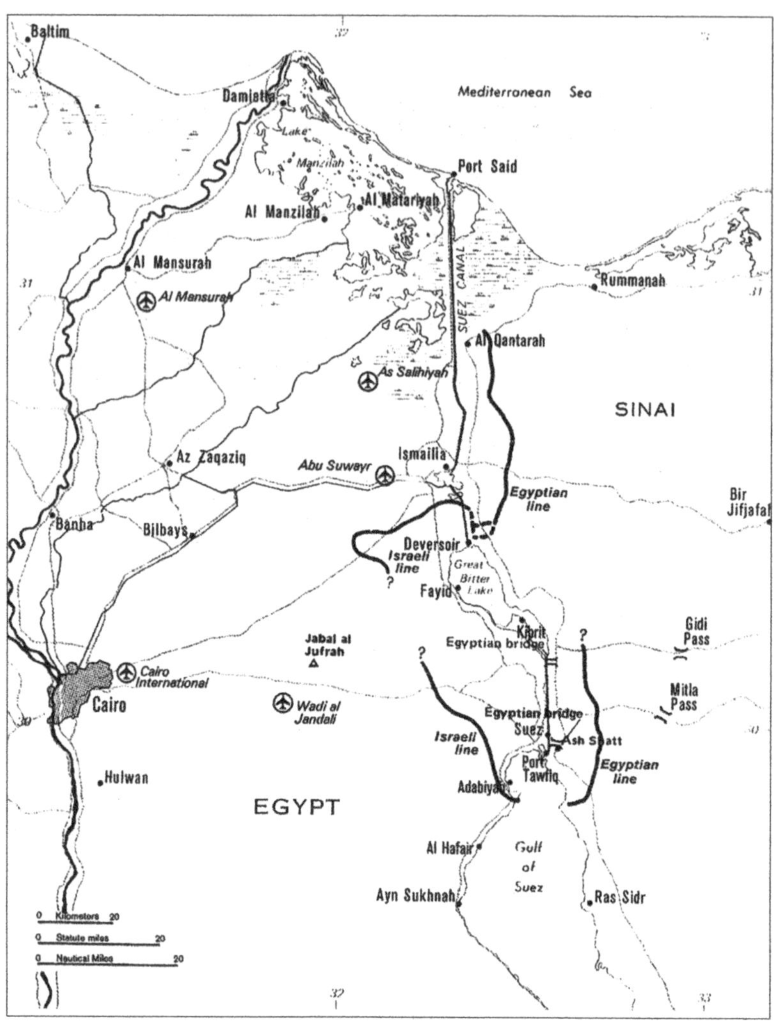

Map of Egyptian air force locations near the Suez Canal zone, 30th October, 1973.

behind a common cause and bring the Egyptian fellahin out of their feudal existence to enfranchise them as citizens in a modern Arab country full of possibility and opportunity. At the same time, the revolution had aimed to break the monopoly of foreign capital, apply the principle of social justice to governance and strengthen the country's military. Nasser had indeed brought about the end of the colonial era in Egypt. The British and French retreat from Suez had marked the moment when, above all others, the British Empire was revealed as threadbare and out of step, its finances turned onto life support, its hard power exposed as fragile and even its most basic values questioned and found wanting. He had, through the political movements of pan-Arabism, Arab nationalism and socialism endeavoured to unite the Arab world around his vision of creating collective power and unity of purpose to achieve greater leverage in the region. He had used the Arab League as his primary project to construct an Arab power base that would punch above its weight in the Cold War Middle East, with Egypt bold and confident enough to harness the twin horses of the United States and the Soviet Union and simultaneously balance the rising hard power of Israel.

The occasion of his death was therefore no time for patriots to deconstruct Nasser's record and enumerate his failures alongside his successes, to reveal the whole man and thus the fallible politician viewed across the trajectory of his career and its sometimes flawed political decision-making. Nasser's performance in some respects undershot his own vaunting ambitions and his fast accelerating legend often failed to take account of some more questionable judgements. Under Nasser and 'Nasserism', Egypt became a one-Party State, it secret police the object of fear amongst the people and its prisons overflowing with dissenters. Its overtly nationalist, 'socialism without socialists' political agenda found little room to accommodate opposition from large and powerful interest blocks such as the Wafd Party, Egyptian Communists, the trade union movement, the Muslim Brotherhood or the various powerful ethnic and religious minorities that made up the entirety of the country's political class. In most respects, neither the Arab League nor brief political union with Syria played out as he wanted or expected but in general failed ideologically and institutionally. Egypt did not quite gain the place it craved or felt it deserved at the head of the Arab table, its progress marred by military involvement in the civil war in Yemen and the messy internal politics of Jordan. It was underplayed but no less true that Nasser offered to resign the Egyptian Presidency after a further terrible military defeat to Israel in June 1967, later dubbed the Six-Day War. Humiliated and disgraced by yet another military reverse, Nasser took the weight of this latest disaster squarely on his shoulders. But, aware of the void that lay beneath them, Egypt's political and military establishment did not allow him to step down. He limped on at the head of Egypt's government for a further three years, in worsening health and increasingly aware that his strategy to back Russia and encourage a dependency on Russian arms had constructed a cul-de-sac from which it had become difficult to exit.

The Six-Day War brought Nasser's bid for regional hard power to a temporary halt. Defeat to the Israelis, the third in a row going back to 1948, was now accompanied by loss of further territory in Gaza, Sinai and east Jerusalem. The failure of Egypt's beefed up, well trained and better equipped military machine to respond to the challenge of engagement with his neighbour's high functioning army and ascendant air force now cast a shadow over his ongoing efforts to recast Egypt's military and security state.

A mere three years after Nasser's death, Egypt again went to war with Israel, as it turned out for the last time before the two countries reached a rapprochement in 1979 with the Camp David Accords. The 1973 war was the final, full-scale crushing encounter between two military machines engaged at full stretch. In this final conflict, which lasted for most of October that year, the Egyptians made a surprise, pre-emptive strike across the Suez Canal and penetrated deep into the Sinai Peninsula, at first catching the Israeli military off guard, causing them considerable damage and pushing their forces back. It was only a second wave of attacks by the Egyptians that created gaps in their own lines which a fast mobilising and more responsive Israeli army was able to exploit, finally crossing the Suez Canal westwards and heading for the city of Suez itself. In the east, Egypt's Syrian ally had also seen initial successes reversed to the point at which Israeli guns reached far enough to be trained on Damascus. The outcome of this 'Yom Kippur' war created the conditions for diplomatic recognition between Egypt and Israel and the eventual operation of common borders with Palestine, through the enclave of Gaza. With the final war between Egypt and Israel over, Egypt started to unwind its arms procurement and licensing arrangements with the Soviet Union, aware that increasing equipment obsolescence, technical weaknesses and difficulties in procurement of spare parts and replacements required a different approach, one which Nasser's successor Anwar Sadat transformed during his own Presidency.

Assessing The German Legacy

It is through the prism of this further defeat that the work of the German military advisers, rocket scientists, engineers and security specialists first contracted to the country's Central Planning Board and ministries in 1952 needs more considered appraisal. What value, temporary or permanent, had this grand and costly Egyptian vision and scheme initiated by King Farouk and developed by Neguib and Nasser yielded over nearly two decades? How much had their advice been heeded by Egypt's political and military establishment, including by Nasser himself? The Egyptians had collectively found it difficult to hear some hard truths which the German experts had delivered over the years, starting with General Artur Schmitt who in 1950 had bluntly criticised Egyptian strategy and tactics in the first Arab Israeli war, characterising them and the leadership of Haider Pasha and Egypt's elitist officer clique as bungling and still anchored in the 19th century.

The volatile Panzer commander Oskar Munzel, preparatory to pulling out of Egypt in late 1954 had slammed his fist down on Nasser's desk and described the Central Planning Board model as being unworkable due to the Germans having no executive authority or battlefield command. His view was that training on its own was a waste of time. What was missing was German leadership and decision-making at the sharp end of tactical deployment and combat itself. To this extent, the engagement of German experts and their advice without the propulsion or authority of official German foreign policy behind it was bound to fail at a strategic level. The failure of the mission was in some respects defined by its own limitations. Fahrmbacher, the generally more supportive and committed number two in the Central Planning Board hierarchy, had first of all focused on getting the

Egyptian soldiers fit and organised. But he rapidly reached the view that Egyptian army units would do best if kept small and only built up slowly over five or six years, their commanders not yet competent to handle the large formations of men and machines required in a modern army extended to the maximum. This view was increasingly borne out by subsequent events over the course of Egypt's wars and to a great degree reinforced British analysis in 1947 that Egypt did not possess an army with large scale offensive capabilities.

The pioneering rocket scientist Rolf Engel, charged with missile and jet engine development for CERVA, had been ground down and beaten back by financial considerations, lack of material resources, a culture of obstruction and poor standards of personnel when he abandoned leadership of the rocket company and returned to Europe in 1957. He recommended preserving the advances made by the programme by turning the great Thalathat factory complex into more dedicated research and training facilities for Egyptian technicians before ramping up any production. And Dr Wilhelm Voss, the highly organised but often abrasive Chief Technical Adviser to the Egyptian Government and in overall charge of the German military mission, had encountered insurmountable personality problems with Nasser. He had also unwisely tripped up over sensitivities in his relationships with West German politicians, some of them like Walter Hallstein at the highest levels of the new federal government. The Egyptian experience in some respects had been a sobering one for the Germans but both they and their methods had nonetheless penetrated Egypt's military and security state widely and deeply, and left their stamp on its culture, systems, processes and some individual moving parts of the country's growing military and intelligence machine.

The German advisers had focused on three principal areas: re-engineering the army, navy and paramilitary forces to make them fit for purpose after the 1948 Arab Israeli War; developing Egypt's arms manufacturing capability, including producing conventional weapons, ammunition and explosives but also carrying forward King Farouk's vision of realising Egypt's first ballistic missile and jet aircraft production; and upgrading the procurement process to initiate a programme of arms acquisition from third party countries in order to supplement domestic production. Through the 1950s, Egypt had subsequently done arms deals with the Russian proxy Czechoslovakia, the United States and the Soviet Union before settling on the Russians, partly for ideological reasons, as sole providers of arms and technical support post-Suez in 1956.

In addition to these key areas and beyond the direct control of the Central Planning Board, German and Nazi expertise propelled by the eminence grise, Reinhard Gehlen, had been widely employed to repurpose the country's intelligence service, its first information department and new internal security and police apparatus. In the process, British analysts determined that Nazi methodology had been applied by introducing a dimension of subversion into Egyptian foreign policy and the associated scheme to build soft power. There had been no attempt to nurture or invest in institutional reform to encourage democratic behaviours, but rather the reverse. The systematic deployment of German knowledge and skills across the institutions of Egypt's government, whilst never wholesale, touched at some time many layers and separate aspects of its generation and projection of hard power over nearly two decades. The German presence and the nature of their advice was judged additionally concerning in the way that it may have helped Egypt counter and in some cases overtake Britain's own efforts to influence regional Arab public opinion and thus generate its own increased soft power.

The reach and penetration of German expertise into Egypt's core institutions had in fact been sufficient for British analysis to conclude that the phenomenon was doing real damage to British interests in Egypt and potentially the wider Middle East. In their confidential critiques over the years, the Foreign Office, the Chiefs of Staff and the Information Research Department flagged up a laundry list of this damage, starting with the perceived authoritarian and militaristic nature of the German character and its potential to disinhibit and stimulate Egyptian government thinking, ambition and risk taking. They had focused on the practical dangers and negative implications of German leadership and training in developing Egyptian paramilitaries and Palestinian Fedayeen and the consequent threat to British bases along the Suez Canal. Indeed, the role played by the German trainers in stimulating full scale guerrilla war and organised resistance in the Canal Zone had altered their own contingency planning for exiting the Zone entirely if necessary in a full scale damage limitation exercise.

The introduction of new West German army operating procedures controversially secured by Dr Wilhelm Voss had raised eyebrows both in Britain and within the highest levels of West German government, along with a new tactical emphasis on speed and mobility of Egyptian forces in the field. Added to this was initial concern over the impact of new technologies, manufacturing capability and production for the development of Egypt's first jet fighter aircraft, its own proprietary jet engines, ballistic missiles and even further into the future, planning for nuclear weapons to counter Israel's own growing though clandestine capability. Their worries were tempered somewhat by US and Israeli scepticism as to just how far these rocket programmes could realistically progress. Nevertheless, Israeli secret service initiatives such as Operation Damocles afforded the Egyptian effort some credibility and traction.

The German and Nazi cohort was instrumental in helping Egypt reach some way towards all these advances in their ambitions and consequently could legitimately claim a role in influencing the country's course, even if such influence was not always translated into a new reality on the ground. Taken as a whole, official analysis shows that the German and former Nazi military influence in Egypt was much greater and reached much deeper than may have been publicly acknowledged at the time or for that matter subsequently. It was also a phenomenon that, though occasionally sensationalised, is now clear was both under reported and under estimated during the 1950s and 1960s, partly because of the controversial nature attached to the advisers' provenance and partly due to the culture of secrecy that surrounded all military and state security issues in Egypt and the inability of domestic media to access information about them and report on or corroborate them independently. It also remains true that the precise extent of the involvement of the 'Allemanni' remains contested history, requiring further evidence, corroboration by formal Egyptian sources or independent verification. However, the subject was one of legitimate inter-governmental concern and it led in turn to many conspiracy theories, most of all centring around the Suez crisis and the subsequent campaign to force Egypt's Jews from their homes, businesses and their adopted country.

Only limited and intermittent media coverage of the German presence and the activities of individual advisers in Egypt provided a route to increased public awareness. Occasional and opportunistic scoops by intrepid or ambitious foreign journalists such as Bill Stephenson, Sanche de Gramont and Diane Sharpley or via unintended leaks often unsupported by first-hand evidence provided tantalising glimpses into the largely hidden world of Egypt's government ministries and its reforming military industrial complex. Whilst Egypt could boast a highly developed media sector, the state information machine has always operated a rigorous system of press censorship, at one time under Nasser imposing an individual censor on each daily newspaper, including the leading daily Al Ahram edited by his own lifelong spokesman Muhammad Heikal. The censorship system which worked to prevent the world knowing too much about the German role in building the state is the same system that today works to prevent timely and accurate reporting of events in post Arab Spring Egypt by newspapers, radio, television, social media and citizen journalists.

A More Militarised Egypt

After the Soviet Union terminated assistance to Egypt in 1975, there was a decline in the country's military capability. This was confirmed in a secret US interagency intelligence assessment of developments in the Egyptian army made in Spring 1984 [1]. However, this temporary dip was to be reversed as US and other foreign military equipment started to arrive. By 1989, Syria would have a larger military capability than Egypt even as Egypt's indigenous military budget reached $US2.5 billion and the country started to modernise its forces after they had been eroded somewhat by dated Russian military equipment. A shadow of the German influence was reflected in Egypt's call for greater mobility and self-sufficiency, with military planners aiming for a smaller, technically more sophisticated force by the late 1980s.

Active duty strength in the Egyptian armed forces reached 447,000 in the mid 1980s, a massive five-fold increase from the position in 1952. 'The Egyptian armed forces are among the largest in the Arab world. Assets include a diversified inventory of modern weapons, a combined-arms organisation and extensive training. Nevertheless, dependence on foreign suppliers for weapons and spare parts, a lack of tactical flexibility and inadequate logistical and maintenance systems continue to impair Egyptian combat effectiveness', the report stated [2]. Egypt's armed forces peaked at 500,000 during the 1973 Yom Kippur war beyond which its force structure remained relatively constant, with major units including 11 manoeuvre divisions, 25 fighter/bomber squadrons and four air defence divisions.

In General Wilhelm Fahrmbacher's original plan back in 1952, worked out in his barracks at Almaza, Egypt's armed forces were to be structured around the old Reichswehr model of 33 divisions. He had called for an interim model based on smaller, more mobile units before moving into major tactical formations. Fahrmbacher's recommendations over time may have been partly realised. Panzer commander General Oskar Munzel, who had decried the poor technical and mechanical state of Egyptian tanks and armoured weapons and the abilities of tank crews back in the mid 1950s, most notably at the Independence Day parade of 1953, might have been gratified some 30 years later by the response to his criticisms. This showed that Egypt's purchase of modern US tanks and armoured personnel carriers (APCs) had led to increased mechanisation of infantry units with a concomitant enhancement of armour capabilities [3]. In an observation that might have brought some sense of vindication to Munzel's analysis, the interagency report found that 'the armoured division has become the primary strike force within the Egyptian army'.

One of the clearest judgements the report made was that foreign military relationships up to the mid 1980s continued to be a determining factor in Egypt's ability to maintain and equip a defence establishment. Once the only major military power in the Arab world, the country had seen its military capabilities erode 'drastically' after the watershed in 1975 when Soviet military assistance ended. It was not long before shortages in spare parts began to have an impact on military readiness, the original lifespan of much of the equipment was exceeded and it became necessary to cannibalise major items such tanks, APCs and artillery pieces.

Egypt's arms Manufacturing Industry

A major component of Dr Wilhelm Voss' remit in 1952 was to help Egypt work towards self-sufficiency in arms and armaments for its expanding military by setting up a domestic arms and armaments manufacturing industry and using third parties to supplement those areas where it could not gain critical mass. German arms experts who Voss brought on board around that time included a number who had served the Third Reich during the Second World War, among them the chemist and high explosives expert Georg Romer, IG Farben tank expert Dr H Andrea and the rocket scientist Kurt Hanisch [4].

In addition, Voss recruited a clutch of arms dealers including some who had already set up partnerships and joint ventures in Egypt. On the list were Special Forces Chief Otto Skorzeny, Albert Gay, Gunter Jackering and Heinrich Blum, a representative of the Egyptian-German Industrial & Trading Company [5]. Arms dealers who the British also flagged up in 1955 included former SS officer Dr W Baisner and former Nazi Party member Joachim Hertslet [6].

To what extent did these former Nazis help realise Voss' objectives? In January 1955, the British Embassy in Cairo confirmed that Egypt had set up a factory for the production of small arms[7]. The beginnings of a domestic arms production industry were now detectable, with the manufacture of rifles, mines and flame throwers amongst other weapons in production in factories and assembly plants across Cairo. Independently, production was in hand on the CERVA programme and other jet engine and rocket assembly lines at the factories in Helwan and Heliopolis which would a decade later produce prototypes for the Al Zahir and Al Kafir rockets and the HA 300 jet fighter.

US analysts were in no doubt that the Egyptian domestic arms industry had made further progress after it abandoned production of domestic rockets and missiles in 1967. 'Egyptian domestic arms production capability has improved somewhat over the past decade…it produces a majority of its small arms, mortars and rocket launchers, and artillery ammunition. In addition it produces limited quantities of air defence artillery and wheeled APCs,' the report asserted[8].

At the end of 1985 a far-reaching US assessment on the state of the Egyptian arms industry was finally able to shed light on some of the facilities and developments started by the Germans and former Nazi scientists in Cairo in the early 1950s. Setting up an arms production programme to manufacture as many Western style arms as possible was part of Nasser's drive from 1954 to generate full employment and economic development in Egypt. Ammunition factories were the first priority, followed by aircraft production at the Helwan complex, armoured vehicle production at the Al Kader factory and surface-to-surface missile production at Heliopolis, the report revealed [9]. Ironically, Egypt only recognised its dependence on Western aerospace technology after West German scientists in Egypt ended their work on advanced aircraft and surface-to-surface missiles and withdrew shortly before the 1967 Arab-Israeli war. It was this overdependence on top of bad planning and poor co-ordination with the military that led Nasser to abolish the Ministry of War Production and declare that arms plants were to manufacture civilian goods under the auspices of the Ministry of Industry. Nasser's purchase of large quantities of Soviet arms in the 1960s was done to match Israeli capabilities as rapidly as possible rather than wait for results from Egypt's own arms industry. But the effect was to shut down the domestic arms industry and cancel the most promising aeronautical research and development programmes. President Sadat's 1979 peace treaty with Israel further stalled the arms industry.

After Nasser's death, President Sadat restored the Ministry of War Production in 1971, initiating new arms and ammunition licensing agreements with Britain and France to supplement Moscow's agreement in December 1970 to permit licensed production of Soviet weapons. Sadat's decision, following the 1973 Yom Kippur War, to use the arms industry to provide employment for a peacetime military and the need to obtain foreign exchange through arms sales in turn provided the impetus for the conception of the Arab Organisation for Industrialisation (AOI) in 1975. The US analysis of 1985 calculated that Egypt's Ministry of Defence operated some 15 military factories in and around Cairo and Alexandria. Between them, these factories manufactured a wide range of arms, armaments and related equipment, some of it Egyptian originated and some under license from French, British and US manufacturers. However, the most startling revelations in the analysis concerned the legacies of Dr Wilhelm Voss and rocket scientists Dr Rolf Engel and Paul Goercke. Their respective projects to kick start the arms production and rocket programmes in Cairo during the 1950s still existed in the arms production landscape of modern Egypt and in some respects were remarkably little changed [10].

The vast, four square-mile factory complex formerly known as Factory 333 (Thalathat) in Almaza outside Cairo which housed Rolf Engel's rocket and missile production for Egypt's CERVA company had been rebranded and in the mid 1980s was now operating as the Sakr Factory for Developed Industries. Just as Engel advised in his exit interviews in 1958, the factory now majored in research and development alongside the production of rockets, missiles and propellants. In line with Engel's suggestion, foreign assistance had been critical to the success of Sakr projects and the German connection had thus survived the intervening decades. Dynamit Nobel supplied at least 15 per cent of rocket propellant used in the Sakr 30 improved 122mm artillery rocket. And the West German firm Bayern Chemie cast the propellants for both the Sakr 30 and the SA7 Sakr Eye missiles. This ongoing involvement of German firms may reflect some of the heritage attached to the facility but it certainly echoes the German fired manufacturing, industrial and technological revolution that supported Nasser's modernising Egypt in the 1950s.

Site 135, the factory complex in Helwan where jet engine genius Ferdinand Brandner toiled on developing the E300 turbojet engine to fit inside Willy Messerschmitt's HA300 jet fighter had also been rebranded. Now known as the Helwan Engine Factory, its purpose directly reflected Brandner's project of some 30 years earlier. In the mid 1980s, the factory had nearly 4,000 employees and was focused on assembling a French jet engine, the Turbomecca 04-C5, for the Alpha Jet. It was also preparing to assemble under license Pratt and Whitney turbo-prop engines for the Egyptian air force Tucano trainer at a planned rate of four a month.

The third of the three major factories set up and occupied by German led arms programmes in the 1950s was Site 36 in Helwan. Here, Paul Goercke and Willy Messerschmitt toiled on the production of the airframes and wings for the HA300 jet fighter and the HA200 jet trainer, both destined to be the spearhead of Egypt's move into jet propelled fighter aircraft to rival Israel's US and French supplied air force. This facility had also been rebranded as the Helwan Aircraft Factory. Here too in the mid 1980s, the factory was engaged in remarkably similar work to its German run predecessor, managing the component assembly, final assembly and flight testing of the French Alpha Jet.

The factory was also scheduled to provide components and assemblies for the Brazilian Tucano trainer once assembly and manufacturing began at AOI's Kader factory, and it had been designated to assemble French Mirage 2000 fighters for the Egyptian Air Force, the US analysis revealed. The Helwan Aircraft Factory became a destination for many of Egypt's top graduate engineers, of whom there were 150 in the mid 1980s out of a total workforce of some 3,500. 'The factory represents a powerhouse for excellence in Egyptian aeronautical projects over the last 20 years, including the design and prototype manufacture of two Egyptian military aircraft in the late 1960s' said the report, in a nod to the last HA300 production line finally abandoned after the Six Day War in 1967 [11].

In an enigmatic coda to its 1985 report, the Directorate of Intelligence referred to the Sakr Factory for Developed Industries 'last major project' which it described as its most interesting, namely the development of a short range ballistic missile. This was under research and development in combination with the Swiss firm Oerlikon-Buehrle which was developing a test stand for Sakr capable of testing solid fuel engines for surface-to-surface missiles [12].

In their findings and judgements on the Egyptian arms industry in 1985, the American analysts confirmed that Egypt at that time was the only Middle Eastern state other than Israel with a significant arms production capability. The issues that were holding it back were lack of a modern technological base and the advanced manufacturing infrastructure necessary for the production of its own advanced tanks, aircraft or missiles. Further inhibiting factors in the drive for self-sufficiency centred on labour shortages and training, planning, logistics, an imperfect procurement process and cultural issues around language, responsibility and management. In general terms, these could be said to resemble the issues that Rolf Engel and Paul Goercke encountered in the 1950s. Used to the meticulous efficiencies and deep resources of German manufacturing industry under the Third Reich, they were defeated by a haphazard approach, lack of financing and skills, and a sometimes obstructionist culture. At that time, the Egyptian vision was in hindsight clearly too grandiose whilst the means to deliver it were limited and lacking maturity. However the German experts, and the work they performed toiling in the factories of Helwan and Heliopolis through the 1950s to the mid 1960s planted seeds which were to bear fruit 30 years later. In some respects they cast the mold and set the tone for an industry which went on to become the most advanced and prolific of its kind in the modern Arab Middle East.

The Arms Race and the Cold War

In February 1963, a US Democratic Senator made a trip to Egypt on official business which was to influence Egypt's reputation in the West for decades to come. Senator Ernest Gruening of Alaska, American son of a German immigrant who had fought in the Union army at the Battle of Five Forks, stood in Tahrir Square during one evening in the Egyptian capital and witnessed preparations for a major speech by Nasser. With its attendant posters, slogans and militaristic posturing, Gruening made the association in his mind between the regalia of Nasser's Egypt and a police state. He later amplified this definition to make direct comparisons between the Egypt he perceived that evening with Kruschev's Russia and Hitler's Germany, using the lack of free speech, state control of the economy, internal police suppression of civilians and the export of a particular brand of economic and political socialism to draw the parallels.

Legitimate or not, or even mistaken, why did his views matter? Gruening was a member of the Senate Committee on US Government Operations, tasked with the mission to look into the operations of the United States foreign aid programme in Egypt. On his return to the US, this Harvard educated politician, former journalist and Executive Editor of the New York Tribune, continued his highly critical and damaging analysis in a formal submission recorded as evidence in the Senate Congressional Record of 30th October 1963 [13]. He accused Egypt of pursuing a subversive campaign to destabilise neighbouring Arab countries, of using American technology provided for under US aid, (namely US aid Project 263-G-22-AA), to facilitate the broadcast of poisonous radio propaganda beyond Egypt's borders and of deploying a large military force to Yemen which had been revamped with the aid of Russian technicians and 'former German Nazis'. Gruening's analysis exposed the tensions, contradictions and practical realities of the Cold War being played out in the Middle East during the 1960s and in the process provided some further context for the presence of the German advisers in Egypt.

Gruening's overarching point was that he could not reconcile the fact that the United States was donating Egypt $200 million a year in wheat subsidies whilst at the same time Egypt was spending an estimated $US920 million a year on arms from the Soviet Union. 'Nasser has undoubtedly been putting a lot of money in arms and a large army which might otherwise be devoted to economic improvement', he said [14]. In the second of two subsequent letters he wrote on his return to US President John F Kennedy, he observed: 'I did not underscore strongly enough the thought that we are supporting an arms race in the Middle East just as surely as though American dollars were used directly to pay for the arms purchased. Under Public Law 480 we are supplying a vital part of the food needs of the Egyptian people. As a consequence Nasser is left free to exchange his cotton for Russia's missiles '[15].

During his trip to Cairo, Gruening met Nasser who told him that after the poor performance of Egyptian forces at Suez against the British, French and Israelis, his officers had demanded that he accept the Russian offer of arms. This had resulted in Nasser's subsequent total dependence on Russian arms supply and technical support, for which he was paying massive sums. Gruening found it difficult to justify America's support of Nasser's government, citing Egypt's evidently subversive foreign policy and the US role in helping encourage its slide 'into the Russian fangs' and thus helping to provoke a possible communist revolution after five or 10 more years of authoritarian state socialism. He admitted there were mitigating circumstances, among them Egypt's joining the General Agreement on Tarriffs and Trades (GATT), its support for the UN efforts to stabilise the Congo and its silence on the US sale of Hawk missiles to Israel. But these were nowhere near enough. He asked US lawmakers to consider the question: where was America's policy vis a vis Colonel Nasser eventually leading?

Moreover it was now apparent that all the time Nasser had been playing the United States and Russia off against each other and 'talking softly', he had been constructing missiles so that he could proudly parade them in Cairo on 23rd July 1963, missiles constructed through the know-how of former German Nazis. To back this up, Gruening quoted from a 24th July report by the US journalist Jay Walz in the New York Times, in which he recorded his impressions of the annual Egypt Independence Day parade: 'The United Arab Republic paraded two rockets today and announced that it has developed 'the first Arab submarine which will be tested at sea within 15 days'. One of the new rockets was a Soviet made SA2 ground-to-air weapon recently demonstrated in the desert near Cairo. The second was the first two-stage missile developed in the United Arab Republic; this missile, called Pioneer, is of ground-to-ground type. A jet fighter that thunderously broke the sound barrier over the Nile was identified as the first faster-than-sound fighter built in the United Arab Republic…the Palestine Army, recruited among refugees at Gaza, participated. This army is being trained to participate in the 'liberation of occupied Palestine (Israel) that President Nasser has promised'.

The final destructive blow to Egypt and Nasser's reputation for double-dealing and morally ambivalent government was dealt by Gruening in his detailed and lengthy take down of the Nazi presence and role in Egypt, leading on to full blown conspiracy theories about the longer term objectives and ambitions of the Germans. Quoting a book provocatively called Behind The Egyptian Sphinx he unrobed 'the full blooded Nazi, SS Colonel Otto Skorzeny as Nasser's chief military and geopolitical adviser, intimate foreign collaborator and confidant, introduced to the Egyptian leader by his father-in-law Hjalmar Schacht, Hitler's former financial wizard now President of a Dusseldorf bank specialising in the promotion of German-Arab trade'. He declared that the Nazis had formed an Arab Foreign Legion to fight against the Jewish State, a claim which he did not support with any evidence. He also named and shamed a long list of former Nazis active in the Nasser Government, including Leopold Gleim, Joachim Deumling, Heinrich Willermann and, with little evidence, Dr Hans Eisele. He did not reveal the source or provenance of these names, many of which were nonetheless authentic.

And he went on to claim that the French with 'their Cartesian sense of realism' thought that the presence of so many Germans in the Nile Valley was an ominous sign and could not be taken lightly or easily explained away. 'Devoid of illusion they rightly concluded that the Germans were in Egypt for the express purpose of re-establishing their power and influence in the Middle East at the expense of the United States, Britain and France', he said.

Whilst some of the evidence concerning the Nazis in Egypt and their role in the persecution and eviction of Egypt's Jews after Suez had been heard in US Congress in 1957, this had been fuelled by Jewish supporting NGOs and other sympathetic organisations active in the US at the time. Gruening, a German by heritage, was a Democratic Party law maker who could not be easily accused of acting as a Zionist or Jewish agent. His engagement was squarely grounded in his formal role of defending the interests of US voters and justifying the expenditure of US tax dollars. Thus his findings, submitted to Congress and summarised and accented in his subsequent letters to President John F Kennedy were highly influential in shaping US political and public opinion about the Nasser regime, its affiliations and objectives in the Middle East. Over time, these perceptions were never fully shifted and to some extent have continued to cast a shadow, shaping some of the negative associations attached to the nearly two decades of Nasser's stewardship of Egypt.

In its reply to Gruening on behalf of President Kennedy, the US State Department set the tone for the years to come in the Middle East arms race. It claimed that between the years 1949 and 1962, the United States had provided Israel and Jordan with financial support of over $US400 and $US190 per capita respectively, whilst providing $US26 per capita to the United Arab Republic [16]. 'The Department has taken and is taking steps designed to reduce or eliminate the tensions underlying the Arab-Israel dispute and to keep to a minimum the flow of arms to the area. The Department seeks to conduct these policies and actions so that they will not of themselves precipitate an adverse chain of events which would be difficult if not impossible to contain and be welcome only to the Soviet Union', Kennedy's arm's length reply ran.

Gaza's Rocket Century

The ineffectual outcome of this policy stance may be judged in one respect by events in Gaza, the Palestinian enclave which now sits in ring fenced isolation between Egypt and Israel with only two functioning entry and exit points, Erez to the east and Rafah to the west. During the 21st century the Palestinian rocket arsenal used in Gaza as a military asset in its wars with Israel has become increasingly significant and includes both home-made and imported missiles. Estimates suggest the Palestinians in Gaza, under a Hamas led government since 2006, may have built, imported and deployed as many as 16 different types of projectile over the last 20 years. Predictably perhaps, one of the principal missiles in this arsenal is called the Al-Nasser, of which two types, the Al Nasser 3 and Al Nasser 4 have been used by the Popular Resistance Committees. Other common types are said to include the Al Quds, deployed by Islamic Jihad, the Arafat, used by the Al Aqsa Martyrs Brigade, the Al Fajr 5, an Iranian artillery rocket, the Katyusha, a Soviet Grad rocket and the Qassem, a Gaza produced rocket used by Hamas. Between them these rockets are sourced in Gaza, the Occupied West Bank, Iran and Syria. Some are transported whilst disassembled into Gaza through highly engineered and secret tunnel complexes originating inside Egypt. There is an ongoing, silent and deadly underground struggle between Israeli forces and Palestinian militias over these highly sophisticated tunnel complexes reminiscent in its way of mine warfare conducted across the western front in the First World War.

Over time, the reach and spread of these various rockets has enabled the Hamas led Palestinian forces to launch co-ordinated attacks into Israeli cities, settlements, farms and civilian areas, affecting conurbations from Ashdod and Ashkelon to Tel Aviv and Jerusalem, causing relatively few deaths but many more, random casualties. The diversity of Palestinian rocket supply and ingenuity of construction has forced Israel to spend more of its defence budget on an anti-missile advance warning network, using home developed systems such as Iron Dome and US defence systems like Patriot to ensure that the threat within Israel can be minimised and thus contained.

Nonetheless, the rocket attacks over the years, the last in 2021 when over 2,000 rockets were deployed over two weeks, have taken a toll on Israeli morale and nerve. Independent medical studies have assessed the impact on the Israeli population as including a range of conditions from Post Traumatic Stress Disorder (PTSD) to depression, children's mental health problems and even miscarriages in pregnant women.

These rocket wars are simply one microcosm of the toxic arms proliferation race underway across the region. The Middle East arms race in all its forms progresses at breakneck speed and has become, at the outer limit, all about managing and containing the threat of the introduction of nuclear weapons to the region. The intention of Iran to enrich uranium and develop its own nuclear warheads as a strategic and battlefield option and Saudi Arabia's response in putting in play the development of its own nuclear deterrent perhaps offers the most conspicuous example of the proliferation dilemma. In a familiar echo of Operation Damocles in the 1960s, Israel in the 2020s is directly connected to this struggle through its programme of remote assassination of Iranian nuclear scientists and weapons programme specialists. Yesterday's Heinz Krug has become today's Mohsen Fakrizadeh.

The potential for regional players to buy tactical or battlefield nuclear warheads on the unregulated 'dirty' market has become a possibility that cannot be discounted or simply relegated to the imaginations of thriller writers. The endgame of the arms race in the Middle East is becoming all the time harder to predict, contingent on the growing intervention of global powers such as Russia, Turkey, Pakistan and China to replace the rapidly contracting US presence on the ground. This arms race, conventional, chemical, ballistic or nuclear, is precipitating an existential crisis in the Middle East and presents amongst the biggest threats to global security.

The opening Chapter of this race was unquestionably written during Nasser's years as President of Egypt during the Cold War that defined the 1950s and 1960s and which brought him to power on a militarisation and rearmament ticket. It was Nasser who started Egypt's nuclear energy programme in 1955, with the creation of Egypt's Atomic Energy Authority. The Egyptians began to operate a two megawatt Soviet supplied research reactor in 1961. Over the next five years Egypt negotiated its first nuclear power plant with American companies GE and Westinghouse before the 1967 war brought these efforts to an end.

In its 2008 report 'Chain Reaction: Avoiding a nuclear arms race in the Middle East'[17], the Committee on Foreign Relations of the United States Senate attempted to quantify and summarise the complex factors driving the potential for nuclear war in the region in order to explain its chief policy considerations. It concluded that the development of a Saudi nuclear weapon represented one of the most serious and most likely consequences of an Iranian acquisition of nuclear weapons. 'If Iran obtains a nuclear weapon, it will place tremendous pressure on Saudi Arabia to follow suit. The factor most likely to dissuade the Saudis from pursuing a nuclear weapon would be a restored United States-Saudi bilateral relationship and a repaired Saudi perception regarding the reliability of the US security guarantee. If the United States does not take deliberate action in the coming years to achieve both of these objectives, an Iranian bomb will almost certainly lead to a Saudi bomb', the report said.

The development of a Saudi nuclear weapon would inevitably spur a regional nuclear arms race, drawing in Iran, Israel and Egypt itself, which would face intense political pressure to respond, either by renouncing its peace treaty with Israel, repudiating its relationship with the United States or initiating an Egyptian nuclear armaments programme. The Egyptian people 'would undoubtedly demand the government take some forceful and substantial action', the report stated. The assessment of the 'Chain Reaction' report concluded that the likelihood of Egypt choosing to cross the nuclear threshold was low, although any Iranian developments would hasten Egypt's nuclear energy efforts. Egypt might follow suit, however, in order to reclaim and maintain its traditional role as a regional power and reassert its position as leader of the Arab world. Were Iran to acquire nuclear weapons, the overriding Egyptian response would not be one of fear of Iran but rather of marginalisation in the region.

In his original vision of a renewed and unassailable fortress Egypt, King Farouk had contemplated the nuclear option as the ultimate endgame in his rearmament strategy, the last piece of the puzzle which would complement conventional armaments, missile and rocket technology. Yet it was to be Nasser who realised this vision of nuclear power within Egypt and Anwar Sadat who took the country's nuclear programme further forward in the 1970s once again.

The German arms and military experts, the scientists and technicians, the arms dealers and security experts were all just a means to an end rather than the end in itself. They were the designers and builders of a bridge from the old to the new. Nasser's vision was of an Egypt that could break free from the years of subservience and plant its own flag in the ground; of a nation that could come together in victory at Suez and seize that moment in history to control its own destiny. Hard power and the leverage of military clout provided the obvious route out of the centuries of servitude, colonial rule and the humiliation of successive defeats by Israel and permanent occupation by the British. It may even have offered a proxy solution to the inferiority complex of the Egyptian leader himself, one identified by the British as essential in accommodating any real understanding of Nasser's and thus Egypt's profile.

If Nasser's German project ultimately failed, it cannot be said to have done so through lack of vision or ambition. In the end the problem did not lie with the vision but in the infinitely complex realisation of it as a practical proposition anchored in actual ways and means. The opportunism that drove this secretive and equivocal episode in Egyptian history was not enough in itself to deliver a defining endgame in the Cold War struggle that engulfed the region, but rather provoked a series of downstream events and their unintended consequences. It certainly provided the spark to ignite the fire of future arms proliferation across the Middle East. The ineluctable growth of the arms race in the region over the ensuing decades of persistent and debilitating conflict has paved the way for an increasingly volatile and unpredictable journey further into the heart of darkness.

Epilogue
ECHOES DOWN A CAIRO STREET

'Rumour came to Cairo of a battle being fought inside Egypt at a railway halt called El Alamein but, it seemed, nothing had been settled. The Germans were still a day's tank drive away and their broadcasts claimed they were merely awaiting supplies. Any day now the advance would begin again. Egypt would be liberated and Rommel and his men would keep their assignation with the ladies of Alexandria'.

Olivia Manning
The Danger Tree, The Levant Trilogy,
Phoenix Fiction 1978.

Search for the Cairo of the 'Allemanni' now and it proves elusive. With every passing decade, the old post-war Cairo becomes a shade more referential, a touch more anecdotal, concealed further beneath the momentum of construction sites, scaffolding towers, booming business districts, shopping malls, traffic gridlock, concrete dust and urban sprawl, the forward march of civic progress in all its shades. But then the colonial Egypt and the European veneer and pretensions that overlaid it in the 1950s and 1960s was never more than a passing interval. Today's Cairo is predominantly an Egyptian city, one whose Arab and Islamic persona relies less on impersonation or mimicry to shape its public spaces and validate its character. It has put history firmly in its place. Twenty first century Cairenes have moved on. The presence of Nasser and his near two decades at the country's helm is not reflected in much visual evidence, either in its statuary, iconography or cultural footprint, although in recent times some banners touting Nasser as 'Leader of the Arab Nation' have again started to appear. During the 2011 Arab Spring uprisings in Tahrir Square demanding the departure of President Hosni Mubarak, Nasser's image once again was spray painted on walls and buildings. Today's metropolis of 21 million people is 10 times the size it was in 1952 and the city is unapologetically the largest in the Middle East and the Arabic speaking world, in turn bearing the weight of Egypt's resource sapping population explosion of the 21st century.

The 'blond German giants' springing from the diving boards and loafing around the pool of the Heliopolis Sporting Club are long gone. There are no eponymous Nazi aircraft designers occupying the top floor of Shepheard's Hotel, and the strains of the Horst Wessel Lied do not float on the air of a balmy summer evening down the leafy Maadi boulevards. In Old Cairo, the German Cemetery lies peacefully behind its high, sun baked brick walls, the neat graves of First World War soldiers and miscellaneous, long forgotten civilian expatriates set out together under the dappled shade of spreading trees amidst well laid and carefully trimmed paths. In Heliopolis, the jewel in Cairo's turn-of-the-century modernist architectural crown, the concrete construction of Baron Empain's Palace, his eccentric and exuberant tribute to Angkor Wat and the Hindu Temples of Orissa, has laid its ghosts to rest and finally been restored with large dollops of heritage funding to its original glory. The expansive hotels, public buildings and palatial houses with their lush gardens are a touch more weathered and worn, hemmed in more closely by utilitarian apartment blocks, shops and small industrial zones thrusting ever outwards from the city centre. Even Groppi's, the legendary watering hole and patisserie go-to destination for foreign residents and castaways in Cairo is something less than it used to be, the shopfront desecrated by vivid green strip lighting. Cairo's Nazi colony, such as it ever was, is not only long gone but these days barely remembered at all.

The German involvement in Egypt's military reconstruction was at first a badly kept secret. The odd sightings, an occasional press conference or interview, a chance briefing alerted the British, the Americans and the perpetually alert Israelis that something was afoot. Change was in the air. But they were all as unsure as each other as to what those changes would mean. After the abdication of King Farouk amidst the coup of the Free Officers in July 1952, the influx of the former Wehrmacht and Nazi officers and scientists into Egypt accelerated and their absorption into the military, security and armaments infrastructure grew more widespread and ominous.

It is now clear that during this period of the early 1950s the Germans were considered to pose a live threat to Israeli and British interests, much more so than may have been generally or openly acknowledged at the time. Israel, though, was rattled enough to launch Operation Susannah as early as 1954 in order to destabilise Egypt and thereby persuade the British to maintain their garrison in the Suez Canal Zone and thus keep a lid on any potential Egyptian regional aggression. For its part, British military intelligence tracked the movements of the German paramilitary specialists in and out of the Suez Canal Zone up to 1956, rightly fearful that the Kateibas of the Muslim Brotherhood and the Liberation Units of the Liberation Rally party were working to exploit the all-too obvious frailties in Britain's militarily shaky and potentially illegal 120-mile long military canton.

The British hatched detailed and highly secret plans, masterminding Operation Rodeo amongst others to deal with all possible outcomes including forced and hurried evacuation of soldiers and civilians from the Zone and Egypt's main cities, including Alexandria. The scale and threat of infiltration and attrition overseen by the German experts in 1953 and 1954 made them temporarily contemplate abandoning their Suez position altogether in favour of a new Middle East base at Gaza. The plan remained still born partly due to its impracticality but mainly its cost and the unacceptability of leaving behind so many valuable military assets to the Egyptians, a solution which Churchill would not contemplate and which the Suez crisis in any case pre-empted.

Whilst the Egyptian initiative to grow its own rocket power, missiles and jet aircraft was only ever taken half seriously by Israel and the United States due to a mixture of budget shortfalls, technical deficiency, logistics hurdles and incompetence, the fact remains that it could never be dismissed completely. Israel's second covert game plan in Egypt and West Germany, Operation Damocles, was a testament to the lethal potential that the German scientists and technicians were working to exploit. The episode of the German advisers in Egypt lasted in the main from 1949 to 1967. In that time some thousands of specialists tried to change both the Egyptian military culture and shape its assets on the ground through a process of strategizing, mentoring, planning, financing, manufacturing and training, even illicitly leading some units from the front in combat from time to time.

Their willing students spanned the Egyptian Army's top planners, general staff, soldiers, sailors, paratroopers, tank commanders, irregulars and paramilitaries along with policemen, intelligence agents, interrogators, diplomats and propagandists. They trained whole cohorts of Egyptian scientists, technical experts and specialists in arms and armaments production, including in some of the world's most advanced, if incomplete, weapons systems. They even took on the training and development of the first Fedayeen, Palestine's 'self-sacrificer' freedom fighters who successfully violated Israel's territorial integrity for the first time and broke the mold in the process, setting the precedent and benchmark for future incarnations of Islamic militias and irregular, insurgent forces across the region to follow in later decades.

The seriousness of this enterprise, despite its obstacles and failures, its lack of finance and endless organisational eccentricities cannot be underestimated or undersold. Had their Central Planning Board contracts not ruled out their licence to impose themselves directly on events, unlike their predecessors in the German military mission in Ottoman Constantinople, it is harder to know where this combined expertise and effort might have led. With the Cairo colony and its German mission just a blink of the eye in Egypt's long military history, the lasting impact of the advisers is tangential, imprecise, their legacy something of an open question. The fact remains however that over 50 years on from the departure of the German advisers, Egypt is now one of the most militarised countries in the world.

Today's Egyptian army is a self-assured, autonomous institution deeply embedded in the country's economy and a major recipient of foreign military aid. It might be reasonably asserted that the strengthening of the country's military, a declared aim of the Free Officers coup in 1952, has finally been achieved. It is 10th in the global league with almost one million regulars and reserves under arms. Its annual budget in January 2021 had swollen to $US7.5 billion [1] with US military aid worth an annual $US 1.3 billion. Egypt both manufactures arms and imports them from all over the world, building an arms industry and related ecosystem spread across multiple factories and assembly sites that is now one of the country's major employers.

Regionally, Egypt's military forces are the largest in Africa and the Middle East apart from Israel. Estimates suggest the Egyptian Air Force has some 216 F-16 fighter jets, and is now the world's fourth largest operator of these state-of-the-art airborne weapons platforms. With 1,373 combat aircraft including helicopters, Mirage V and MIG fighter jets, Egypt is much closer to reaching General Artur Schmitt's recommended levels of 2,000 aircraft, made in 1949 during his inspection tour of the country's armed forces. The Egyptian Navy, once the despair of Baron Theodor von Bechtolsheim in his Alexandrian exile, is now the sixth largest in the world measured by its 128 vessels, including two aircraft carriers and eight submarines. Egyptian Special Forces are amongst the best trained in the world and provide a sharp cutting edge to the country's rapid response capability.

Ironically, the role played by Major Gerhard Mertins in establishing and training Egypt's first paratroopers in the early 1950s may have finally been overtaken by advances in modern warfare, which are increasingly rendering this form of fighting obsolescent. In November 2019, the Egypt Defence Review reported that the paratroop corps had become of little use, with neither the capacity nor capability to deploy by air in contemporary conventional environments and 'a litany of structural hurdles that impede special operations potential together creating a paratrooper crisis of identity'.

Egypt also possesses general security and central security forces numbering some 400,000 which come under the control of the Ministry of the Interior. Within the Egyptian State the Armed Forces enjoy almost unlimited power, prestige and authority with the ability to override almost every government representative or bureaucratic process. It is also true that during the history of the Egyptian Republic, from 1952 to the present day only once has the Head of State not been an active or retired military officer. The psychological profile and style of the country's leadership remain predominantly associated with the trappings, visual tropes and mechanisms of authoritarianism and militarism. The one democratically elected civilian who served as the head of the Egyptian State, Muhammad Morsi, was removed in 2013 after only one year in power by yet another military coup d'état.

Egypt's military powerbase, finances and estate are secretive, but it is widely known that this 'people's army' has its own hospitals, factories and clubs and engages on its own account in business, housing, construction, resort management and real estate. Young Egyptians, uneducated or not, will invariably be conscripted between the ages of 19 and 34 into the Armed Forces for a period of time, sometimes as much as three years. The military culture, infrastructure and ethos fostered by Dr Wilhelm Voss, General Wilhem Fahrmbacher and their colleagues from 1952 has if nothing else become embedded deeply within Egypt's national life and hard wired into the collective psyche of a people caught on the wrong end of too many past military defeats and determined not to repeat the experience. In some respects, Egypt's military and its role in the Egyptian revolution and national government still remains a prototype for other developing states seeking political alternatives.

The work of Johann von Leers and other German imports in the information department of Egypt's Ministry of National Guidance, toiling away through the Suez years and into the 1960s in Cold War Cairo, has since moved through the generational gears along with the ongoing struggle for Palestinian national identity. This running sore remains unhealed despite numerous international efforts at reconciliation. It still plays a predominant part in the ongoing instability of the Middle East region as a whole. Through successive Intifadas and wars in Gaza, the advent of Hamas missile launches from underground silos and the Al-Qassam Brigade suicide bombers, Egyptian public opinion has echoed much of the Arabic speaking world in rejecting Israel's expansionism, military occupation and oppression of the Palestinian population. Despite a formal rapprochement with the State of Israel that has lasted since 1979, part of this prevailing zeitgeist has been expressed through a continuing and corrosive strain of anti-Semitism, an echo of the post-Suez era of 1956 when Nasser's government moved against the Jewish population of Egypt with punitive citizenship, nationalisation and sequestration laws that encouraged and enabled a wholesale Jewish exodus from Egypt.

Some independent writers and journalists working in Cairo, representatives it has to be said of a profession increasingly under pressure from personal restrictions and eroding press freedoms, have reported on specific incidents that have marked the continuing and occasional presence of Nazi images and anti-Semitic propaganda. These have included copies of the notorious *Mein Kampf* on sale at street corner newsstands, banners flown at political demonstrations and graffiti plastered on city walls and buildings [2]. Amidst all of the uniforms, hardware, parades and military strutting, the National Police and General Intelligence Service in Egypt are doing booming business. Both these instruments of state control are large and growing in numbers all the time, dealing with an army of political dissidents, civil rights and human rights protestors and even those who have chosen to voice an opinion which might qualify as simply unorthodox and thus unwelcome.

Whereas back in the 1950s Nasser mobilised his German trained state security cadre against the Communists, trade unionists, Muslim Brotherhood, political activists and dissenters, today's at-risk Egyptians can simply be mainstream social media commentators, influencers, writers, young professionals, rights campaigners, women's activists, students and ordinary citizens with something to say about their world. Like Cairo dentist Muhammad Abdelatif, who chose to raise his head above the parapet to demand better wages for doctors and a better flow of medical supplies to deploy with his patients. Early one morning in September 2019, some 50 security agents stormed his family home entirely unannounced. He was subsequently accused of starting a social media campaign using the Twitter hashtag '#egyptiandoctorsareangry'. The security forces interrogated him for two hours at his home, then took him to an undisclosed police building where he was interrogated for nine days, blindfolded, handcuffed and not allowed to wash, move or talk, wearing the same clothes in which he was arrested and with almost no food or drink [3].

Human rights in today's Egypt are a growing problem and

increasingly attract world attention, nearly always for the wrong reasons. An estimated 60,000 political prisoners now populate Egypt's jails and many ordinary citizens, from businessmen to students, gay people to poets, live in fear of torture and lengthy imprisonment. Egypt has built a further 19 prisons since 2011 to house its growing dissident problem [4]. It is now reported that plans are underway to build a new 'supermax' prison facility north-west of Cairo with the capacity to house over 30,000 inmates. And yet once imprisoned, there is paradoxically no guarantee a prisoner will move through the judicial and court system. Some detainees appear never to face trial or judicial process, condemned to pre-trial detention in perpetuity. Hunger strikes, prison protests, deaths in custody and simply speaking out are all met with the same iron fist, official stonewalling and lack of action. The involvement of the UN and international human rights NGOs, even foreign governments including the United States, does not seem to exert much leverage on an intransigent leadership.

The ebullient and explosive expressions of democratic aspiration and intent displayed in Cairo's Tahrir Square during the 2011 Arab Spring uprisings and the subsequent departure of a humiliated President Hosni Mubarak now lie far behind in the national narrative, fast receding to a vanishing point in the collective rear view mirror. Instead, the authoritarian state has become an existential intrusion into daily life for most Egyptians, independent minded or otherwise. It affects their thinking, their actions, professional choices, relationships, conversations, social connections and economic status. This repressive grip that embraces thought and speech is enabled by a pervasive and sophisticated machinery of state. The military, police, intelligence, judiciary, prison system, interrogation methodology and the sinister 'Nacht und Nabel' knock on the door in the dead of night perhaps offer some clues as to the origin of a long ago imported security infrastructure and style that still enables and empowers today's Egyptian regime. The scale and culture of this mode and apparatus of repression might be said to have transcended time and place. If there are now no longer any Nazis on the Nile, perhaps their abiding legacy lies in the currency of fear and despair in which they so assiduously traded.

Acknowledgements

In 'Nazis on the Nile' I have attempted to find out and reconstruct in as far as possible the often obscured or secretive events that ensued when the post-war leadership in Cairo invited a cohort of German advisers to modernise and expand Egypt's military state, security infrastructure, arms industry and information apparatus. The general facts, circumstances and some specialist corners of this opaque episode have been hinted at, written about or referred to for many years.

'Nazis on the Nile' was conceived and written primarily as a history book, albeit one encasing a singular and unlikely drama. I should state from the outset that I am not a trained historian let alone a professional one, so I acknowledge any technical shortcomings in the book as mine. I have no doubt that I have left myself open to accusations of lack of academic rigour and opportunistic fact selection as far as my historical account and perspective goes. The book is perhaps best approached as a popular history in a sometimes academic wrapping, written for a general readership interested in the activities of post-war Nazis, former Wehrmacht professionals and German scientists and engineers directly engaged in shaping the affairs of Egypt between 1949 and the Six-Day War in 1967 when Nasser lost his big throw of the dice against Israel.

Some excellent authors, including Roger Howard in 'Operation Damocles' and Barry Rubin and Wolfgang Schwanitz in 'Nazis, Islamists and the Making of the Modern Middle East' have already exposed the detail of some of these events. The film maker Géraldine Leach's work, 'The Nazi Exiles' needs acknowledging for its visual story telling, as does the ground breaking investigative study into fugitive Nazi doctor Aribert Heim in 'The Eternal Nazi' by Nicholas Kulish and Souad Mekhennet. I have referenced and duly acknowledge these, and other, excellent works accessed in the course of writing the book.

There are always a variety of sources on which to draw in pulling together an account like this, but my primary sources of information have been archival, both analogue and digital. I have drawn heavily on the British official account of these events through the close examination of many associated files in the National Archives at Kew in London, including the Foreign Office, Information Research Department, War Office, Staff

Officers' Committee, Prime Minister's Personal Minutes and Defence Department. Since much of this research was carried out during London's first and second lockdowns, I want to acknowledge and pay tribute to the staff of the National Archives at Kew who managed to make it possible for at least some of the time to continue to access their physical files, even if on occasions it became a somewhat testing and solitary activity as the building temperature was turned down and the windows were opened to reduce the possibilities of Covid 19 transmission.

I want too to acknowledge the extensive and meticulous facilities offered through the electronic reading room and open access system of the US Central Intelligence Agency. Following the passing of the Nazi War Crimes Disclosure Act in the US in 1998, a wealth of formerly classified information about certain individuals associated with the Third Reich and their movements has increasingly been made available to researchers and the general public. Over eight million pages of these records have now been published, with some additional material published as late as 2009 and more to follow in time. I have extensively mined these files, some redacted and some of which, like the 60,000 pages accounted for by Adolf Eichmann alone, are intimidatingly large. However, it turns out that the CIA maintained a close and enduring interest in the former Nazi and German advisers in Egypt, along with other countries in the Middle East, and built a wide network of informers and intelligence gatherers on the ground in the country to keep an eye on their comings and goings. Without these files and associated ones relating to Nazi activities in Argentina, Syria and West Germany, the book would not practically have been possible.

I have used one CIA file in particular, of the Nazi anti-Semitic propagandist and racial theorist Johann von Leers to establish a foreground character and narrative spine for the book. Von Leers' long and infamous career included a senior wartime role in Berlin masterminding an anti-British, anti-Semitic Arabic language propaganda campaign to disseminate across the Middle East, first revealed in astonishing detail by the academic and historian Geoffrey Herf. It encompassed pro-Nazi efforts in Buenos Aires during his five year residency there in the early 1950s and culminated in the near decade he spent in Cairo as the head of anti-Semitic propaganda at Nasser's Ministry of National

Guidance in Cairo from 1956. His file thus enables the reader to trace his personal journey from post war Germany to Italy, Sweden, then to Argentina and finally to Cairo and his at times flamboyant and openly defiant lifestyle there as a German exile.

Whilst a biography of this pivotal figure has been written in the German language by Marco Sennholz, the details of his life intersect with the story of post-war Egypt in a way which invites some further expansion. Starting with von Leers himself, I have tried throughout the book to construct fuller portraits of some of the key characters who appear in it, mostly individual stories and personal motivations that have never been fully explored. The process of compilation and visualisation of these character studies has been helped by the availability of photographs held in the Bundesarchiv library. I pay tribute to the massive effort to digitise this huge photographic archive and organise it in such a way that a lay person can navigate the endless possibilities it presents. Of course some central characters in the book remain impossible to represent pictorially, but the events in which they were involved happened a long time ago and most often out of sight.

Part of my approach and plan for 'Nazis' was to visit some places of interest in Cairo and elsewhere in Egypt that relate directly to events, people and places portrayed in the book. Lockdown and the lack of international travel options made this impossible during the two years spent researching and writing the book. In the process of opening up the subject matter, it also became apparent that any Egyptian archive or official record covering the intervention of the Germans in the country's governance over the relevant years are not available, or perhaps do not exist in any accessible form. The official Egyptian perspective remains therefore enigmatic or incomplete at best.

There are unquestionably tensions that are attached to any account of this period. Parts of it remain contested history and some important threads remain uncorroborated or verified. I have though attempted to convey an Egyptian side to the story revealed through contemporary press coverage and eye witness accounts of the time. It is the intelligence reports however, often cross-referenced against each other, that provide the documentary information we have. Further insight as to the reach and influence of the Nazi exiles will emerge when archives in the related Middle East countries are finally opened.

I want to gratefully acknowledge help I have had with some technical aspects of the book. With a zero capability in written or spoken German, I relied on the kindness of friends to translate some original material from German to English, including picture captions and letters. These included Alex Küng, Peter Küng and Charlotte Aldridge. Help with some translations from Arabic to English was kindly given by former colleague and friend Haider Shakiry. I have had endless help and support with the concept, struggles, blind alleys and occasional triumphs involved in writing the book from my wife Sue Kinross and I pay tribute to her endless patience, encouragement and belief in the project. I also acknowledge the help and support of those who have read parts of the book and given some selective feedback on it, including my brother Julian Kinross and David Perkins, along with many others who remain nameless but whose goodwill I have leaned on when talking about the book and what I have been trying to achieve with it. However, I must particularly acknowledge the help and support, along with copious professional advice I have received from my publisher Max Scott and editor Michael Karam who have both made important contributions to the structure and content of the book itself. In particular, the many suggestions, observations, recommendations, structural improvements and alternative routes to expression that Michael Karam put forward, together with a very high degree of encouragement and enthusiasm, have made a material difference to the final text and I thank him most particularly.

CHAPTER NOTES

Chapter One

1. Nasser's Blessed Movement, Egypt's Free Officers and the July Revolution, Joel Gordon, Oxford University Press 1992, ISBN 9789774167782, p163
2. TNA/PREM11/392/86940 Prime Minister's Personal Minutes
3. Ibid
4. Letter to Colonel Gamal Abd Al Nasser from General Muhammad Neguib. Written in town 'S' on Monday 2 Rabia Al-Thani 1276 Islamic, falling on 5th November 1956.
5. TNA/PREM11/392/86940 Prime Minister's Personal Minutes

Chapter Two

1. USArch11, RG263, CIA, NF, EnZZ-16, B80, von Leers, 'Statement of Cesar Ugarte Jr', April 29, 1965
2. Society for the Prevention of WW111, Summer issue, 1957, CIA-RDP88-0131R000400480017-1
3. Congressional Record, 1957. Extension of Remarks of Hon James Roosevelt of California in the House of Representatives, pA6143
4. Nazi Propaganda for the Arab World, Jeffrey Herf, Yale University Press, 2009, ISBN 9780300168051
5. The Anglo-French Aggression Against Egypt, Egypt Today, 1956, IWM Collection, COI 582
6. CIA/RDP62/8th July 1953/German Nationalist and Neo-Nazi Activities in Argentina
7. Ibid
8. CIA 4th September 1952, Germany: Frankfurt am Main, JI-2911B, 'Johann von Leers'
9. Report from Buenos Aires, 4-7-1-222/GW-072, 11th February 1952, 'Who's Who in the German Argentine Junta'
10. CIA 4-7-1-249/HAB680, 23rd April 1954 'Committee formed to

Obtain Residence Permit for Former Admiral Karl Doenitz'
11. 19th April, 1954, Field Information Report, Argentine Origin of Movimiento Revoluconario Obrera La Escoba in Uruguay, HAb-650
12. CIA,CS-3/390,421, Propaganda Activities of Dr Johannes von Leers against Israel and West Germany, 12th March 1959
13. CIA, Dispatch EGOA-12892, NFCA, 30 December 1960, to Chief of Station Germany
14. The Post-War Career of Nazi Ideologue Johan Von Leers, aka Omar Amin, 'the first ranking German in Nasser's Egypt, Joel Fishman, Jerusalem Center for Public Affairs, July 10, 2016
15. Operation Paperclip: the Secret Intelligence Program to Bring Nazi Scientists to America, Annie Jacobsen, Little, Brown and Co, 2014
16. Ibid
17. Operation Damocles, Roger Howard, Pegasus Books, 2013, ISBN 978160598438, p83
18. Ibid
19. Ref: Into That Darkness, Gitta Sereny, 1974
20. Rat lines – the hunt for Nazi War Criminals Mark Felton Productions May 15, 2020
21. Nazis, Islamists and the Making of the Modern Middle East, Barry Rubin and Wolfgang Schwanitz, Yale University Press, 2014, ISBN 9780300140903, p211
22. CIA/RDP62/8th July 1953/German Nationalist and Neo-Nazi Activities in Argentina

Chapter Three

1. The Listener, The Quest for Skorzeny, W Stanley Moss, June 28th 1951
2. Ill Met By Moonlight, William Moss, Harrap, 1950
3. Ill Met By Moonlight, Emeric Pressburger, The Archers, 1957
4. The Listener, The Quest for Skorzeny, W Stanley Moss, June 28th 1951
5. CIA Information Report, B-33806, 5th June 1951
6. Ibid
7. TNA/Prem 11/392/86940/Prime Minister's Personal Minute
8. CIA/RDP62/8th July 1953/German Nationalist and Neo-Nazi Activities in Argentina
9. TNA/FO 371/113694, German Advisers To The Egyptian Army
10. TNA/ Prem 11/392/ 86940, Re-Deployment of Egyptian Army
11. Ibid
12. CIA RDP65-007 1999/09/07, April 1945
13. CIA RDP65-007 1999/09/07, April 1945

14. TNA DEFE/5/46/254 German Military Influence in Egypt
15. The Nazi Exiles: Promise of the Orient, Géraldine Leach, Artline Films, France Television, 2014
16. Wiki
17. Marefa.org
18. Secret Biographic Sketch of Reinhard Gehlen, CIA report, declassified and released, Nazi War Crimes Disclosure Act 2001
19. Ibid
20. CIA/Report of Initial Contacts with General Gehlen's Organization by John R Boker Jr, 1st May 1952
21. The Beast Reawakens, Martin A Lee, Routledge, Taylor & Francis, 2011, ISBN 0415925460, Ch 3, p86
22. Ibid
23. CIA, Otto Ernst Remer, Declassified and Released, Nazi War Crimes Disclosure Act, 2001/2008
24. Ibid
25. Ref: Prevent World War 111, Summer issue, 1957, 'Der Weg'
26. Ibid
27. Newsweek Magazine: 'The secret history of Israel's war against Hitler's scientists', 4th December 2018
28. Wiki
29. 'El Hombre Más Peligroso de Europa, Otto Skorzeny En España', dir Pedro de Echave Garcia, Pablo Azorin Williams

Chapter Four

1. Nasser and the Missile Age in the Middle East, Owen L Sirrs, Routledge, 2006, ISBN 0415370036
2. TNA/DEFE/5/46/254/German Military Influence in Egypt
3. Ibid
4. Ibid
5. Ibid
6. Ibid
7. TNA/FO 371/113694/German Advisors to the Egyptian Army
8. wilsoncentre/digitalarchive/209376/March 31, 1947, Telegram: Reports Written by Dr Wilhelm Voss
9. Enemy Personnel Exploitation Centre, Fiat EP.092-76/5/27th March 1947
10. TNA/FO 371/102869 German Military Advisers in Egypt
11. CIA/JX-5911/The German Advisory Group in Egypt
12. CIA/RDP62/18th July 1953, German Nationalist and Neo-Nazi Activities in Argentina

13. CIA/JX-5911/The German Advisory Group in Egypt
14. Operation Damocles, Roger Howard, Pegasus Books, 2013, ISBN 9781605984384, p27
15.TNA/DEFE/5/46/254/German Military Influence in Egypt
16. TNA/FO/371/113687/Manufacture of Arms & Military Aircraft in Egypt
17. Ibid
18. A Game of Birds and Wolves, Simon Parkin, Sceptre 2019, ISBN 9781529353037
19. Thenationalinterest.org/blog
20. The Times, Shreveport, Louisiana, 14th December 1952, p66: 'Egypt Hires German War Specialists'
21. Operation Damocles, Roger Howard, Pegasus Books, 2013, ISBN 9781605984384, p36
22. TNA/FO371/113694/German Advisors To Egyptian Army
23. TNA/PREM 11/392/86940 Prime Minister's Personal Minutes
24. Operation Damocles, Roger Howard, Pegasus Books, 2013, ISBN 9781605984384, p35
25. TNA/FO 371/ 102869/German Military Advisors in Egypt
26. TNA/PREM 11/392/86940/Prime Minister's Private Minutes
27. TNA/WO 208/5216 Bechtolsheim, Theodor von Humpert
28. Ibid
29. Ibid
30. Operation Damocles, Roger Howard, Pegasus Books, 2013, ISBN 9781605984384, p36
31. TNA/DEFE/5/46/254/German Military Influence in Egypt
32. Ibid

Chapter Five

1. TNA/PREM 11/392/86940 Prime Minister's Personal Minutes
2. TNA/PREM 11/392/86940/Onward Telegram from Commonwealth Relations Office
3. TNA/PREM 11/392/86940 Prime Minister's Personal Minutes
4. Ibid
5. National Army Museum, Suez Canal Zone
6. paradata.org.uk/event/canal-zone-egypt
7. The Suez Emergency: The forgotten war of the conscript soldier, BBC News, Pamela Parkes, 24th October 2016
8. National Army Museum, Suez Canal Zone
9. Conditions in the Canal Zone, HOC Debate 11th March 1954
10.TNA/PREM/11/392/86940

11. Ibid
12. Defining the enemy as Israel, Zionist, Neo-Nazi or Jewish: The propaganda war in Nasser's Egypt, 1952-1967, Michael Sharnof
13. The Nazi Exiles, dir. Geraldine Leach, Artline Films, 2014
14. TNA/DEFE/5/46/254/German Military Influence in Egypt
15. TNA/DEFE/5/46/COC/201-290/The Egyptian Situation
16. Ibid
17. TNA/DEFE/5/46/254 German Military Influence in Egypt
18. Ibid
19. Ibid
20.TNA/DEFE/5/46/COC/201-290/The Egyptian Situation

Chapter Six
1. TNA FO 371/121774 Egyptian Fedayeen
2. Ibid
3. Ibid
4. CIA/RDP62/8th July 1953/German Nationalist and Neo-Nazi Activities in Argentina
5. TNA/FO 371/113694, German Advisers To The Egyptian Army
6. TNA/FO371/102869 German Military Advisers in Egypt
7. Jerusalem Post, 7th June 2016
8. Daniel Pipes/Islamo-Nazis/Factual history
9. Wikiwand
10. TNA/FO371/102869/Military Advisers in Egypt/Egyptian Para-Military Forces
11. Ibid
12. Nazis, Islamism and the Making of the Modern Middle East, Barry Rubin, Wolfgang Schwanitz, Yale University Press, p25
13. Ibid
14. Ibid
15. Propaganda for the Arab World, Jeffrey Herf
16. Nazis, Islamism and the Making of the Modern Middle East, Barry Rubin, Wolfgang Schwanitz, Yale University Press, p196

Chapter Seven
1. TNA/ FO 371/69289/Egypt and Sudan
2. Ibid
3. Ibid
4. TNA FO/371/69289/ Egypt and Sudan/J 8290
5. TNA/PREM11/392/86940/Prime Minister's Personal Minutes

6. TNA/FO 371/113694/German Advisers to the Egyptian Army
7. Ibid
8. CIA/RDP70/Daily Worker/November 29th 1953
9. Ibid
10. TNA/FO 371/113694/German Advisers to the Egyptian Army
11. Ibid
12. TNA/FO 371/113687/Manufacture of Arms and Military Aircraft in Egypt 1955
13. Ibid
14. Ibid
15. TNA/PREM 11/392/86940 Prime Minister's Personal Minutes
16. FO 371/115571 Israeli-Egyptian Tension and the Middle East Arms Race
17. Jewish Telegraphic Agency, Daily News Bulletin, New York, December 31, 1957
18. FO 371/115571 Israeli-Egyptian Tension and the Middle East Arms Race
19. FO 371/121774 Israel-Egypt Arms
20. National Security Archive/CIA collection/EngelDrRolf/ark:/13960
21. Ibid
22. Ibid
23. Operation Damocles, Roger Howard, Pegasus Books, 2013, ISBN 9781605984384, p 36
24. Newsweek Magazine, The Secret History of Israel's War Against Hitler's Scientists, Ronen Bergman, 4th April, 2018
25.CIA/OSI-SM/63-3
26. Operation Damocles, Roger Howard, Pegasus Books, 2013, ISBN 9781605984384, p 36

Chapter Eight

1. Nazis in Egypt, the Exposé That Nasser Couldn't Take, New York New York Daily Post, 25th August 1956
2. CIA/DIR 28463/Dr Johann von Leers/19 Sept 1956
3. Washington Daily News, Thursday, September 13th, 1956
4. periscope.com
5. CIA, Dispatch, Chief of Station, Egypt, March 1960
6. CIA/CS-3/397,379, 20th October 1958, Frankfurt, Activities of Professor Johannes von Leers and Dr Hans Eisele
7. The Anglo-French Aggression Against Egypt, Egypt Today, 1956, IWM Collection, COI 582

8. IWM Collection/COI/340
9. Egypt's Nazi Exiles: Promise of the Orient, Géraldine Leach, Artline Films, 2014
10. Ibid
11. TNA/FCO/168/519/Propaganda Attitudes Towards Nasser and the UAR
12. Ibid
13. Ibid
14. Ibid
15. TNA/FCO 168/519 Egyptian Propaganda and Subversion in the Middle East and Africa
16. Ibid
17. Ibid
18. London Daily Telegraph, 20th January 1960
19. tandfonline/Nazis In Cairo, Vol 1, Issue 3
20. Nazis, Islamism, and the Making of the Modern Middle East, Barry Rubin & Wolfgang Schwanitz, Yale University Press 2014, p247
21. Wiki
22. Nazis, Islamism, and the Making of the Modern Middle East, Barry Rubin & Wolfgang Schwanitz, Yale University Press 2014, p77

Chapter Nine

1. Defining the Enemy as Israel, Zionist, Neo-Nazi or Jewish: The Propaganda War in Nasser's Egypt 1952-1976, Michael Sharnoff, Associate Professor of Middle East Studies, Daniel Morgan School, Security Studies
2.The Backbench Diaries of Richard Crossman, Hamish Hamilton & Jonathan Cape, 1981, p287
3. The Times, Shreveport, Louisiana, 14th December 1952, p 66: 'Egypt Hires German War Specialists'
4. Operation Damocles, Roger Howard, p34
5. The Plight of the Jews in Egypt, A Fact Sheet from the American Jewish Committee, March 1957
6. CIA Name File/Record Group 263/box 14-15/ Dir of Ops/File 1/ Vol 1/ Doc 19/ Adolf Karl Eichmann Espionage FBI Memorandum
7. The Jews of Egypt before Nasser, A Fact Sheet from the American Jewish Committee, March 1957
8. New York Post, William Richardson, 18th December 1956
9. The New York Times, editorial, 29th November, 1956
10. Journal d'Égypte, 10th December 1956
11. New York Times, 13th December 1956

12. Nasser's four-pronged attack against the Jews, A Fact Sheet from the American Jewish Committee, March 1957
13. The New York Post, William Richardson, 8th January 1957
14. Nasser's four-pronged attack against the Jews, A Fact Sheet from the American Jewish Committee, March 1957
15. The Suez Crisis and the Jews of Egypt, Fathom, Lynn Julius, 2017
16. Congressional Record 1957, Ext of remarks of Hon James Roosevelt of California in the House of Representatives, Tuesday 30th July 1957
17. 'From Dachau to Cairo', Prevent World War 111, Summer issue, 1957
18. Ibid
19. Ruth Kimche, "Politi, Elie", in: Encyclopaedia of Jews in the Islamic World, Executive Editor Norman A. Stillman. Consulted online on 19 February 2021
20. From Dachau to Cairo, National Jewish Monthly, February 1957, reprinted in 'Prevent World War 111, published by Society for the Prevention of World War 111, Summer Issue, 1957
21.Ibid
22. The Wisconsin Jewish Chronicle, Friday, April 4th, 1958, p20
23.Congressional Record, Proceedings and Debates, House of Representatives, p A4412, 30th August, 1967, Hon Theodore Kupferman of New York
24. Nazis, Islamists and the Making of the Modern Middle East, Barry Rubin and Wolfgang Schwanitz, Yale University Press, 2014, p221
25. From Kafr Al-Dawwar to Kharga's 'Desert Hell Camp': the repression of communist workers in Egypt, 1952-1965. Derek Ide, Vol 1, Number 7, 2015, International Journal on Strikes and Social Conflicts'
26. Ibid
27. Ibid
28. Ibid
29. Defining The Enemy as Israel, Zionist, Neo-Nazi, or Jewish: The Propaganda War in Nasser's Egypt 1952-1967, Michael Sharnoff)
30. The Dispersion of Egyptian Jewry, Joel Beinin, University of California Press, 1998, p108
31. 'Egypt's Last Jews, BBC News, 21st September 2014

Chapter Ten

1. Adolf Eichmann Name File, Record Group 263, CIA Names Files, Director of Operations File Vol 1, Doc 6, SS Obersturmbannführer Adolf Eichmann - Chief of Group IV B 4 of the Reichssicherheitshauptamt, the So-Called Judenreferat, June 17, 1946. Report from

Berlin
2. The Nazi Exiles, Géraldine Schwarz, Artline Films, ZED, 2014
3. Obituary, New York Times, 'Walter Rauff, 77, ex-Nazi, dead, was an accused war criminal'. Robert D McFadden, New York Times, Obituary, 15th May 1984
4. Nazis, Islamists and the Making of the Modern Middle East', Barry Rubin and Wolfgang Schwanitz, Yale University Press 2014, p9
5. New York Times 'Old Nazis Never Die', Nicholas Kulish, 10th January 2015
6. Central Intelligence Agency Report number RSD-323, Damascus, Syria, 2nd September 1949
7. Ibid
8. 'Walter Rauff, Obituary, New York Times,15th May 1984. Robert D McFadden
9. The Eternal Nazi, Nicholas Kulish and Souad Mekhennet, Doubleday, New York, 2014, ISBN 978038553244, p70
10. Ibid
11. Ibid
12. CIA/Directorate of Intelligence File/Doc 73/Reuters/Adolf Eichmann Dies On The Gallows
13. Irish Times, 13th January 2017, Lara Marlowe, 'Nazi War Criminal Allegedly Dies in a Syrian Dungeon'
14. Revue XX1 Magazine, 11th January 2017
15. CIA/Directorate of Intelligence file/Document 4/Adolf Eichmann Name File/ Record Group 263/CIA Names File/Box 14-15
16. Ibid
17. Ibid
18. CIA/Directorate of Intelligence file/Document 2/Senator Kennedy letter to Ambassador on Nazi War Criminal Alois Brunner July 3rd 1991

Chapter Eleven

1. Operation Damocles, Roger Howard, Pegasus Books, 2013, ISBN 9781605984384, p 123
2. The Eternal Nazi, Nicholas Kulish and Souad Mekhennet, Doubleday, 2014, ISBN 9780385532440, p93
3. Cairo – the City Victorious, Islamic Empires, Fifteen Cities that Define a Civilisation, Justin Marozzi, Allen Lane,ISBN9780241199046, p127
4. Operation Damocles, Roger Howard, Pegasus, ISBN 9781605984384, p36
5. Wiki
6. CIA Report Number CS-3/397,379, 1st May 1959

7. The Champagne Spy, Wolfgang Lotz, Valentine Mitchell, ISBN 9780853036531, p63
8. The Post-War Career of Nazi Ideologue Johan Von Leers, aka Omar Amin, 'the first ranking German in Nasser's Egypt, Joel Fishman, Jerusalem Center for Public Affairs, July 10, 2016
9. The Eternal Nazi, Nicholas Kulish and Souad Mekhennet, Doubleday, 2014, ISBN 9780385532440, p112
10.Field Information Report, Egypt/West Germany, EGF-2435, 24 October 1957 'Activities of Dr Johann von Leers'
11. TNA/FO 371/113694/German Advisers To The Egyptian Army
12. 'When Doctor Goebbels Came To Town, Egyptian Mail, Samir Raafat, 30th September 1995
13. Journal of Contemporary History, Katherine Pence, 2011, 47 (1) 69-95
14. 'German Rockets For Nasser', Der Spiegel, May 8th 1963
15. Ref: Saturday Evening Post July 28th 1963
16. 'The enduring charm of Café Groppi in Cairo, Vivian Salama, Newsweek, 20th August 2012
17. 'When Doctor Goebbels Came To Town, Egyptian Mail, Samir Raafat, 30th September 1995)

Chapter Twelve

1. CIA RDP87T004/Interagency Intelligence Assessment, 6th April 1984, 'Developments in the Egyptian Armed Forces'
2. Ibid
3. Ibid
4. TNA/FO 371/113694/German Advisers to the Egyptian Army
5. Ibid
6. Ibid
7. TNA/FO 371/113687/Manufacture of Arms and Military Aircraft in Egypt 1955
8. CIA RDP87T004/Interagency Intelligence Assessment, 6th April 1984, 'Developments in the Egyptian Armed Forces'
9. The Egyptian Arms Industry, Directorate of Intelligence, NESA 85-1091, September 1985, CIA-RDP06T004
10. Ibid
11. Ibid
12. Ibid
13. Congressional Record, Senate, 30th October 1963, p20571
14. Congressional Record, Senate, 30th October 1963, p20572
15. Congressional Record, Senate, 30th October 1963, p20576
16. Ibid

17. 'Chain Reaction: Avoiding a nuclear arms race in the Middle East', the Committee on Foreign Relations of the United States Senate, One Hundred Tenth Congress, Second Session, February 2008

Epilogue

1. military weapons channel/Youtube
2. Cairo Scene, Conor Sheils, 23rd July 2014
3. Guardian 'Threat of jail looms over even mildest critics', 24th January 2020
4. Ibid

BIBLIOGRAPHY

Adolf Eichmann Name File, Record Group 263, CIA Names Files, Director of Operations File Vol 1, Doc 6, SS Obersturmbannführer Adolf Eichmann - Chief of Group IV B 4 of the Reichssicherheitshauptamt, the So-Called Judenreferat, June 17, 1946. Report from Berlin).

'Chain Reaction: Avoiding a nuclear arms race in the Middle East', the Committee on Foreign Relations of the United States Senate

CIA/Directorate of Intelligence File/Doc 73/Reuters/Adolf Eichmann Dies On The Gallows.

CIA/RDP62/8th July 1953/German Nationalist and Neo-Nazi Activities in Argentina

CIA/ RDP65-007 1999/09/07, April 1945

CIA/Report of Initial Contacts with General Gehlen's Organization by John R Boker Jr, 1st May 1952

CIA 4th September 1952, Germany: Frankfurt am Main, JI-2911B, 'Johann von Leers'

CIA, CS-3/390,421, 'Propaganda Activities of Dr Johannes von Leers against Israel and West Germany', 12th March 1959

CIA Report from Buenos Aires, 4-7-1-222/GW-072, 11th February 1952, 'Who's Who in the German Argentine Junta'

CIA 4-7-1-249/HAB680, 23rd April 1954 'Committee formed to Obtain Residence Permit for Former Admiral Karl Doenitz

CIA/ 19th April, 1954, Field Information Report, Argentine Origin of Movimiento Revolucionario Obrera La Escoba in Uruguay, HAb-650).

CIA 4-7-1-222/GW-072, 11th February 1952, Report from Buenos Aires, 'Who's Who in the German Argentine Junta'

CIA 4-7-1-249/HAB680, 23rd April 1954 'Committee formed to Obtain Residence Permit for Former Admiral Karl Doenitz'

CIA, Report number RSD-323, Damascus, Syria, 2nd September 1949

CIA, Otto Ernst Remer, Declassified and Released, Nazi War Crimes Disclosure Act, 2001/2008

CIA-RDP06T004/The Egyptian Arms Industry, Directorate of Intelligence, NESA 85-1091, September 1985

CIA Information Report, B-33806, 5th June 1951

CIA/OSI-SM/63-3), 'The United Arab Republic Missile Program', compiled by the Office of Scientific Intelligence of the CIA in February 1963

CIA Reading Room: Leers, Johannes von, CIA complete file, released 2008: www.archive.org/details/LeersJohannesVon/FileComplete

CIA/RDP62/8th July 1953/Gezrman Nationalist and Neo-Nazi Activities in Argentina

CIA, Dispatch EGOA-12892, NFCA, 30 December 1960, to Chief of Station Germany

CIA/Directorate of Intelligence file/Document 2/Senator Kennedy letter to Ambassador on Nazi War Criminal Alois Brunner July 3rd 1991

Defenders of Fortress Europe, The Untold Story of the German Officers during the Allied Invasion, Samuel W Mitcham Jr, Potomac Books, 2009

Egypt, A Place In The Sun for the Nazi Elite, Peter Lust, September 1, 1967. Macleans Archive https://archive.macleans.ca

Enemy Personnel Exploitation Centre, Fiat EP.092-76/5/27th March 1947.

Grand Mufti of Jerusalem's funeral in Beirut, 1974. Source pictures.

'Hitler's Arab & Black Soldiers, the Free Arabian Legion'. Film: Mark Felton Productions: Aug 2019, Four mins, 10 secs.

Hitler's Shadow, Nazi War Criminals, US Intelligence and the Cold War, National Archives, Richard Breitman, Norman J W Goda

Huntley Film Archive. Youtube.com, Cairo, Egypt in the 1950s, film 3955,

IMG Entertainment, WMR Productions; History Channel: May 10, 2012: Haj Amin Al Husseini recruitment of 30,000 Bosnian Muslims to Handzar Waffen SS 13th Division. Hunts down resistors in Yugoslavia

Inside the Muslim Brotherhood – the truth: Youssef Nada, Douglas Thompson, Metro Publishing 2012

Irish Times, 13th January 2017, Lara Marlowe, 'Nazi War Criminal Allegedly Dies in a Syrian Dungeon'

Israel's Secret Wars, Ian Black, Benny Morris, Futura 1991

Johann von Leers, Ein Propagandist des Nationalsozialismus, Marco Sennholz, Bebra Verlag, 2013

Nasser & The Missile Age in the Middle East, Owen L Sirrs, pub 2006, Routledge ISBN 0415370035

Nasser's Blessed Movement, Egypt's Free Officers and the July Revolution, Joel Gordon, Oxford University Press 1992, ISBN 9789774167782

Nelles Map Egypt. 1 : 750,000/1 : 2,500,000ISBN 978-3-86574-221-6 www.nelles.com

Nazis, Islamists and the Making of the Modern Middle East, Barry Rubin and Wolfgang G Schwanitz, Yale University Press, 2014, pp 217, ISBN 9780300140903.

Nazi Propaganda for the Arab World, Jeffrey Herf, Yale University Press, 2009, ISBN 9780300168051).

Nile River and People of the River, 1950, Academy Films, www.Youtube.com

New York Times, 15th May 1984 obituary, of Walter Rauff, Robert D McFadden. 'Walter Rauff, 77, ex-Nazi Dead'

New York Times, January 10th 2015 'Old Nazis Never Die' Nicholas Kulish

Operation Damocles: Israel's Secret War Against Hitler's Scientists, 1951-1967, Roger Howard, Pegasus Books, 2013, ISBN 978-1-60598-438-4

Operation Paperclip: the Secret Intelligence Program to Bring Nazi Scientists to America, Annie Jacobsen, Little, Brown and Co, 2014

Operation Osoaviakhim, Cold War Channel, Youtube, accessed 10th December 2021 www.youtube.com

Panzer Tactics: Operations in the East, 1941-42, Oskar Munzel, Die Wehrmacht in Kamp, Casemate Publishing

Simon Wiesenthal Centre, Vienna

Society for the Prevention of WW111, Summer issue, 1957, CIA-RDP88-0131R000400480017-1

The Anglo-French Aggression Against Egypt, Egypt Today, 1956, IWM Collection, COI 582.

The Aftershock of the Nazi War against the Jews, 1947-1948: Could War in the Middle East Have Been Prevented? Author(s): Matthias Küntzel, Source: Jewish Political Studies Review, Vol. 26, No. 3/4 (Fall 2014), pp. 38-53, Published by: Jerusalem Center for Public Affairs, Stable URL: https://www.jstor.org/stable/43922001, Accessed: 08-05-2020 10:09 UTC

The Beast Reawakens, Martin. A Lee, Routledge, 1997, ISBN

0415925460

The Champagne Spy, Israel's Man in Egypt, Wolfgang Lotz, Valentine & Mitchell

The Egyptian Arms Industry, Directorate of Intelligence, NESA 85-1091, September 1985, CIA-RDP06T004.

The Eternal Nazi: From Mauthausen to Cairo, the relentless pursuit of the SS Doctor Aribert Heim. Nicholas Kulish, Souad Mekhennet, Doubleday Random House, 2014, ISBN 978-0-385-53243-3

The Game of Nations, Miles Copeland, Simon & Schuster, May 1970, ISBN 9780671205324

The Postwar Career of Nazi Ideologue Johann von Leers, aka Omar Amin, the "First-Ranking German" in Nasser's Egypt, Author(s): Joel Fishman, Source: Jewish Political Studies Review, Vol. 26, No. 3/4 (Fall 2014), pp. 54-72, Published by: Jerusalem Center for Public Affairs, Stable URL: https://www.jstor.org/stable/43922002, Accessed: 08-05-2020 10:07 UTC

The Odessa File, Frederick Forsyth. Pub (name) Frederick Forsyth

The Listener, The Quest for Skorzeny, W Stanley Moss, June 28th 1951

The Nazi Exiles, Géraldine Schwarz, Artline Films 52 mins, (ZED,FR 2014)

TNA/PREM11/392/86940 Prime Minister's Personal Minutes

TNA/FO 371/108358/German Military Advisors in Egypt 1954

TNA/FO 371/127789 Military Equipment for Syria and Egypt from Soviet Union

TNA/WO 216/849 Reports on Military and Political Situations in Egypt

TNA/FO 371/113687 Manufacture of Arms and Military aircraft in Egypt, 1955

TNA/FO 371/113694German Military Advisers to Egyptian Army, 1955,

TNA/FO 371/108489 German Military Advisers with Egyptian Army, 1954

TNA/FO 371/102869 German Military Advisers in Egypt, 1953

TNA/ DEFE 5/46/254 Memorandum 254 of 1953, German Military Influence in Egypt

TNA/FO 371/69289 Egyptian Request for British Military Aid to resist Jewish forces invading Egypt

TNA/ FO 371/121774/1091/104 Egyptian Fedayeen

TNA/FO 371/121774/1091/103 Egyptian Fedayeen, 1956

TNA/ FO 371/90117/ Political Situation in Egypt, 1951

TNA/FO 371 115571/1192/468 Israeli-Egypt Tension and Middle East Arms Race, 1955

TNA/FO 371/115551/1192/14 Possible production of jet aircraft, 1955

TNA/WO 28/5575 Weapons and Equipment of the Egyptian Army, 1951

TNA/FO 371/118911/1094/193 Egyptian Propaganda, 1956

TNA/FO 371/118922/1094/425 Samples of Egyptian Propaganda

TNA/ FO 371/119087/14211/291 Canal nationalisation

TNA/FCO 168/519 Propaganda stance

TNA/ FO 371/115867/1076/60G Egypt's Defence

TNA/PREM11/392/86940 Prime Minister's Personal Minutes

TNA/ British Chiefs of Staff Committee, C.O.S (53) Memoranda 201-290, Vol 111, 1953

TNA/WO 208/5216/Theodor von Bechtolsheim

TNA/ FO 371/96984 Reports of German Nationals as Military Advisers

TNA/FO 371/103914/1015/304 Dr Naumann with Voss & Skorzeny

US Congressional Record, 1957. Extension of Remarks of Hon James Roosevelt of California in the House of Representatives, pA6143).

US Congressional Record April 23rd, 1958 (p7131), Proceedings and Debates, Vol 104, part 6 'Prevent World War Three'

US Congressional Record, Senate, 30th October 1963, p20572

US Congressional Record, US Senate, 30th October 1963, p20576

USArch11, RG263, CIA, NF, EnZZ-16, B80, von Leers, 'Statement of Cesar Ugarte Jr', April 29, 1965

wilsoncentre/digitalarchive/209376/March 31, 1947, Telegram: Reports Written by Dr Wilhelm Voss

INDEX